The
Life
of
Christ

by

Ralph M. Riggs

III

Contents

UNIT ONE

Introduction... 3

PART 1—BEFORE HIS BIRTH

Lesson 1.. 5
Before the World Was
At the Creation of the World
Theophanies

Lesson 2.. 9
Messianic Prophecies
Messianic Types
Messianic Expectations

Lesson 3.. 13
Jewish Life When He Came
World Scene When He Came
Purpose and Plan of His Coming
Difficulties to Overcome

PART 2—BIRTH AND CHILDHOOD

Lesson 4.. 19
Genealogies
Announcement of John's Birth
Announcement of Jesus' Birth
Birth of John the Baptist

Lesson 5.. 23
Birth of Jesus
Circumcision and Presentation

Lesson 6 29
   Visit of the Wise Men
   Flight into Egypt
   Slaughter of Innocents

Lesson 7 33
   Return to Nazareth
   Visit to Jerusalem
   Eighteen Silent Years

PART 3—YEARS OF BEGINNINGS

Lesson 8 38
   Ministry of John the Baptist
   Jesus' Baptism
   Temptation of Christ

Lesson 9 46
   John's Witness of Jesus
   Jesus' First Disciples
   Marriage at Cana

Lesson 10 51
   Cleansing of Temple
   Discourse with Nicodemus

Lesson 11 56
   John's Further Witness
   John Cast into Prison
   Conversation with Samaritan Woman

Map 62

Study Questions, Unit One 63

UNIT TWO

PART 4—EARLY GALILEAN MINISTRY

Lesson 12 67
   Arrival in Galilee
   Second Miracle at Cana
   Preaches at Nazareth

Lesson 13... 73
    Leaves Nazareth
    Miraculous Draught of Fishes
    Calls Fishermen
    Casts Out Demon at Capernaum
    Heals Peter's Wife's Mother
    Heals Many
    Rises Early to Pray

Lesson 14... 78
    Tours Galilee
    Heals Leper
    Heals Palsied Man
    Calls Matthew
    Eats with Sinners
    Concerning Fasting
    Parables of Garment and Bottles

Lesson 15... 83
    Heals Impotent Man
    Witnesses Concerning Himself
    Concerning the Sabbath
    Heals Man with Withered Hand

Lesson 16... 88
    Heals Multitudes
    Names Twelve Apostles
    Sermon on the Mount
    Heals Centurion's Servant
    Raises Widow's Son

Lesson 17... 93
    John the Baptist Sends Disciples to Jesus
    Jesus Condemns That Generation
    Sinful Woman Anoints His Feet
    Preaches Throughout Every City and Village
    The Unpardonable Sin
    A Woman's Blessing
    The Sign of Jonas

PART 5—LATER GALILEAN MINISTRY

Lesson 18.. 98
    Parables by the Sea
    Jesus Stills the Storm
    Delivers the Gadarene Demoniac
    Heals Woman and Jairus' Daughter
    Heals Two Blind Men and a Dumb Demoniac
    Rejection at Nazareth
    Sends Out Twelve Disciples
    Herod Kills John

Lesson 19.. 104
    Feeds Five Thousand
    Walks on the Sea
    Heals at Gennesaret
    Discourse Concerning Bread of Life
    Rebukes Tradition of Elders
    Heals Syrophenician Woman's Daughter
    Heals Deaf Mute and Multitudes
    Herod Fears

Lesson 20.. 109
    Feeds Four Thousand
    Pharisees Demand a Sign
    Beware of Leaven
    Heals Blind Man
    Peter's Confession
    Foretells Death
    Value of a Soul

PART 6—LAST GALILEAN MINISTRY

Lesson 21.. 113
    The Transfiguration
    Heals Lunatic Son
    Foretells Death
    Coin in Fish's Mouth

Lesson 22.. 116
   Sermon on a Child
   Discipline in the Church
   Parable of Forgiveness
   Rebukes Sectarianism
   Warns of Hell

Lesson 23.. 119
   Cost of Discipleship
   Sends Seventy Forth
   Upbraids Certain Cities and Rebukes Herod
   Return of the Seventy
   His Brothers Deride Him
   Heals Ten Lepers
   Parable of Good Samaritan

Study Questions, Unit Two............................... 123

UNIT THREE

PART 7—JERUSALEM AND PEREAN MINISTRY

Lesson 24.. 129
   Attends Feast at Jerusalem
   Forgives Adulterous Woman
   Discourse Concerning Himself
   Concerning Freedom
   Mary and Martha

Lesson 25.. 133
   Man Born Blind
   The Sheepfold
   Rebukes Pharisees and Lawyers
   The Rich Fool

Lesson 26.. 137
   The Importunate Friend
   Watching for the Wedding
   Repent or Perish
   Parable of Barren Fig Tree
   Woman Loosed from Infirmity
   Healing of Man with Dropsy

Lesson 27.. 140
  The Ambitious Guest
  The Great Supper
  The Unfinished Tower
  The Lost Sheep and the Lost Coin
  The Prodigal Son
  The Unjust Steward

Lesson 28.. 144
  The Rich Man and Lazarus
  A Word to His Disciples
  The Unjust Judge
  Lazarus Raised from the Dead
  Pharisees Plot to Kill Him

PART 8—LAST JOURNEY TO JERUSALEM

Lesson 29.. 149
  Beginning to Journey
  Teaching and Journeying
  Pharisee and Publican
  Teaching on Divorce
  Blesses Little Children

Lesson 30.. 152
  The Rich Young Ruler
  The Apostles' Place in the Kingdom
  Laborers in the Vineyard
  Foretells Death
  Who Will Be the Greatest?

Lesson 31.. 156
  Blind Bartimeus
  Zaccheus
  Ten Pounds
  Anointed by Mary

PART 9—LAST PUBLIC MINISTRY

Lesson 32.. 159
  Triumphal Entry
  Weeps Over Jerusalem
  Cleanses Temple
  Curses Fig Tree

Authority Questioned
Parable of Two Sons

Lesson 33... 163
Parable of Householder Demanding Fruit
Marriage of the King's Son
About Tribute Money
Answers Sadducees
The Greatest Commandment
Questions the Pharisees

Lesson 34... 167
Pharisee Religion
Denounces Pharisees
The Widow's Mite
Greeks Come to See Him
His Soul Troubled
Last Appeal to the Jews

Lesson 35... 171
The Olivet Discourse
Ten Virgins
Parable of the Talents
Living Nations Judgment
Jews Plot to Kill Him

Study Questions, Unit Three............................... 176

UNIT FOUR

PART 10—FAREWELL MINISTRY

Lesson 36... 181
Passover Prepared
Passover Observed
Washes Disciples' Feet
Betrayer Revealed
A New Commandment
Predicts Peter's Denial
Last-Minute Instructions
Final Words of Comfort and Encouragement

Lesson 37... 185
The Vine and the Branches
The Disciples' Relationship to the World
Ministry of the Holy Spirit
Disciples' Personal Reaction to His Going Away
The High-Priestly Prayer
Christ Prays for His Disciples

PART 11—TRIAL AND CRUCIFIXION

Lesson 38... 190
Gethsemane
The Betrayal
The Arrest
Peter Smites Malchus
First Jewish Trial
Peter's Denial

Lesson 39... 194
Second Jewish Trial
Judas' Remorse
Third Jewish Trial
First Roman Trial
Second Roman Trial

Lesson 40... 198
Barabbas Released
Third Roman Trial
On the Way to Calvary
The Crucifixion
Title and Garments

Lesson 41... 203
Ridiculed
Last Words

Lesson 42... 207
Invisible Accomplishments at Calvary
His Side Pierced
Temple Veil Rent and Graves Opened
The Burial
The Watch Set

XI

PART 12—RESURRECTION

Lesson 43.. 212
The Resurrection
The Women Come to the Tomb
Peter and John Come to the Tomb
Appearance to Mary and the Other Women
The Watch Report
Appearance to Peter

Lesson 44.. 216
Appearance to Two Disciples on Way to Emmaus
Appearance to Ten Disciples
The Plan of Salvation
Appearance to Eleven Disciples

Lesson 45.. 220
Appearance to Seven Disciples
Appearance in Galilee
Appearance to James and All the Apostles

Lesson 46.. 224
Many Infallible Proofs
The Ascension
Our Identification with Christ
Christ's Arrival in Heaven

Lesson 47.. 228
High Priestly Ministry
The Second Advent
The Millennial Reign
The Great White Throne Judgment
Eternity

Study Questions, Unit Four 232

UNIT ONE

Lessons 1 through 11

BEFORE HIS BIRTH

BIRTH AND CHILDHOOD

YEAR OF BEGINNINGS

Introduction

"I am Alpha and Omega, the beginning and the ending, saith the Lord, which is, and which was, and which is to come, the Almighty" (Revelation 1:8). "I am Alpha and Omega, the beginning and the end, the first and the last" (Revelation 22:13).

The life of Christ covers a tremendous scope. "Even from everlasting to everlasting, thou art God" (Psalm 90:2). In the words of the inspired writer, the "things which Jesus did, . . . if they should be written every one, I suppose that even the world itself could not contain the books that should be written" (John 21:25).

This attempt to sketch the life of Christ will consist of four units. Unit One, *The Beginning,* will trace from the absolute beginning until Christ is well launched on His earthly ministry. Unit Two will describe the events which constitute the various phases of *His Galilean Ministry.* Unit Three, *His Judean Ministry,* will concentrate upon His activities and teaching in the latter part of His earthy life. Unit Four, *The End,* will take up the story as He enters Jerusalem the last time and the shadows of Calvary gather around Him. Tracing these tragic events until the glorious resurrection and ascension, some attention will then be given to His high-priestly ministry, His millennial reign, and the part He will play in the future eternity, the infinite "Omega."

3

Lesson 1

BEFORE THE WORLD WAS

The Absolute Beginning. "In the beginning was the Word, and the Word was with God, and the Word was God. The same was in the beginning with God" (John 1:1, 2). This is the absolute beginning. The Bible record goes back no further than this. It would be impossible for the finite mind to penetrate into the eternity of the past any further. The New English Bible translates this passage, "When all things began, the Word already was."

"The Lord possessed me in the beginning of his way, before his works of old. I was set up from everlasting, from the beginning, or ever the earth was. . . . Then I was by him, as one brought up with him: and I was daily his delight, rejoicing always before him" (Proverbs 8:22, 23, 30). Here Christ is presented as the personification of wisdom, and as such He was indeed from the very beginning.

Creation of Heaven. "For by him were all things created, that are in heaven, and that are in earth, visible and invisible, whether they be thrones, or dominions, or principalities, or powers: all things were created by him, and for him: And he is before all things, and by him all things consist" (Colossians 1:16, 17). Here is a declaration that by the Lord Christ the very heavens were made. He made the throne upon which He and His Father sit. He created the angels in all their serried ranks which surround that eternal throne. All these things were created by Him and for His pleasure.

Eternal Love and Glory. "And now, O Father, glorify thou me with thine own self with the glory which I had with thee before the world was . . . for thou lovedst me before the foundation of the world" (John 17:5, 24). This is Christ's comment about the reciprocal

5

relations between Him and His Father from the absolute beginning. They shared in the glory of unaccompanied omnipotence and basked in mutual love from the very beginning.

The Lamb Slain, ". . . Whose names are not written in the book of life of the Lamb slain from the foundation of the world" (Revelation 13:8). We are here introduced to the plan of redemption which was conceived and thoroughly thought out before ever the world was made or men were brought into existence, to say nothing of before their sin and need of redemption. The plan for a redeemed group of people to constitute His body was made by God the Father before the foundation of the world. "He hath chosen us in him before the foundation of the world, that we should be holy and without blame before him in love" (Ephesians 1:4). Thus the whole plan of redemption, including Calvary and its magnificent end results, was spelled out in the mind of God from the very beginning.

AT THE CREATION OF THE WORLD

Christ Was there. "When there were no depths,, I was brought forth; when there were no fountains abounding with water. Before the mountains were settled, before the hills was I brought forth: while as yet he had not made the earth, nor the fields, nor the highest part of the dust of the world. When he prepared the heavens, I was there: when he set a compass upon the face of the depth: when he established the clouds above: when he strengthened the fountains of the deep: when he gave to the sea his decree, that the waters should not pass his commandment: when he appointed the foundations of the earth: then I was by him" (Proverbs 8:24-30). This represents Christ as being present at the creation of the world. "Before the mountains were brought forth, or ever thou hadst formed the earth and the world, even from everlasting to everlasting, thou art God" (Psalm 90:2).

Christ Creates This World. "All things were made by him; and without him was not any thing made that was made" (John 1:3). This is a distinct reference to Christ, the Word, who was with God at the beginning. When the profound announcement came in Genesis 1:1, "In the beginning God created the heaven and the earth," the word "Elohim" was used. This is the plural form of the noun translated "God." Verse 2 tells of the action of the Holy Spirit in creation: "And the Spirit of God moved upon the face of the waters." Thus Father, Son, and Holy Ghost were occupied in the creation of the world. The passage in Proverbs 8 refers to Christ as being with God in that creation. John 1:3 declares that He was the active Agent in that creation. Colossians 1:16 also states that all things which are in earth were made by Christ. Romans 11:36 summarizes by saying, "For of him, and through him, and to him, are all things: to whom be glory forever. Amen." Thus we have the great revelation that our Lord Jesus Christ himself was the divine Agent in the creation of this earth and all things that are therein.

THEOPHANIES

Christ Was Manifested in Old Testament Times. A theophany is a visible manifestation of God. It was Christ who created this world and who gave himself in advance to be its redeemer. From earth's inhabitants the members of His eternal body would come. It was also He who was to be the revealer of God in His earthly ministry (John 1:18; 6:46; 12:45; 14:9). And He is himself the very image of the Godhead (Hebrews 1:3). We should not be surprised, therefore, to discover that He visited the earth from time to time long before His incarnation.

To Isaiah and Abraham. John tells us (12:41) that Isaiah saw Christ's glory and spoke of Him. "In the year that King Uzziah died I saw also the Lord sitting upon a throne, high and lifted up, and his train filled the temple. Above it stood the seraphims: each one had six wings; with twain he covered his face, and with twain he covered his feet, and with twain he did fly. And one cried unto another, and said, Holy, holy, holy, is the Lord of hosts: the whole earth is full of his glory. And the posts of the door moved at the voice of him that cried, and the house was filled with smoke" (Isaiah 6:1-4). Christ himself said, "Your father Abraham rejoiced to see my day: and he saw it, and was glad. . . . Verily, verily, I say unto you, Before Abraham was, I am" (John 8:56, 58). Here is the association of Christ with Abraham, and it encourages us to conclude that it was Christ with whom Abraham interceded on behalf of Lot and Sodom (Genesis 18:17-33).

To Jacob, Hagar, Moses, Joshua, and Manoah. It was Christ who wrestled with Jacob until the break of day. Jacob said, "I have seen God face to face, and my life is preserved" (Genesis 32:24-30). It was He also whom Hagar saw when she declared, "Thou God seest me" (Genesis 16:13). And it was He who appeared to Moses in the burning bush and announced himself as the Great "I am . . . the

God of Abraham . . . Isaac and Jacob' (Exodus 3:2-6). (He called himself the "I am" in John 8:24, 28, 58 and 18:5.) It could have been none other than He also who continued His contact with Moses on the holy mount and revealed His glory to him particularly as described in Exodus 33:18-23. Manoah likewise saw Him (Judges 13:22), and it was He who revealed himself to Gideon as described in Judges 6. Who else was the captain of the Lord's host that appeared to Joshua at the beginning of the conquest of Canaan? (Joshua 5:13-15).

References to Christ in the Old Testament. In the New Testament description of Old Testament activities there also shines through (it might even seem accidentally) references to Christ in Old Testament times. Hebrews 11:26 states that Moses esteemed "the reproach of Christ greater riches than the treasures in Egypt." In Paul's description of the Old Testament covenant he declared that the covenant to Abraham was confirmed "before of God in Christ" (Galatians 3:17). He stated also (1 Corinthians 10:4, 9) that the spiritual Rock that followed the Israelites in the wilderness was indeed Christ, and it was Christ whom they tempted.

Lesson 2

MESSIANIC PROPHECIES

Made to First Family. The Christ who planned the redemption of the world before man ever sinned came quickly on the scene when they did sin to inform them of His plan of redemption. Genesis 3:15 is the great Protoevangelium (or first form of the gospel). In this Scripture, which pronounces God's curse upon the serpent, is contained the germ and gist of all prophecy. The first and second coming of Christ are included as well as His virgin birth. The seed of the woman (Mary) will crush the serpent's head eventually (at His second coming). This appears to us as a cryptic announcement, but we are sure it was fully explained to our first parents.

"By faith Abel offered unto God a more excellent sacrifice than Cain, by which he obtained witness that he was righteous, God testifying of his gifts" (Hebrews 11:4). "So then faith cometh by hearing, and hearing by the word of God" (Romans 10:17). This means that Abel heard God's word concerning His plan of redemption by way of the great sacrifice of His Son, which was to be typified by the shedding of the blood of innocent animals. By conforming to this symbolism and making a gift of this kind to God, man was to receive forgiveness of sins and obtain righteousness. This was in anticipation of the great sacrifice of the Lamb of God who would atone for our sins and whose righteousness could become ours by faith (John 1:29; 2 Corinthians 5:21).

To Noah, Abraham, Jacob, Moses, and Balaam. The initial and basic prophecy of a coming Redeemer through the seed of the woman was repeated and delimited in subsequent revelations and announcements. To Noah God intimated that his son Shem was the one through whom the Redeemer would come (Genesis 9:26, 27). Isaac, the son of Abraham, was in the divine genealogy, and Judah was the fortunate son of Jacob in this regard (Genesis 17:19; 49:10).

9

Even Balaam joined in to declare, "There shall come a Star out of Jacob, and a Sceptre shall rise out of Israel. . . . Out of Jacob shall come he that shall have dominion" (Numbers 24:17, 19). Moses tells us, "The Lord thy God will raise up unto thee a Prophet from the midst of thee, of thy brethren, like unto me; unto him ye shall hearken; . . . I will raise them up a Prophet from among their brethren, like unto thee, and will put my words in his mouth; and he shall speak unto them all that I shall command him. And it shall come to pass, that whosoever will not hearken unto my words which he shall speak in my name, I will require it of him" (Deuteronomy 18:15, 18 19). (See also Acts 3:22, 23.)

To David, Micah, and Hosea. Many centuries later David was designated as a father of the great Redeemer (2 Samuel 7:13). Isaiah's prediction of the coming Redeemer (Isaiah 9:6, 7) identified Him as a son of David. In Gabriel's announcement to Mary concerning the birth of the Christ he declared, "The Lord God shall give unto him the throne of his father David" (Luke 1:32). Micah told of His being born in Bethlehem (Micah 5:2), and Jeremiah (Jeremiah 31:15) spoke of the weeping in Ramah for the children that were to be slaughtered (Matthew 2:17, 18). Hosea prophesied concerning His trip into Egypt (Hosea 11:1).

Other Prophecies. The predictions concerning the suffering of the Messiah are almost too numerous to indicate in detail. The 22nd Psalm is a vivid picture of the Crucifixion. Isaiah 50:6 and the great 53rd chapter of Isaiah give us a picture of what happened when Jesus died, some details which even the New Testament does not mention. Isaiah 7:14 tells us He was to be born of a virgin and be known as Immanuel, which means "God with us." David predicts at some length the treacherous betrayal by Judas, His companion (Psalms 41:9; 55:12-14; 109:8). Zechariah foretells His humble ride into Jerusalem (9:9), His being sold for thirty pieces of silver (11:13), and His being pierced and smitten (12:10; 13:7).

MESSIANIC TYPES

Types in Eden. To supplement and illustrate the prophecies of the coming Redeemer, God gave man pictures and symbols of that redemption. When man sinned in the garden and foolishly attempted to hide his nakedness with fig leaves, soon to wither, the Lord immediately shed the blood of an animal and took of its skin to provide a more permanent covering for His embarrassed, sinning creatures. The double significance of this symbolic action was surely explained to Adam and Eve, for it was faith in that explanation which caused Abel to follow the prescribed pattern for the expression of faith in the coming Redeemer (Hebrews 11:4). Thus Abel's lamb also became a type of the great Lamb of God. Noah, Job, Abraham, Isaac, and Jacob were all careful to build their altars and offer sacrifices to God.

In Passover and Tabernacle Worship. The paschal lamb of the Passover feast is possibly the most outstanding type of substitutionary sacrifice which we have in the Old Testament (Exodus 12:3, 13). This shedding of blood became the great basic ritual of the tabernacle and temple worship. The significance of this symbolism was surely clear to believing Jews for John the Baptist declared, pointing to Jesus, "Behold the Lamb of God, which taketh away the sin of the world" (John 1:29).

The Cloud and the Glory. "The Lord went before them by day in a pillar of a cloud, to lead them the way; and by night in a pillar of fire, to give them light; to go by day and night" (Exodus 13:21). This cloud is referred to by Paul (1 Corinthians 10:1, 2), thus emphasizing its significance. It was to cover the tabernacle and to be their signal for marching or remaining in their tents. It was identified also with the glory of the Lord which filled the tabernacle and became the Shekinah glory of the holy of holies (Exodus 40:34-38). Thus the cloud and the glory of Old Testament time was a picture of the overshadowing and guiding presence of the Lord God to His people.

The Smitten Rock. Paul tells us that the Rock which Moses smote and from which an abundance of water flowed was typical of Christ (1 Corinthians 10:4). This provided the water to which Israel sang, "Spring up, O well" (Numbers 21:17). When Moses smote the rock the second time he spoiled the type and offended God, for Christ was not to be smitten subsequent to the great blow which fell upon Him on the cross of Calvary (Numbers 20:9-12; Romans 6:10).

The Brazen Serpent. Another outstanding type of the coming Redeemer and His substitutionary work is found in Numbers 21:5-9. Jesus confirmed the significance of this type when He declared (John 3:14 15), "As Moses lifted up the serpent in the wilderness, even so must the Son of man be lifted up: that whosoever believeth in him should not perish, but have eternal life."

MESSIANIC EXPECTATIONS

Confused First and Second Comings. The Messianic prophecies indicated earlier in this lesson were related to the first coming of Christ. There are many more prophecies in the Old Testament which relate to His second coming. Inasmuch as these have to do with the victory and triumph of the Messiah they were much more pleasing to the Jews than the prophecies which related to His suffering and death. They therefore bypassed and overlooked the prophecies of His first coming (being willingly ignorant of them— 2 Peter 3:5). They built their Messianic hope and expectation exclusively on the prophecies of the second coming of Christ. Their scribes and religious leaders elaborated on these prophecies, and their interpretations became valid and a part of their Messianic hope.

Ignored His Sacrificial Death. Their ignoring of the Scriptures which related to the offering of Christ as the great Substitute for their sins and their insistence that their Messiah was to be their national deliverer was basic and deep rooted in the consciousness of the whole Jewish nation. This formed the basis for their rejection of Jesus since he did not meet their expectations of what the Messiah should be. This Messianic conception persisted in the consciousness of His own disciples until the very last. Just a few days before His crucifixion the mother of Zebedee's children asked that her sons should sit on either side of Him in His great triumph (Matthew 20:20, 21). Even following the crucifixion and resurrection His disciples asked Him, "Lord, wilt thou at this time restore again the kingdom to Israel"? (Acts 1:6).

Lesson 3

JEWISH LIFE WHEN JESUS CAME

Long Declension. Through the long centuries of the declension of the Jewish people, from the high peak of the reign of David and Solomon, there appeared periodically great men of God who called the people back to repentance and true religion. But these prophets of God were trampled upon and rejected. As Jesus said, "Ye are the children of them which killed the prophets" (Matthew 23:31). The first martyr of the gospel era climaxed his great defense with this statement: "Which of the prophets have not your fathers persecuted? and they have slain them which shewed before of the coming of the Just One" (Acts 7:52). Expulsion from Canaan and deportation to foreign lands began first with the northern tribes in 721 B.C., and was followed eventually in 586 B.C. by Judea and the Southern Kingdom.

After seventy years of Babylonian captivity, Zerubabel as governor and Joshua the high priest led a remnant of Jews back to Jerusalem. Under the godly leadership of the prophets Haggai and Zechariah, the temple was rebuilt. About two generations later Ezra and Nehemiah led back other groups and made further attempts to restore pure worship.

When these leaders passed from the scene the Jews again fell into apostasy and sin. The last messenger of God in Old Testament times was Malachi, who prophesied about 400 B.C. In the four hundred years which followed the extinguishing of the lamp of this last prophet, the Jews passed through many vicissitudes. They were overrun by foreign conquerors, from the Persians and Grecians to the Romans. A brief brave effort was made by the Maccabean family to return to the worship of Jehovah and escape the domination of their foreign

13

oppressors. However, this too subsided and the Jewish nation sank in defeat and under God's displeasure.

Synagogues and Legal Religion. Strangely enough a pseudoreligiousness prevailed. The nation maintained an external orthodoxy, and the temple services and annual feasts were observed regularly in Jerusalem. To supplement and foster their religious life, the institution of the synagogue had been invented. Wherever Jews were (and they were scattered throughout the world), these places of worship were established and were filled with worshipers. Rabbis, the appointed leaders, instructed the people in the externals of the law. To the commandments of Moses there had been added a great number of regulations which Jesus called "the tradition of the elders." This amplification and interpretation of the law became a part of the binding requirement which was laid heavily upon the people. No wonder Peter later said (Acts 15:10) that this was a yoke which neither they nor their fathers were able to bear.

Pharisees. Foremost among the interpreters of this superimposed law was the sect of the Pharisees. They were very punctilious in their observance of the externals, but they utterly disregarded purity of heart and the mercy, love, and faith which were inherent in the true law of God. They nourished the Messianic hope, but it was interwoven with a strong nationalism. They chafed under the leadership of foreign armies and were eager to rise in rebellion. They were looking for a Messiah who would lead them in such a revolt.

Sadducees and Herodians. Another segment of Jewish life appeared in the sect of the Sadducees. They rejected the yoke of the Pharisees and professed no belief in a resurrection, angels, or spirits (Acts 23:8). They were usually the wealthy class, and some of them were known as Herodians for they were supporters of Herod, their overlord. Below these two distinct classes there were the common people who admired and tried to follow the Pharisees. There was also the lowest class who were shunned and derided by all the others.

A Faithful Remnant. We must not forget that there was hidden in this great mass a few people who looked for redemption in Jerusalem (Luke 2:38). The shepherds to whom the angels appeared, and Anna and Simeon, to say nothing of Joseph and Mary, were acceptable in the sight of the Lord and were ready for His appearing.

THE WORLD SCENE WHEN JESUS CAME

Judaism Everywhere. The time of Christ's first advent found representatives of the Jewish nation throughout the then-known world. "For Moses of old time hath in every city them that preach him, being read in the synagogues every sabbath day" (Acts 15:21). On the Day of Pentecost there were devout Jews who had gathered together "out of every nation under heaven." Sixteen distinct nations are enumerated (Acts 2:5, 9-11). The Jews had carried with them the conception of the one God and their version of the Messianic hope. Ancient religions and philosophies had begun to crumble, and it seems the world was ready for the arrival of the Christian message.

Rome's Universal Rule. In a political sense the world was united. The great Roman Empire held sway. To facilitate their military control the Romans had constructed excellent roads which expedited easy transfer and interchange between all nations. Their laws also bound the world together in one great unit.

Greek Language Well Known. Not the least of the international conditions which prepared the world for the advent of our Lord is the fact that the Greek language was the vehicle of international thought. This language was understood, thus making it convenient for the gospel to be carried to all peoples everywhere. At the moment of Christ's advent universal peace also prevailed. So God had brought all things into preparation and readiness for the arrival of His Son.

THE PURPOSE AND PLAN OF HIS COMING

To Fulfill Prophecy. "My Father worketh hitherto, and I work" (John 5:17). A magnificent display of the cooperative work of the Father and the Son now lies before us. It might be considered that the first occupation of the Father in connection with the arrival of His Son was the meticulous fulfillment of all prophecy concerning His first advent. The predictions cited in Lesson Two (Messianic Prophecies) were carefully and faithfully fulfilled from point to point in the wonderful life of His Son. Events beyond Christ's control were nevertheless under His Father's control, and between the two the obligation was perfectly discharged. The virgin birth, in the town of Bethlehem, the slaughter of the infants, and the flight into Egypt were within God's providence and unfolded in proper sequence. The whole Roman empire was set in motion ostensibly at Caesar's edict but really at the command of the great eternal Governor, who set in motion all peoples simply to bring the prospective mother of His Son to the village (about eighty miles from her home) where her Baby was to be born. The Gospel writer, Matthew, takes particular pains to cite case after case of the fulfillment of the Messianic prophecies. He specifically declares nineteen events in the life of Jesus to be fulfillment of prophecy and makes twenty-five other Old Testament quotations. He quotes Jesus as saying, "But how then shall the scriptures be fulfilled, that thus it must be?" (Matthew 26:54). Even on the cross, that the Scripture might be fulfilled, Jesus said, "I thirst" (John 19:28). This was one of the objectives which He and His Father had and carefully fulfilled in His first advent. They were careful that not one jot or tittle should pass from the law till all was fulfilled (Matthew 5:18).

To Reveal God. It seems that one of the chief purposes and occupations of the life of Christ was to reveal His Father to the sons of men. To satisfy the groping of the human heart as to the personality and nature of the Supreme Being, as well as to correct the gross misconceptions which prevailed in this regard, Christ set himself immediately to portray His Father as He really is. John the Baptist, even before the beginning of Christ's ministry, announced, "No man hath seen God at any time; the only begotten Son, which is in the bosom of the Father, he hath declared him" (John 1:18). Jesus was called the Word of God (John 1:1, 14). A word is an audible expression of an inaudible thought. Thus Christ was to take the inaudible, invisible God and clothe Him in such a way that men could hear and see Him. In this way His coming would reveal His Father. "For I came down from heaven, not to do mine own will, but the will of him that sent me" (John 6:38). "And he that sent me is with me: the Father hath not left me alone; for I do always those things that please him" (John 8:29). "He that hath seen me hath seen the Father; . . . the Father that dwelleth in me, he doeth the works" (John 14:9, 10). The revelation of the Father displayed the love, compassion, tenderness, humility, and great condescension which is inherent in His nature. Also the display of power and truth which shone forth from the life of Christ was derived from His Father and represented Him truly.

To Save the World. One of the most loved and appreciated expressions of God which came to us through Jesus is given in Luke 19:10, "For the Son of man is come to seek and to save that which was lost." In teaching true humility He cited His own life as an example. "Even as the Son of man came not to be ministered unto, but to minister, and to give his life a ransom for many" (Matthew 20:28). This brings us to the great culmination and consummation of the mission of Christ on the earth. He came to pay the ransom price for the redemption of all mankind. "But God commendeth his love toward us, in that, while we were yet sinners, Christ died for us" (Romans 5:8). This was the great objective from which He would not be swerved. It was the supreme accomplishment of His first advent.

It will be seen as the life of Christ unfolds that He was careful to demonstrate and declare His eternal deity. This was necessary to establish faith in Him without which man cannot be saved. "But these are written, that ye might believe that Jesus is the Christ, the Son of God; and that believing ye might have life through his name" (John 20:31).

DIFFICULTIES TO OVERCOME

Wrong Conception of Messiah. Possibly the most stubborn mental block as a hurdle in His pathway was the built-up anticipation in the Jewish mind of what the Messiah should be. Persistently the Jews sought to make Him a king, ignoring the necessity of their personal cleansing from sin and His great plan for the redemption of mankind. But He pushed steadfastly on, preaching His doctrine of the pure in heart, and persisted in offering Himself as the Lamb to be slain.

National Pride. The national pride which prevailed in such extreme form throughout the Jewish nation was also a great roadblock in Christ's way. Samaritans and Gentiles were but dogs in the Jewish mind, and Christ's attention to the Samaritans and His occasional ministry to the Gentiles did not meet with Jewish approval. Social distinctions also were deep and pronounced and ran counter to His attitude and practice. They complained, "This man receiveth sinners, and eateth with them" (Luke 15:2). His reply was, "For I am not come to call the righteous, but sinners to repentance" (Matthew 9:13). With vigorous opposition He collided with the hypocrisy and deep-rooted sin of the Pharisees.

He Humbled Himself. We hesitate even to intimate that He had any problem at all with His own will. If there were such it was not apparent, save possibly His Gethsemane prayer: "O my Father, if it be possible, let this cup pass from me: nevertheless not as I will, but as thou wilt" (Matthew 26:39; Luke 22:42). "Now is my soul troubled; and what shall I say? Father, save me from this hour: but for this cause came I unto this hour" (John 12:27). He drank the bitter cup of Gethsemane to the very dregs, and went forward to the utter pouring out of His soul and life unto death. "He humbled himself, and became obedient unto death, even the death of the cross" (Philippians 2:8).

Lesson 4

GENEALOGIES (*Matthew* 1:1-17; *Luke* 3:23-38)

There are two genealogies of Christ. The one given by Matthew traces His ancestry on the side of Joseph. "Joseph the husband of Mary, of whom was born Jesus, who is called Christ" (v. 16). This is to establish His legal right to the throne of His father David, of whom Joseph was a lineal descendant. Luke's genealogy traces Mary's ancestry back to Nathan, the son of David, and on back to Abraham, Noah, and Adam. Thus Mary also was in the actual physical line of David. Luke emphasizes His being the Son of man rather than merely the Son of David.

ANNOUNCEMENT OF JOHN'S BIRTH (*Luke* 1:5-25)

Angelic Ministry. Here is the introduction of the ministry of angels in connection with the earthly life of Christ. It is to be followed by the angelic announcement to Mary (Luke 1:26), and the great proclamation of the angel to the shepherds in connection with Christ's actual birth (Luke 2:9). Angels ministered to Him on the mount of temptation (Matthew 4:11) and stood ready for His call in the garden of Gethsemane (Matthew 26:53). Angels also stood by as Jesus ascended into heaven.

An Angel Predicts. A devout priest by the name of Zacharias was burning incense in the temple when there appeared unto him "an angel of the Lord." Very naturally Zacharias was troubled and afraid. But the angel encouraged him not to fear, assuring him his prayer was heard. Evidently Zacharias and his wife Elisabeth, both advanced in years, had nevertheless prayed for a child, remembering that God had met Abraham and Sarah almost two thousand years before in the same miraculous fashion. The angel's assurance to

19

Zacharias that their prayer was heard carried with it a description of the nature and ministry of the child who was to be born unto them. He was to be a Nazarite from his birth and was to be filled with the Holy Ghost from his mother's womb. He was to be a forerunner of the Messiah and serve in the spirit and the power of Elias. Zacharias hesitated to believe this announcement and asked for proof. The proof given was in the nature of a rebuke for his unbelief. He was smitten dumb until the birth of the child.

Fulfillment of Prophecy. Here is the first fulfillment of prophecy in connection with the advent of Christ. The last Old Testament prophet had predicted, "Behold, I will send you Elijah the prophet before the coming of the great and dreadful day of the Lord: and he shall turn the heart of the fathers to the children, and the heart of the children to their fathers" (Malachi 4:5, 6). Notice also the introduction of the ministry of the Holy Spirit in God's great program in connection with the coming of the Son. His forerunner was to be filled with the Spirit as no other person ever was.

ANNOUNCEMENT OF JESUS' BIRTH (*Luke* 1:26-38)

The Angel Again Predicts. The same angel, Gabriel, six months later appeared to Mary, a maiden of the village of Nazareth in upper Galilee. He saluted her as one highly favored and blessed among women. Her reaction also was one of fear. The angel told her not to fear and went on to explain how highly favored she was. He told her that she was to be the mother of the Son of the Highest, who was to reign on the throne of His father, David. This was double identification of His Messiahship, Son of God and Son of David. She was indeed to be the mother of the Messiah. Gabriel gave her the further information that the Holy Ghost would come upon her and God's power would overshadow her, thus announcing the great Virgin Birth.

The Virgin Birth. The fact that Jesus was born without an earthly father was confirmed to Joseph to whom Mary was engaged (Matthew 1:18-20). It is also specifically stated that His birth was the fulfillment of Isaiah's prophecy (7:14) that "a virgin shall be with child, and shall bring forth a son, and they shall call his name Emmanuel, which being interpreted is, God with us" (Matthew 1:23). Here is a further statement also that He was the Son of God and God in the flesh. The virgin birth of Christ is consistent with and explanatory of the whole miraculous life which followed. One can better understand the supernatural life of Jesus Christ when one knows that He was born as the Son of God.

Mary Believes. In contrast to Zacharias, Mary accepted and believed the word of the angel. Upon her visit to her cousin Elisabeth, in Judea, she announced that Jehovah had done to her great things (Luke 1:49). Elisabeth declared, "Blessed is she that believed" (v. 45). This is the supreme quality in men which is acceptable with God. "Without faith, it is impossible to please Him" (Hebrews 11:6) and "all things are possible to him that believeth" (Mark 9:23).

THE BIRTH OF JOHN THE BAPTIST (*Luke* 1:57-80)

Holy Ghost Ministry. Immediately upon Mary's conception she made the long journey into the hill country of Judea, a distance of some ninety miles. She went to visit her cousin Elisabeth to share with her the good news and to talk over her own prospects of becoming a mother according to the word of the angel Gabriel. Immediately upon her entry into the home of Elisabeth a wonderful thing happened. Elisabeth's unborn babe moved in her womb, and according to the Scripture, she, as well as her babe-to-be, was filled with the Holy Ghost (Luke 1:15, 41).

Here is another beginning in this wonderful story. These are the first two individuals in the New Testament dispensation who were filled with the Holy Ghost in connection with the birth and life of Christ. This was to be followed by the experience of Mary who spoke out under prophetic anointing (vv. 46-55), and Zacharias' being filled with the Holy Ghost on the occasion of the birth of his son (v. 67). Upon the prophet Simeon the Holy Ghost also came and revealed unto him the approaching appearance of the Messiah (Luke 2:25, 26). By the same Spirit he was guided into the temple just as the infant Christ was being brought in for official presentation (v. 27). Anna, the prophetess, also "gave thanks likewise unto the Lord" (v. 38). Here were eight distinct references to the Holy Spirit and His ministry in connection with the birth of John the Baptist and of Jesus.

Miracles. Another "first" now meets us in connection with the birth of Christ. The first miracle was that a child should be born to Zacharias and Elisabeth in their old age. Zacharias had said, "I am an old man, and my wife well stricken in years" (Luke 1:18). Nevertheless it came to pass according to the word of the angel that a child was born unto them. Whereupon "her neighbors and her cousins heard how the Lord had shewed great mercy upon her; and they rejoiced with her" (Luke 1:58). At the circumcision of the child on the eighth day they called his name John in obedience to the instruction of the angel. This was contrary to the Jewish custom of naming the child after his father.

Prophetic Utterance. But many new things were beginning to happen in these days. Upon this obedience to the angel the miracle of the temporary dumbness of Zacharias was lifted and he opened his mouth and praised the Lord. The Scripture records that Zacharias was filled with the Holy Ghost on this occasion and spoke out in the gift of prophecy. Elisabeth had spoken out under divine inspiration when she was filled with the Holy Ghost. Who can deny that the great "Magnificat" of Mary recorded in Luke 1:46-53 was a revelation and inspiration of the Holy Spirit? This also is a pattern, begun in Old Testament times when the seventy elders received the Spirit and prophesied (Numbers 11:25). It followed likewise on the Day of Pentecost (Acts 2:4), and thereafter as people were filled with the Holy Ghost (Acts 10:46; 19:6).

Prophecy of Zacharias. Zacharias prophesied that the birth of his son and the Son of the Highest that should follow would fulfill the words of the holy prophets. There shone through his prophecy the great national conviction that the Messiah would be their deliverer from all their enemies. But Zacharias faithfully added that holiness and righteousness must attend the deliverance wrought by the true Messiah. His son John likewise was to give knowledge of salvation and remission of sins (Luke 1:77). Indeed the Messiah and His forerunner were on the threshold of history. Here was the great and long expected Messiah and righteousness would be the girdle of His loins (Isaiah 11:5).

Lesson 5

THE BIRTH OF JESUS (*Luke* 2:1-20; *Matthew* 1:25; *John* 1:14)

The Fulness of Time. Now the fulness of time had come and God sent forth His Son to be made of a woman (Galatians 4:4). The onward march of God and His eternal purposes is inexorable. From the time of Adam's sin and the promise of the Redeemer which followed immediately, on down through the centuries and millenniums, He filled the sacred pages of Holy Writ with countless types and prophecies that His Son would eventually come to redeem mankind and lead many sons to glory. Canon Liddon has said there are 332 distinct predictions of Christ's coming, all of which were literally fulfilled in the coming of Jesus. "One jot or one tittle shall in no wise pass from the law till all be fulfilled" (Matthew 5:18). Not a sparrow falls to the ground without the Father's knowing (Matthew 10:29), and "heaven and earth shall pass away but my words shall not pass away" (Matthew 24:35). Relentlessly the events of the ages moved forward and were now to climax in the birth of Jesus Christ.

Humility in His Birth. Here was the most auspicious event that had ever happened in the history of mankind. The great Creator of the earth and of the entire universe was about to clothe himself with the garment of human flesh and be born on earth as the Son of man. And yet there was not the pageantry, ostentation, or material splendor which man would expect of his fellowmen on an occasion like this. The very lowliness and lack of splendor in connection with this great event is itself a revelation of the character of the God who is its main Actor. "I am meek and lowly in heart" the Word says concerning Christ, and His every action reveals this beautiful characteristic. This must be the nature of the Father as well, although it was difficult for Him to display this quality from the omnipotence of the sovereign throne of the universe which He occupied. It must

23

have been a satisfaction to the Father to be able to reveal to mankind this quality of His which had been hidden so long. This unexpected characteristic of His, however, brings Him down to human level and appreciation and enables us to draw nearer to Him.

God Moves an Empire. Without recognizing the great hand of Almighty God that moved him, the mighty Caesar of the Roman Empire sent forth his edict that "all the world" should enroll for taxation, each at the place of his ancestral home. This set in motion hundreds of thousands of pilgrims all over the Roman world who went back to the place of their own birth or that of their ancestors. Unseen and unknown in that great moving of Roman masses, a humble carpenter of Nazareth took his expectant wife on the weary pilgrimage to Bethlehem, their ancestral home. They both were of the house and lineage of David, which explains their return to the city of David for their enrollment. It was of no interest to Caesar or his functionaries that this was a difficult, delicate time for Mary to be traveling. Their wish was law, but the prophecy of Almighty God also was supreme law and had to be fulfilled. "But thou, Bethlehem Ephratah, though thou be little among the thousands of Judah, yet out of thee shall he come forth unto me that is to be ruler in Israel; whose goings forth have been from of old, from everlasting" (Micah 5:2). God's prophecies are both inexorable and faithful. We can always count on their fulfillment, regardless of the price or obstacle.

His Birth. Neither did it matter that "there was no room in the inn." A place must be found for the birth of His only begotten Son. All things are holy to Him and nothing too lowly for Him. He accepted the manger in a humble stable which the innkeeper offered as the only place which was yet available. The exertion of the long journey had been too much for the expectant mother and here, without the attention of physician, midwife, or kindly woman, she gave birth to the Son of God. By her own hand she wrapped Him in swaddling clothes and laid Him in the manger. It was this same type of cloth that was to be wrapped around Him again as He was laid to rest in a cave-tomb in the hillside (Matthew 27:59, 60).

Angels Announce It. But this event did not escape the notice of the heavenly host. With the permission of God the Father they celebrated the first advent of His Son. Upon the hills of Judea surrounding the little town of Bethlehem, shepherds kept watch over their flocks by night. In the stillness of the night these devout men could well have been musing upon the Great Shepherd with whom David himself had communed upon the same hillside a thousand years before. The God who communed with the shepherd boy chose these humble shepherds as the audience who would hear the great heavenly concert. The leader of the angelic host made his great proclamation: "For unto you is born this day in the city of David a Saviour, which is Christ the Lord" (Luke 2:11). A great multitude of the heavenly host burst out in praise to God, saying, "Glory to God in the highest, and on earth peace, good will toward men" (v. 14). The simple shepherds responded immediately and came with haste into the village of Bethlehem. There they found Mary, and Joseph, and the Babe lying in a manger, just as the angel had said they would. And when they had seen, they returned to their flocks and accustomed duties and told all their friends and neighbors the wondrous events of that historic night. The neighborhood was stirred only temporarily, but it was all sweet confirmation to Mary that her Babe was indeed the Son of God and that she was now the mother of the Messiah.

Varied Human Reactions. Let us pause for a moment to take a quick glance at the human scene which surrounded the birth of the Christ. There were many actors upon this stage, and they all reacted in characteristic fashion. We have seen the part of reverent worship and praise which the angels played as their great Creator entered the earthly scene. The humble shepherds likewise glorified and praised God for all the things they had heard and seen. But the businessmen, the religious leaders, and common people of Bethlehem, were not even conscious of the momentous event which had taken place.

Later there came Wise Men from the East seeking Him who had been born King of the Jews. Here is Gentile participation and reverence at the great event. In their search for the "Star" these men came first to Jerusalem and told the Pharisees there of their quest. These religious men at least knew the Scriptures and were able to give the needed information to the Wise Men. But they themselves were unmoved, even by curiosity, to see the fulfillment of Micah's prophecy. How deep in religiosity, sanctimonious pride, and unbelief these men were. Their Messiah and Saviour meant nothing to them as they pursued their religious ritual and received the acclaim of the populace as being "men of God." Herod was more concerned about the birth of Christ than were these calloused Jews. But instead of welcoming Him and doing Him sincere honor (as he professed to the Wise Men he wanted to do), Herod schemed His destruction even as a babe. Here we see active, violent antagonism as the reaction of one element of society.

In contrast to the professional religionists of the day we find Simeon and Anna, godly people of the temple, who knew the leading of the Holy Spirit and who broke forth in prophetic utterance upon beholding the Baby Messiah. After Anna had contacted the holy couple and their divine Babe, she too went to tell others about Him. She "spake of him to all that looked for redemption in Jerusalem" (Luke 2:38). Here is an indirect glance at a group of godly people known to God and to Anna who doubtless met together to encourage themselves in their hope of the coming Messiah. "Then they that feared the Lord spake often one to another: and the Lord hearkened, and heard it, and a book of remembrance was written before him for them that feared the Lord, and that thought upon his name" (Malachi 3:16).

All these people represent varying attitudes which mankind took and ever afterward has taken toward the Son of God. In which group are you?

The Incarnation. It is very clear in this story as recorded by the Gospel writers that Jesus was born of a virgin and is indeed the very Son of God. It remained for the apostle Paul, however, to describe the incarnation in these words: "Let this mind be in you, which was also in Christ Jesus: who, being in the form of God, thought it not robbery to be equal with God: but made himself of no reputation, and took upon him the form of a servant, and was made in the likeness of men" (Philippians 2:5-7). The writer to the Hebrews said, "For unto which of the angels said he at any time, Thou art my Son, this day have I begotten thee? And again, I will be to him a Father, and he shall be to me a Son? And again, when he bringeth in the first begotten into the world, he saith, And let all the angels of God worship Him" (Hebrews 1:5, 6). David wrote, "I will declare the decree: the Lord hath said unto me, Thou art my Son; this day have I begotten thee" (Psalm 2:7). The mystery of the incarnation of the Lord Jesus Christ is beyond human understanding or explanation. In the one person, Jesus Christ, there are two natures, a human and a divine. "And the Word was made flesh, and dwelt among us, (and we beheld his glory, the glory as of the only begotten of the Father,) full of grace and truth" (John

1:14). Human birth itself is a miracle beyond human comprehension, and so we do not hesitate to accept the great miracle of the divine birth of Jesus, the Son of God. God sent "his own Son in the likeness of sinful flesh" (Romans 8:3), but He "did no sin, neither was guile found in his mouth" (1 Peter 2:22). The whole life of Christ, His nature, His word, and His deeds became Him as the Son of God. His virgin birth and true incarnation were the great introduction and explanation of the supernatural life that followed. We stand amazed at the beauty and logical unfolding of this divine revelation.

CIRCUMCISION AND PRESENTATION (*Luke* 2:21-39)

The Law Fulfilled. Paul said that when Christ was born of a woman He was made under the law (Galatians 4:4). As a true son of Israel His parents did for Him according to the instruction of the Mosaic law: "And in the eighth day the flesh of his foreskin shall be circumcised" (Leviticus 12:3). As John had been given the name which the angel had designated for him, so Christ was called Jesus, the name given by the angel before He was conceived in the womb (Luke 2:21; Matthew 1:21). The name Jesus means "the Lord is salvation," "for he shall save his people from their sins" (Matthew 1:21). It is the Greek form of "Joshua," who was the great deliverer of the children of Israel. The circumcision of Jesus marked Him as a son of the Jews, an identification He deliberately and gladly assumed. It is to the eternal glory of the Jewish nation that the Son of God chose to be born as a Jew.

Simeon's Prophecy. Again the law of Moses was to be observed. The same Levitical code which called for the circumcision of the male child on the eighth day required that his mother should bring an offering to the Lord at the end of forty days after the birth of the child (Leviticus 12:4-8). Preferably she should bring a lamb of the first year, but a young pigeon or a turtle dove would be acceptable if she could not afford a lamb. Mary brought a pair of turtle doves, or two young pigeons, which indicated her lowly station. As she came into the temple to present the Babe to the Lord, she was greeted by the prophet Simeon. This man was not a professional religionist, for he prophesied under the inspiration of the Holy Ghost. He had been promised by the Holy Ghost that he should not see death until he had seen the Lord's Christ. The same Holy Spirit directed him to go into the temple at the very time when the baby Christ was being brought in. He went immediately to Him, took Him into his own arms, and blessed God. He spoke under the anointing of the Holy Spirit. "For mine eyes have seen thy salvation, which thou hast prepared before the face of all people; a light to lighten the Gentiles, and the glory of thy people israel" (Luke 2:30-32). The Gentile Wise Men worshiped Him when He was still in Bethlehem, but even before their coming the Holy Ghost gave through Simeon the prediction that Christ was to be a blessing to the Gentiles as well as to the people of Israel.

In faithful anticipation of the full life of Christ, Simeon spoke of the shadow that was to fall upon that light and the sword which was to pierce the soul of Mary, His mother. The division of Israel on the issue of Jesus as the Messiah was predicted by the prophet Simeon. Many were to fall because of this "child." But likewise many would rise again in Israel because of Him. Could this be the rising to walk in newness of life with Him of those who had been dead in trespasses and sin? Or does it refer to the great resurrection with which Christ identified himself when He said to Martha, "I am the resurrection, and the life: he that believeth in me, though he were dead, yet shall he live: and whosoever liveth and believeth in me shall never die"? (John 11:25, 26). The revelation of the thoughts of many hearts was also predicted by the prophet. How many events were wrapped up in the short sentence which he uttered when he saw the Christ!

Anna's Contribution. Womankind was also represented on this occasion. Anna, the prophetess, stood at Simeon's side to welcome the Babe upon His presentation in the temple. She too had come in providentially at that instant, and now she joined with Simeon in giving thanks unto the Lord. It was she who returned to tell the good news to the humble group of those that looked for redemption in Jerusalem (v. 38).

Lesson 6

VISIT OF THE WISE MEN (*Matthew* 2:1-12)

Gentiles Seek Him. Another important event in connection with the birth of Christ was the visit of the Wise Men. The record tells us that "when Jesus was born in Bethlehem of Judea in the days of Herod the King, behold, there came wise men from the east to Jerusalem, saying, Where is he that is born King of the Jews? for we have seen his star in the east, and are come to worship him" (Matthew 2:1, 2). We are not told how many there were nor the particular country from which they came. Tradition has it that there were three Wise Men. This is doubtless assumed by the fact that there were three gifts which they brought Him: gold, frankincense, and myrrh. Their country was usually considered to be Babylon and its vicinity. The men were scientists of their day for they were students of the stars. Something phenomenal had occurred; a new star had appeared which in some way they considered to be the star of the King of the Jews.

Babylon was the country of Daniel the prophet. He had predicted some five hundred years previously that the Messiah would come after the return of the Jews from Babylon to Palestine and the going forth of the commandment to restore and build Jerusalem (Daniel 9:25). It could be that these devout men were believers in the Jewish religion of which Daniel was the outstanding prophet of their country. This would give them a clue as to the time of the appearance of the Messiah, and some unusual event in the heavens at such a time would confirm the prediction to them. It could also be that Balaam's prediction of the rising of the Star out of Jacob might have been associated in their minds with Daniel's prediction and the appearance of the unusual star (Numbers 24:17). In any event these were devout men who valued the fulfillment of prophecy and con-

29

sidered the arrival of the King of the Jews so great an event that
they left their homeland to make the long wearisome journey to the
land of Palestine. They must have been men of means as well, for
the offering which they brought the new King was of considerable
worth.

Indifferent Jewish Leaders. It is worthy of note in this connection
that the chief priests and the scribes who served in Herod's court
were able to tell the Wise Men where the King of Israel was to be
born. They simply quoted Micah 5:2 which declared that Bethlehem
was to be the birthplace of the new King and Governor. One cannot
help but observe that these men were striking examples of how it
is possible to know the Scriptures intellectually and yet be utterly
unmoved by them in one's heart. One would think that they would
thrill at the news of the arrival of the Wise Men with their story of
the birth of the King of the Jews and the appearance of the phenomenal star. However, there is no record of their accompanying
the Wise Men to Bethlehem or of any interest at all which they
evidenced in the birth of their Messiah. Religious, yet perfectly calloused and dead to spiritual realities.

They Find Him. The Wise Men however were not to be discouraged or deterred by the attitude of the Jews concerning the
birth of their King. They went to Bethlehem to find the new King,
and again God graciously accorded them the signal of the star which
led them to the very house in which the young child was. They did
not arrive conjointly with the shepherds, for the shepherds arrived
the very night of His birth and found Him lying in a manger. In
the meantime Joseph had secured a house in which to keep his little
family until they were able to travel again. It was into this house
that the Wise Men came (Matthew 2:11). Upon their entry into the
home they fell down and worshiped Him, bringing the sincere acclaim and acknowledgment of the Gentiles of the Messiahship and
Kingship of this newborn Babe.

They Present Their Gifts. Now it was time for them to open their
treasures. This is the instinctive response of those who really find
their Lord. Our dearest treasures are gladly laid at His feet. The
Wise Men presented unto Him gifts, gold, frankincense, and myrrh.
Throughout the Bible these elements always have a beautiful significance.

The gold, representing deity, indicated that these men recognized
it was the Son of God whom they now worshiped.

Frankincense was the part of that specially compounded perfume used in the tabernacle worship which represented the rare richness and fragrance of the presence of the Lord. The common people were forbidden to make it, for it was to remain very sacred and holy (Exodus 30:34-38). The meal offering was to have frankincense put thereon, but all the frankincense thereof was to be burnt upon the altar as a sweet savor unto the Lord (Leviticus 2:1, 2). Again the Wise Men realized that this Child in whose presence they knelt was deity personified and the very fragrance of heaven.

As Simeon had been faithful to warn that the sword was to pierce Mary's heart and that this Child would be for the fall of many in Israel, so the Wise Men faithfully presented myrrh among their gifts, for myrrh was always a type of suffering. God though the Baby was, myrrh was to be a true symbol of the new life into which He was now born: "a man of sorrows and acquainted with grief" (Isaiah 53:3), who "poured out his soul unto death" (v. 12). But to avoid a premature death at the hands of the wicked king, God warned the Wise Men in a dream not to return to Herod. Again they obeyed the divine leading and returned to their own country another way.

FLIGHT INTO EGYPT (*Matthew* 2:13-15)

Upon the departure of the Wise Men, the angel of the Lord appeared to Joseph also in a dream. He warned Joseph that Herod would seek the young child to destroy Him. He instructed him therefore to arise immediately and take the young child and His mother and flee into Egypt. That very night Joseph arose and departed. He came into Egypt and remained there until the death of Herod when the angel brought him word to return again to Palestine. Here it was not the innocent edict of Caesar that all the world should be taxed which determined the movement of Mary and the place of the birth of His Son. Here it was the wicked, murderous hand of a cruel, bloodthirsty king whom God used to control the movement of His Son and the fulfillment of prophecy. Some 750 years before, the Lord had said through His prophet Hosea (11:1) that He would call His Son out of Egypt. How unerring and how mighty are the moves of our great God, and how careful He is to fulfill every word of divine prophecy.

SLAUGHTER OF THE INNOCENTS (*Matthew* 2:16-18)

No sooner had Herod sensed that the Wise Men were ignoring

his command to return and tell him where the young child was, than he proceeded immediately in a cruel, villainous effort to destroy the young Babe. From the information the Wise Men had given him, Herod concluded that if he killed all the children under two years of age he would surely destroy the Baby-King in the slaughter. It might be assumed from this that Joseph had remained in Bethlehem for two years after the birth of Jesus and it was during that period of time that the Wise Men came. In any event, all the babies under two years of age in the city of Bethlehem and in all of its environs were slaughtered by the soldiers of King Herod.

This horrible event had been foreseen by the holy prophets. Jeremiah had written, "A voice was heard in Ramah, lamentation, and bitter weeping, Rachel weeping for her children refused to be comforted for her children, because they were not" (Jeremiah 31:15). This did not occur because God had predicted it, but He predicted it because He knew it would occur.

Lesson 7

RETURN TO NAZARETH (*Matthew* 2:19-23; *Luke* 2:39, 40)

Nazareth. "The steps of a good man are ordered by the Lord: and he delighteth in his way" (Psalm 37:23). More particularly would the way of Joseph be ordered by the Lord for by that instruction the channel of the life of His Son was marked out. Again an angel of the Lord appeared in a dream to Joseph, instructing him to leave Egypt and return to the land of Israel, for the tyrant Herod was dead. In obedience to the divine instruction, Joseph returned to his native land. He did not return to Bethlehem for he feared that Archelaus, the son of Herod, might also attempt to slaughter the Baby. The Lord confirmed his fear by another dream and directed him to go back to Galilee, to his own city of Nazareth. Matthew declared that this move was also a fulfillment of prophecy: "He shall be called a Nazarene" (Matthew 2:23). It does not seem that this is a quotation from one of the Old Testament prophets, but some take this as a reference to the word *Branch* (Hebrew, *netser,* corresponding to Netseret, still the Hebrew name for Nazareth today). This theme set in Isaiah 11:1 is carried on in Jeremiah 23:5; 33:15; Zechariah 3:8; 6:12. In any event Nazareth gave Him this beautiful title.

His Early Childhood. Of His early childhood in the city of Nazareth the Holy Spirit merely gives us the comment, "And the child grew, and waxed strong in spirit, filled with wisdom: and the grace of God was upon him" (Luke 2:40). Here is a condensed commentary upon His physical growth, His mental growth, and His growth in spirit. In addition to these natural developments the grace of God is mentioned as resting upon Him. Thus He was a natural human boy, developing in the ordinary fashion but especially accompanied by the presence and grace of His Father.

33

Visit to Jerusalem (*Luke* 2:41-52)

His Childhood Education. The faithful devotion to the faith of
their fathers on the part of Joseph and Mary is revealed by the fact
that every year they went up to Jerusalem at the Feast of the Passover. They felt they must as a family eat the Passover lamb in
memory of the death angel passing over their homes in Egypt,
sparing the firstborn sons. Then, through the following seven days,
the Feast of Unleavened Bread, they would celebrate Israel's deliverance from Egypt. In this orthodox religious atmosphere Jesus
was reared. This annual pilgrimage was particularly important to
Jesus when He was twelve years of age. The education of Jesus
began when He was six as He followed the Jewish custom of attending the local synagogue school. Thus His education was based
on and permeated by a study of the Old Testament law. This was
the textbook of His school. At the age of twelve He graduated from
what one might call primary school and became a "son of the law."
"He then experienced what some circles would now call "confirmation." He was allowed to go to Jerusalem and enter into conversation with the great rabbis there.

When He Was Twelve. It was on this occasion that the development in the mind of this Child became so apparent that it disturbed the routine pilgrimage (Luke 2:42-47). It is shown here that
even the Child Christ had begun to penetrate the deeper meaning
of the law and revel in its rich significance. To a later generation of
Pharisee-rabbis Jesus chided, "But go ye and learn what that meaneth, I will have mercy, and not sacrifice" (Matthew 9:13). He had
already gone somewhere to learn that meaning. It could be that He
had fellowship and communion with His Father even as a little child
and from Him directly had learned the deeper meaning of the law.
But He listened respectfully to these doctors of the law and asked
them searching questions. They in turn asked Him questions and
were astonished at His understanding and answers. Thus He enjoyed to the full His initiation into intercourse with the doctors of
the law and took His place among them with ease.

In the Temple. Jesus had become so absorbed in His conversation
with these older men, teachers of the law, that He was oblivious to
the fact that Joseph and His mother had started on their return
journey to Nazareth without Him. Three days later He was still in
the temple sitting in the circle of the doctors of the law. Joseph and

Mary had turned back from their journey homeward to search for their missing Son. They were amazed at discovering where He was, and Mary chided Him gently with having occasioned their sorrow in seeking Him for three days. His response was an expression of open-eyed wonder that they would not have known where He was. "Wist ye not that I must be about My Father's business?" (Luke 2:49).

His Father's Business. What a revelation this was of the thinking and experience of this Lad. It revealed that He was already conscious of the fact that He was the Son of Almighty God. One cannot say when this consciousness dawned upon Him, but here it is revealed that when He was twelve years old He was living under the influence of that consciousness. With it also went a conviction that His Father had a business to perform and that He already was a partner in that business. This took precedence over every other relationship and consideration. He was faithfully discharging His duty to His heavenly Father, <u>for time</u> was the most important thing in all His life.

Back to Nazareth. But the human side of His nature was not to be ignored. He immediately followed Joseph and Mary back to the home town of Nazareth where, the Record says, He was "subject unto them." This was His characteristic attitude toward His heavenly Father and also His earthly parents. A significant comment on the proper attitude of all children of God! Jesus' explanation of His staying behind in Jerusalem served as a reminder to Mary of the unique nature of her Son, and she kept all these things in her heart.

EIGHTEEN SILENT YEARS (*Luke* 2:41-52)

His Textbooks. From the age of twelve until He was thirty, the Bible is completely silent concerning Christ's record. The only comment on His life during these eighteen years was, "And Jesus increased in wisdom and stature, and in favor with God and man" (Luke 2:52). In the years before He was twelve He had grown and become filled with wisdom. Now after twelve and on into maturity He still increased in wisdom and stature. It could have been that His contact with the elders in Jerusalem had revealed to Him the quality and caliber of the Jewish leaders. He had added them to His textbooks. The Holy Scripture was basic to His knowledge, and the world of nature also lay open all around Him. Every jot and tittle of the sacred Word was precious to Him as well as to His

Father. He declared that not one such jot or tittle would pass away until all would be fulfilled (Matthew 5:18).

And it was not merely the technical, literal meaning of the law which He learned. He understood the significance of David's being allowed to eat the shewbread even when it was not lawful for him to do so. He knew also how the priests in the temple could profane the Sabbath and be blameless. In the great realm of common sense and reason He moved with respect and appreciation. He declared that the Sabbath was made for man, and not man for the Sabbath (Mark 2:27). It was logical and easy for Him to conclude that if the Pharisees could pull a sheep out of the pit on the Sabbath day, He could heal a man with a withered arm on the Sabbath day and be blameless. The inherent law of justice and the common-sense comparison of values between men and beasts were sacred to Him and recognized as placed by His Father in the human mind and nature.

His Education Complete. All of the parables which followed throughout the preaching ministry of our Lord were drawn from observations of nature and common human experience. All these were the textbooks in which He was steeped and thoroughly informed. They gave Him complete and sufficient equipment with which to launch upon His career. Even the Pharisees admitted, "How knoweth this man letters having never learned?" (John 7:15). He had not frequented their halls of learning and so His education was not formal. It was nevertheless thorough and complete and included all the things that were really worthwhile in human knowledge.

In Favor with God and Men. His own integration into human experience is also revealed by the expression that He grew in favor with God and man. He could not have been eccentric or a hermit or a constant critic of His fellowmen. The time had not arrived for His ministry and His frank appraisal of human conduct. He was merely to become thoroughly informed as to the behavior of men and to manifest the greatest humility of a true Son of man. This He did in such a way that He enjoyed the favor of His fellowmen. Most important of all, from the early years when the grace of God was upon Him, He continued in ever-deepening fellowship with His heavenly Father. Here was His great Teacher. It was doubtless true that every moment of His days was spent in the consciousness of His Father's presence, whether in His sessions in the rabbinical school, His attendance at the synagogue, working in Joseph's carpenter shop, walking in the fields, or communing with His Father alone on the hilltop. Even as a lad and a young man He did always those things that pleased His Father (John 8:29). This merited the terse report in Luke 2:52 that "He increased in favor with God and man."

Lesson 8

PART 3—THE YEAR OF BEGINNINGS

THE MINISTRY OF JOHN THE BAPTIST (*Luke* 1:80; *John* 1:6-8; *Luke* 3:1-18; *Matthew* 3:1-12; *Mark* 1:3-8)

Thirty Silent Years. The eighteen silent years in the life of Jesus Christ corresponded with the thirty silent years in the life of His forerunner, John the Baptist. The summary of the story of these years is found in Luke 1:80, "And the child grew, and waxed strong in spirit, and was in the deserts till the day of his showing unto Israel." (It was said of Christ also that He waxed strong in spirit.) This we can take to refer to John's spiritual life and to be a sufficient statement in that regard. The fact that he was in the desert till the day of his showing to Israel tells us that he was largely shut up to the direct teaching of God himself. Although his desert life resulted in his wearing a garment of camel's hair and subsisting on a diet of locusts and wild honey, yet our Lord himself later in His ministry revealed something of what had taken place in the heart life of His forerunner.

A Sent Messenger and Witness. Seven distinct words were used to define and describe John in his relation to God. First of all, he was *sent* (John 1:6, 33). This implies a choice on the part of God among all the men of his generation. John alone received a divine commission and went forth in obedience to that commission. The Lord placed a message within his mouth and sent him to deliver it to the children of Israel. He thus became the messenger of Jehovah (Mark 1:2). The fact that he was also called a witness (John 1:7) implies that a revelation had been given to him, as in the case of the apostle Paul, "Thou shalt be his witness unto all men of what thou has seen and heard" (Acts 22:15). The great Christ of whom

John was the forerunner declared of himself, "What he seeth the Father do . . . these also doeth the Son likewise" (John 5:19). Again, "He shall not judge after the sight of his eyes, neither reprove after the hearing of his ears" (Isaiah 11:3). John thus qualifies as a true witness and messenger of Jehovah, for he too had been given the heavenly vision and went forth to bear witness of what he saw.

A Voice and a Light. Another feature of the ministry of John the Baptist was so prominent in the vision of Isaiah that he wrote it out and included it in his prophecy of John's coming. "The voice of him that crieth in the wilderness" (Isaiah 40:3). This is a figurative way of indicating that the words and the thought of John's message were not his own. He simply lent his voice to the great God who was speaking, so much so that he was designated simply as "The *voice*" (John 1:23). How eloquent and significant is this description. This should indeed be the ambition of every man of God. Another figure with the same connotation is used by Christ, "He was a burning and a shining light: and ye were willing for a season to rejoice in this light" (John 5:35). Christ Himself is the great Light of the world (John 8:12). He stated that all Christians are the light of the world (Matthew 5:14). Christ said, "As long as I am in the world, I am the light of the world" (John 9:5). Christ becomes resident and dominant in the life and experience of His children, and through them He, the great Light, shines forth. This quality and experience reached such a degree of perfection and fullness in John the Baptist that Jesus reported "he was a burning and shining *light.*"

A Reed. It is considered by many that when Christ asked the multitude concerning John (Matthew 11: 7-9), "What went ye out into the wilderness to see? A reed shaken with the wind?" that it was a rhetorical question implying a negative answer. Christ followed by another question concerning soft raiment, and the answer indeed was no. But He followed with a third question, "But what went ye out for to see? A prophet? Yea, I say unto you, and more than a prophet." Thus the answer in the third case was affirmative. There is a beautiful sense in which the answer to the first question was also yes. John the Baptist was not a helpless, insignificant reed, tossed about with every wind of doctrine. But there was a sense in which he was a pliable conduit such as a reed, planted by the rivers of water (Psalm 1:3), and constantly moved by the wind of the Holy Spirit. Contrasted to the posts which some people are, dead and motionless, regardless of the wind, John the Baptist was very much alive. His roots were connected with the streams of living water, and he was constantly under the sway and control of the wonderful Spirit of God.

More Than a Prophet. The climax of Christ's complimentary description of John, His great forerunner, was His declaration that he was *more than a prophet,* that there had not arisen among them that are born of women a greater than he (Matthew 11:11). Thus John was the climax and high consummation of God's production of the great line of prophets from Enoch until His Son who came in fulfillment of Deuteronomy 18:15, the prophet like unto Moses. As Moses had been forty years on the backside of the desert in God's postgraduate school, developing into the great friend and mouthpiece of God to his generation, so John the Baptist attended this same desert school. Paul's three silent years in Arabia and Damascus, and Christ's eighteen silent years in Nazareth, complete the picture of how God often trains His workers in silence and solitude.

His Message. When Isaiah predicted the coming of this great voice, he went on to declare what that voice would cry. The message of John the Baptist was to be, "Prepare ye the way of the Lord, make straight in the desert a highway for our God" (Isaiah 40:3). His announcement of the coming of the Messiah would carry with it instructions to the children of Israel as to how to prepare their own heart for that coming. The mountains and hills and the pride of men's hearts should be brought low. The crooked things in their lives should be made straight, and the rough places should be made smooth and plain. The coming and revelation of Christ was to be the coming and revelation of the Lord's glory (Isaiah 40:4, 5).

Repentance. When John began his ministry he developed the theme which Isaiah had put in his mouth. He applied it to the people of Jerusalem, Judea, and all the region around Jordan who came to hear him. In essence his message was of repentance. To the Pharisees and Sadducees, he called, "Bring forth therefore fruits meet for repentance" (Matthew 3:7-10). He struck at their entrenched pride of ancestry and warned them not to say, "We have Abraham to our father." Personal righteousness would be required of every individual, he said, or else the axe would be laid to the root of the trees, and the evil trees would be cast into the fire. He applied this appeal for righteousness to the case of the soldier and the publicans who asked for that application. Great numbers responded to the preaching of this man of God and were baptized by him "unto repentance."

Forerunner of Christ. In John's evangelistic ministry which called for repentance he did not forget the main burden of his mission. He continually announced that One was coming after him who was mightier than he, "the lachet of whose shoes I am not worthy to stoop down and unloose" (Mark 1:7). But his prediction of the coming of the Christ extended beyond His advent. John even anticipated the great baptism in the Holy Ghost which Christ would bestow on the Day of Pentecost, fifty days after His resurrection. "He shall baptize you with the Holy Ghost, and with fire: whose fan is in his hand, and he will throughly purge his floor, and gather his wheat into the garner; but he will burn up the chaff with unquenchable fire" (Matthew 3:11, 12). This should emphasize to us that the baptism in the Holy Ghost (Acts 2:33) is of tremendous importance. As the ministry of John and of Christ called for repentance and righteousness, even so the ministry of the coming Holy Ghost would thoroughly purge His floor.

JESUS' BAPTISM (*Matthew* 3:13-17; *Mark* 1:9-11; *Luke* 3:21-23)

Thirty Years Old. The Christ who had been "made under the law" (Galatians 4:4), conformed to the law as to the year in which He began His priestly ministry (Numbers 4:30; Luke 3:23). Although He was not of the tribe of Levi, He was nevertheless a priest and conformed to the priestly pattern in this regard. Thirty years of age was legal maturity for those who served in the tabernacle. It also represented the maturity of His own development and training in preparation for His great ministry.

Significance of His Baptism. At this age Jesus appeared at the banks of Jordan to present himself to John for baptism. This was a crisis also in the life of John the Baptist. It was the moment for which he had been called and for which he was waiting. He testified that he had not known Christ personally up until that moment (John 1:33). Although they were cousins it appears that John's isolation in the desert had resulted in their complete separation from each other. But John knew from the heavenly Father of his cousin, Jesus, and had received from Him instructions about the coming of His Son to him for baptism. "And I saw the Spirit descending from heaven like a dove, and it abode upon him . . . He that sent me to baptize with water, the same said unto me, Upon whom thou shalt see the

Spirit descending, and remaining on him, the same is he which baptizeth with the Holy Ghost. And I saw, and bare record that this is the Son of God" (John 1:32-34).

When Jesus presented himself for baptism, apparently as one of John's converts, John immediately recoiled. He knew this was no convert but was indeed the very Son of God. He declined to baptize Jesus, declaring, "I have need to be baptized of thee, and comest thou to me?" (Matthew 3:14). Jesus replied, "Suffer it to be so now: for thus it becometh us to fulfill all righteousness. Then he suffered him" (v. 15). Peter shrank from letting the Lord wash his feet, but Jesus insisted on washing Peter's feet, explaining to him, "What I do thou knowest not now; but thou shalt know hereafter" (John 13:7). Likewise, John the Baptist did not understand the significance of Christ's baptism at his hand. But Christ knew that although He had no sins to wash away, He had come to be the great pattern for His people. He took His place with them and identified himself as one of them, walking ahead in the pathway that they should follow.

The Holy Ghost Descends. A wonderful thing happened at this time. The One who had sent John and who had given him the signal concerning the identity of Jesus was now on hand to fulfill that sign. He was also there to give an audible witness, "This is My beloved Son in whom I am well pleased." At this moment the Spirit of God descended upon Jesus and remained upon Him (Matthew 3:16; John 1:33). Here were all three members of the Trinity: the Father speaking from heaven, the Holy Ghost descending from heaven, and Jesus the Son receiving the Holy Ghost and having His Father's blessing pronounced upon Him.

Power for Service. Up until this time Jesus had performed no miracles. The turning of the water into wine at Cana of Galilee shortly thereafter was called "the beginning of miracles" (John 2:11). Peter declared that it was following the anointing of Jesus with the Holy Ghost and power that He "went about doing good, and healing all that were oppressed of the devil" (Acts 10:38). This visitation of the Holy Ghost upon Him was His equipment for public ministry and signaled the beginning of that ministry. John the Baptist explained that God had given the Holy Spirit unto Jesus without measure (John 3:34). The fullest possible anointing and infilling was needed and was bestowed for the tremendously important ministry that followed.

THE TEMPTATION OF CHRIST (*Matthew* 4:1-11; *Mark* 1:12, 13; *Luke* 4:1-13)

Into the Wilderness. At this point we are introduced to an unusual situation. Since Christ's baptism in the Holy Spirit was His equipment for service, and since He had been introduced as the Messiah, the Son of God, one would expect that He would launch immediately upon His ministry in that capacity. However, three of the Gospel evangelists record that the first act of the Holy Spirit in His leadership and direction of the life of Christ was to take Him into the wilderness to be tempted of the devil. The control of the Spirit over Christ in this regard was so strong that "immediately the Spirit driveth him into the wilderness" (Mark 1:12). He retired so far into the wilderness that He was surrounded by wild beast denizens of that area. But, as in the case of Daniel of old, the beasts were restrained from harming Him, possibly recognizing in Him their great Creator. Here was a foretaste also, in the presence of the great Millennial-King, of conditions that will be normal at that time. "The lion shall eat straw like an ox" (Isaiah 11:7) and "a little child shall lead them" (v. 6).

Meets Satan. The Scriptures record that in these days He fasted and ate nothing. Only at the end of this fasting period did He hunger. Among the beasts of this area was one called the serpent, the dragon, the lion that goeth about seeking whom he may devour. It was natural to find him with the other beasts. But he was no ordinary beast. He was the great Satan who rebelled against God and was expelled from his high position as Lucifer, the son of the morning. This is the one who tempted Eve in the Garden of Eden and effected the fall of the whole human race. The first Adam had fallen before him, and now he was face-to-face with the great Second Adam. He sought nothing less than the overthrow and fall of this Adam also.

Lust of the Flesh. Satan seized upon the fact that Christ was physically weakened by His long fasting and that now He hungered. He knew that Christ had just recently been proclaimed as the Son of God. Here was his chance to test Christ's own faith in His divine sonship. How easy it would be for Christ to demonstrate to Satan that He had divine power and at the same time satisfy the hunger of His body. Steeped in the Scripture as He was, the Holy Spirit brought to His remembrance the word of Moses, "Man doth not live by bread only, but by every word that proceedeth out of the mouth of the Lord" (Deuteronomy 8:3). There was something more important to Christ than bread (see John 4:32). And it would be a needless expenditure of divine power to demonstrate to Satan that He was the Son of God.

Lust of the Eyes. But Satan was not finished with his temptation. In some way which is not explained to us, he took Christ up into an exceeding high mountain and showed Him all the kingdoms of the world and the glory of them. Here was a panoramic and penetrating view of the splendor of earthly power as extended all over the world. This had high value to Satan but he was willing to trade it for something that was of still greater value. He offered to give these things to Christ if He would fall down and worship him. This was no vain promise and he did not lie when he said, "That is delivered unto me; and to whomsoever I will give it" (Luke 4:6). It would have been an idle boast and a waste of time if it had been otherwise. This dominion of the world had been given to Satan by Adam's forfeiture of that dominion. The Holy Spirit confirmed that Satan is indeed the god of this world and the prince of the power of the air (2 Corinthians 4:4; Ephesians 2:2; 1 John 5:19). But Jesus was the great Creator of all things and the One to whom His Father had promised personal lordship over all kings and nations (Psalm 2:8, 9). It was unthinkable therefore that He should desert His Father, forsake His promise, and worship the great enemy of Almighty God. Again He used Scripture to refuse Satan's offer (Luke 4:8).

Pride of Life. In the same mysterious way Satan transported Christ to Jerusalem and set Him on a pinnacle of the temple. He now challenged Christ to display His divine status and power by casting Himself down from hence. He sought to make his appeal more effective by quoting the Scripture in Psalm 91. But in this quotation Satan omitted the very important phrase, "in all thy ways." "He shall give his angels charge over thee, to keep thee in all thy ways. They shall bear thee up in their hands, lest thou dash thy foot against a stone" (Psalm 91:11, 12). Christ recognized this for what it was, a tempting of the Lord God. He declined to yield to Satan's temptations and quoted its scriptural prohibition (Luke 4:12). Whereupon Satan left Him. This drama had been observed by the angels in heaven and now they flocked to minister unto Him. Angels brought food to the prophet Elijah (1 Kings 19:5, 6). It could be that they now brought Christ food from heaven and the Man Christ Jesus did eat angel's food (Psalm 78:25).

Lesson 9

JOHN'S WITNESS OF JESUS (*John* 1:15-34)

His Deity. The scene is on the banks of Jordan where John had baptized Jesus forty days before. We find him proclaiming to the people concerning the Christ whom He had baptized, "This was he of whom I spake, He that cometh after me is preferred before me: for he was before me" (John 1:15). This is not only a comment concerning the place of Jesus in comparison to John's but also a statement concerning His eternalness. Jesus himself said later, "Before Abraham was, I am" (John 8:58). He antedated John the Baptist. John also declared that Christ is the great Fountain from which all of His people drink, receiving grace upon grace. This was amplified later by the Lord Jesus himself. "If any man thirst, let him come unto me, and drink. He that believeth on me, as the scripture hath said, out of his belly shall flow rivers of living water" (John 7:37, 38). Then followed an announcement that Christ was to be the great turning point of dispensations. "The law was given by Moses, but grace and truth came by Jesus Christ" (John 1:17). This was the beautiful prospect ahead under the ministry of Christ. Then John declared the purpose of Christ's coming as it related to His Father. He said, "This man is the only begotten Son of God, who dwells in the very bosom of the Father. God the Father is invisible to man all the time, but His Son has come to declare and reveal Him" (see v. 18).

Who Was John? John was evidently interrupted at this time by the priests and Levites whom the Jews had sent from Jerusalem to interview him. They asked, "Who art thou?" Knowing that the Jews were expecting the Christ and would probably be willing to accept him as such, John immediately informed them, "I am not the Christ." They pressed the question further, "Art thou Elias or that prophet?"

(like unto Moses, Deuteronomy 18:15). Again he denied and then told them plainly, "I am the voice of one crying in the wilderness, Make straight the way of the Lord, as said the prophet Esaias" (v. 23). John was definitely a fulfillment of prophecy and a part in the great plan of God. That part was to prepare the way for the Messiah. He went on to say the Messiah had arrived but they did not know Him. "He it is, who coming after me is preferred before me, whose shoe's latchet I am not worthy to unloose" (v. 27).

Jesus the Lamb of God. The very next day Jesus appeared on the banks of the river Jordan. He had returned from His victory over Satan in the wilderness. His personal appearance among the people gave John the opportunity to point Him out and introduce Him to the multitude. As Jesus approached, John said, "Behold the Lamb of God, which taketh away the sin of the world" (John 1:29). "This is the One about whom I have been speaking. He is the One whom God has told me is the great Messiah. When I was sent by the Lord to baptize in water, He told me that the individual upon whom I would see the Spirit descending and remaining upon Him, the same is He which baptizeth with the Holy Ghost. And I saw and bare record that this is the Son of God" (see John 1:30:34).

Here was a double announcement to the Jews. Their Messiah had arrived; but He was not immediately to be the great deliverer whom they had anticipated. He must first serve as the substitutionary sacrifice, not for their sin only but for the sin of the entire world. The Gentiles in all parts of the earth were to be embraced in the atonement which He would make. The significance of this announcement was easily understood by his Jewish audience. Lambs were slain every year in the temple and blood was sprinkled upon the mercy seat, signifying redemption by shed blood. How easy then for them to understand that this Man, the Son of God, their Messiah, was to be offered up as God's Lamb, and His death was to be the atonement for the sin of all the world. What excuse then could the Jews have for misunderstanding the mission of the Messiah? The Jews were willing for a season to rejoice in the light of John the Baptist (John 5:35). Why then did they not accept the statement John made that this Person, who was their Messiah, would be offered up as a sacrifice for sin? Instead, they rejected Him as Messiah and actually called for His crucifixion, thus becoming the slayers of the Lamb of God.

THE FIRST DISCIPLES (*John* 1:35-51)

John, Andrew, and Peter. Immediately Christ began His ministry. The first thing for Him to do would be to assemble certain disciples whom He could train and use as His co-workers. The day after John's historic public introduction of Him, He came again to where John was. At this time two of John's disciples were standing with him. Again John declared to these disciples, "Behold the Lamb of God." It is not recorded what had been the effect of John's proclamation the previous day, but now the two disciples to whom John spoke concerning Christ turned immediately and followed Jesus. They had been prompted by the Father who had chosen them for this relationship (John 6:44). Christ turned and invited them to come to where He was staying that they might get acquainted with Him. Andrew was one of these disciples and John was doubtless the other. Andrew then found his brother, Simon, and told him of his faith in this Person, that He was indeed the Messiah. He was accepting John's statement concerning Christ which had been confirmed in his own personal contact with Him. Simon went with him to see Jesus and immediately became one of His followers. As the Man wrestled with Jacob centuries before and changed his name to Israel, which meant "prince" (Genesis 32:24-28), so now this Man changed Peter's name from Simon to Cephas which meant "a stone."

Philip and Nathanael. The following day Jesus was ready to start on His journey into Galilee. It was at this time that He found Philip, whom He invited to follow Him. As Andrew had found his brother Peter, so Philip also found a convert. When he approached Nathanael concerning Jesus and mentioned incidentally that He was from Nazareth, Nathanael protested that no good thing could come out of Nazareth. However, he accompanied Philip to Jesus whereupon Christ demonstrated His omniscience, declaring that He had seen Nathanael under the fig tree before Philip had called him (v. 48). This confirmed the testimony of Philip and convinced Nathanael that Jesus was indeed the Son of God, the King of Israel. Whereupon Jesus predicted that Nathanael would have greater evidence than this. He laid bare to him the whole purpose and future of His program. Jesus would open heaven itself and provide the way for intercourse between heaven and earth (v. 51). As He said later, "I am the way, the truth, and the life: no man cometh unto the Father, but by me" (John 14:6).

THE MARRIAGE AT CANA (*John* 2:1-12)

Jesus Attends. With these five followers (John, Andrew, Peter, Philip, and Nathanael), Jesus traveled across to Cana, a distance of about twenty-five miles from Bethabara, the point in the Jordan River where Jesus had been baptized. They arrived in time to attend the marriage feast at which His mother also was present. Nazareth was only about five miles from Cana and it could have been that some acquaintance or relative of Jesus was being married and that Mary was assisting in the preparation for the feast. The omission of any mention of Joseph would indicate that he had died sometime during the eighteen silent years. He is not mentioned later in the narrative, and when Jesus died on the cross He made arrangements for John to take care of His mother (John 19:26, 27).

Mary's Faith. Mary's remark to the Lord concerning the supply of wine being exhausted revealed something of her attitude and expectation in connection with her Son. She had pondered many things in her heart for many years. She had also doubtless heard of John the Baptist's proclamation concerning Him, and now she fully expected that He would launch upon His divine ministry. Jehovah had multiplied the oil in the cruse under the ministry of the prophet Elisha (2 Kings 4:1-7), and Mary expected a similar miracle now.

Jesus Waited. However, Jesus was not influenced by external conditions. He was awaiting the leading of His Father. When His brothers later urged Him to show himself at the feast (John 7:1-9), He replied to them as He did to His mother on this occasion that His hour had not yet come. Not one minute or day would He move ahead of His Father's plan (John 8:28). His use of the word "woman" in addressing His mother was not disrespectful, though it sounds so in present-day usage. It could have been that Jesus was calling attention to the fact that the promise given at the fall of man, that the seed of the woman should bruise the head of the serpent, was about to be fulfilled and that Mary was the woman referred to. On the cross also He addressed her as "woman" when He made that tender and filial provision for her in the hour of His suffering and death.

Jesus Turns Water into Wine. His mother was not rebuffed but gave orders to the servants to do whatever Jesus told them to do. This confirms the assumption made above that she had to do with the management of the feast. Six great waterpots stood near at hand.

Each contained about twenty gallons of water, evidently used for the bathing of the feet of the guests. But this water too was exhausted. Jesus turned to the servants and told them to fill the waterpots with water. They obeyed Him as Mary had instructed them. It could have been that they too were expecting a miracle at His hand. This is why they did not hesitate to follow His instruction to take portions of the water with which they had just filled the waterpots and actually present it to the governor of the feast as if it were wine. This was faith on their part in the expected miracle on Christ's part.

The water indeed was made wine by the time the governor tasted it, so that he remarked concerning its excellent quality.

His First Miracle. This first miracle of Christ is typical of His whole mission on earth. He was to take the commonplace elements of human existence and enrich them by His word. By this first miracle Jesus manifested His glory, and it confirmed the faith of the disciples who were with Him. It doubtless made a deep impression also upon the servants, the governor, the guests, and the principals of the marriage feast at Cana of Galilee.

A simple statement follows that after this feast He and His mother, His brethren (again no mention is made of Joseph), and His disciples went down to Capernaum. This was a metropolis on the shores of Galilee, about twenty miles from Cana and Nazareth. We are told that they continued there a few days.

Lesson 10

CLEANSING OF THE TEMPLE AT JERUSALEM (*John* 2:13-25)

Another Passover. It was at a feast of the Passover that we got a glimpse of the Boy Christ on that memorable visit to Jerusalem. He doubtless accompanied His parents on subsequent annual visits. Now another Passover time had come. Again Jesus went up to Jerusalem, but this time in an entirely different capacity. He had learned of the corruption of the court, and the hour had arrived at His Father's command that He should take action about it.

Desecration of the Temple. The leaders among the Jews, and the whole Jewish nation for that matter, had sunk so low in their religious life that they did not hesitate to desecrate the very temple of God. They used the temple court as an open market place. It was indeed necessary that animals be provided the pilgrims with which to make their sacrifices, but it was not proper that these animals should be kept in the very presence of the divine sanctuary. The pilgrims had come from all nations of the world, bringing the money of their respective nations. This money had to be changed into the currency of the Jews for use in Jerusalem. Exorbitant profit was being made by these money-changers, for the Bible calls them thieves and robbers (Luke 19:46; Jeremiah 7:11).

God's Judgment Revealed. The righteous judgment of the heavenly Father flared forth in revelation through His Son. The Christ to whom the Father had committed all judgment (John 5:22) gave a little preview of His action in that capacity, and the people upon whom His wrath fell seemed to recognize the justice of His condemnation and His authority to express it so dramatically. He made a scourge of small cords, drove them out of the temple, overthrew the tables, and spilled the changers' money on the ground. He commanded those who sold doves to take them out and cease making His Father's house a house of merchandise. His disciples evidently

51

were with Him on this occasion for immediately the prophecy of
David found in Psalm 69:9 came to their mind: "The zeal of thine
house hath eaten me up."

A Sign Given. The only protest which the Jews made against His
action and their eviction was the question, "What sign showest thou
unto us, seeing that thou doest these things?" (v. 18). This question
they were to ask of Him many times, and it was not to go without
an answer. His life was to be filled with signs and proofs of His
deity, and they all were to be climaxed with the great miracle of
His resurrection. It was this great sign to which He now pointed
them, although it was to be three years until it was fulfilled. He
said, "Destroy this temple, and in three days I will raise it up." The
literal-minded Jews could think of nothing but the temple which
they were desecrating. Evidently they were rather sensitive about
that subject at the time. But He, of course, referred to the temple
of His body which they would desecrate and destroy and which He
would raise up in three days. It was not until His actual resurrection,
however, that even His disciples understood the significance of His
remark. "When . . . he was risen from the dead, his disciples remembered that he had said this" (v. 22).

Miracles Performed. But this is not all He did when He was in
Jerusalem at the Passover feast. He performed many miracles in
the sight of the people, and many believed upon Him as a result.
However, Jesus did not completely reveal himself in His Messiah
capacity for He knew how the Jews would react to such a revelation,
particularly if it were made prematurely. He had not yet had time
to emphasize the righteousness which was an essential part of His
kingdom nor the fact that He must first be offered as the great Lamb
of God. He knew what was in man and therefore He did not commit
Himself unto them (v. 24).

DISCOURSE WITH NICODEMUS (*John* 3:1-21)

Importance of This Record. While Jesus was in Jerusalem at this
time He came in contact with a certain ruler of the Jews whose
name was Nicodemus. His conversation with this religious leader
was so important that it is recorded in full in the Gospel of John.
It was so fundamental in its teaching that it has become the very
base of the gospel itself. The conversation which Christ had with
this man contained two great texts which have been used by gospel

preachers possibly more often than any others. They are found in John 3:3 and John 3:16.

A Believer. Evidently Nicodemus was among those who believed when they witnessed the miracles which Jesus did during the Passover feast. That he came to Jesus by night is taken by many to indicate that he was ashamed to be seen in Christ's presence. This does not accord with his frank confession of faith in Christ as "a teacher come from God." It could be that, like Zacchaeus, he had difficulty in contacting Christ, although for a different reason. He chose the quiet of the nighttime when Christ was not so crowded by the multitude.

Needed the New Birth. His introductory confession of faith in Christ as the divine teacher was followed immediately by Christ's explanation of the whole matter which Nicodemus needed to know. His standing as a ruler among the Jews did not influence Christ. He was one of a world full of sinners who needed the Saviour in whose presence he now was. Jesus made very plain to him the way to get saved. "Except a man be born again, he cannot see the kingdom of God" (v. 3). The kingdom of God is what Nicodemus really was seeking, and what all men need. Thus Christ's teaching was for Nicodemus and all men everywhere.

A Spiritual Birth. Nicodemus had no spiritual comprehension. He did not understand the new birth. Patiently Christ explained and referred to a "birth of the Spirit." He contrasted the two in verse 6 and insisted that the second birth "of the Spirit" was essential to entry into the kingdom of God. He illustrated the matter by citing the action of wind. Wind is real and even produces sound, but it is invisible, and it is impossible to determine whence it comes and whither it goes. "So is every one that is born of the Spirit" (v. 8).

Should Have Known. When Jesus expressed surprise that Nicodemus could be a master in Israel and not know these things, He implied that it was the will of His Father that Nicodemus and all teachers of the Jews should have had a spiritual comprehension of the Old Testament Scriptures. He would chide other Pharisees later, "Go ye and learn what that meaneth" (Matthew 9:13) or "Have ye not read in the law?" (Matthew 12:3, 5). Christ himself had read and understood under the teaching of His heavenly Father. The Spirit of God, who had given these Scriptures in the first place, was available to its readers to enable them to understand.

Heavenly Things. Here Jesus gave Nicodemus a glimpse of the realm in which He himself lived. He was then telling Nicodemus of matters which one on earth could know. But He knew of heavenly things which of course Nicodemus could not receive. "We speak that we do know, and testify that we have seen; and ye receive not our witness" (v. 11). He then testified (v. 13) to Nicodemus that He had come down from heaven—that heaven was the realm in which He lived. See also John 5:19, 20.

Prediction of Calvary. Then Jesus cited to Nicodemus the Old Testament story with which he was well acquainted. All the Jews knew the record of the wandering of the Israelites in the wilderness on the way to Canaan. They had become rebellious on one occasion, and the Lord sent fiery serpents to punish them. When Moses prayed on their behalf, the Lord instructed him to make a serpent of brass and put it on a pole, promising that all who looked on that brazen serpent would be healed of their poisonous snake bite (Numbers 21:5-9). Jesus told Nicodemus, "Even so must the Son of man be lifted up" (v. 14). He was beginning now to foretell His own death and call attention to the great purpose of His coming into the world. He had hesitated to commit himself in this regard to the throngs that surrounded Him (John 2:23-25), but He was making this commitment to Nicodemus, an attentive listener.

The Gospel. Then follows the golden text of the Bible. "For God so loved the world that he gave his only begotten Son, that whosoever believeth in him should not perish, but have everlasting life" (John 3:16). This is the gospel in a nutshell. In this statement Christ presents His Father as not only a God of power, far removed from His creatures, but also a God of love that impelled Him to give the life of His only Son to effect the salvation of men. John the Baptist's statement (John 1:29) concerning the world nature of God's plan was here confirmed as well as its Calvary (sacrifice-to-death) provision. He added that His death would provide the alternative between perishing and living forever.

A New Condemnation. Next He assured Nicodemus (and all of us) that His mission on the earth was not to condemn the world but rather to save it. Men were already on the way to eternal death, but He had come to save them and to give them everlasting life. Condemnation already rested upon unbelievers but would be lifted from those who believed in Him. Now a new feature was introduced. Instead of the condemnation being because of their inherent evil or their having broken the ten commandments, it was because they refused to believe on Him who came to save them. This then is the cardinal sin, that men prefer to live on in darkness and condemnation rather than to follow Him who is the Light of the world. He came to call those who prefer light over darkness.

Lesson 11

JOHN'S FURTHER WITNESS OF JESUS (*John* 3:22-36)

Judean Ministry. From Jerusalem Jesus moved out into the land of Judea, continuing His miracles and His teachings. He too began to baptize, although the actual baptizing was performed by His disciples (John 4:2), thus perpetuating the ministry of John the Baptist, Christ also preached repentance unto baptism (Matthew 4:17). There was a period of time in which these two preachers of repentance ran parallel in their ministry. John continued to preach and to baptize farther up the river Jordan in the eastern part of Samaria.

John's Disciples. At least two of John's disciples had left him to follow Jesus, but evidently he still had many others. The Book of Acts tells us (18:25; 19:3, 4) that the ministry of John's disciples was quite extensive. A certain Jew named Apollos, who had been born at Alexandria, knew the baptism of John and was fervent in preaching and teaching what he had learned. Either Apollos or another disciple of John had so preached in Ephesus that there were at least twelve men who had been baptized unto John's baptism.

Certain of John's disciples now got into an argument with the Jews about the question of purifying. John was baptizing with water unto repentance, and the Jews evidently questioned the orthodoxy of this procedure. At this time they took occasion to tell John that Jesus whom he had baptized was now in turn also baptizing and that great crowds were flocking to Him. Whether or not their motive was to provoke John to jealousy their comment did not produce this result. It gave John occasion to continue his wonderful testimony to the Lord Christ.

Christ Greater than John. First of all, John laid down the basic principle, "A man can receive nothing, except it be given him from heaven" (v. 27). "In other words," John said, "neither I nor He

56

could do anything except by the enabling of God from heaven, therefore comparisons are useless." He then proceeded to talk about the Christ. He repeated that he had merely come to precede Him. He likened his relationship to Jesus to that of the friend of the Bridegroom. He was happy in the good fortune which the Bridegroom was enjoying. He predicted Christ's increase and his corresponding decrease. Another comparison which he cited was the disparity between earth and heaven. "He that cometh from heaven is above all" (v. 31).

Christ's Exalted Place. John then repeated the testimony which Christ had given concerning Himself in John 3:11-13. "We speak that we do know, and testify that we have seen." John knew that he had been sent of God, but now he declared that Christ also had been sent of God and as such was speaking the words of God. He testified that the Holy Spirit, whom he had seen descending like a dove and remaining upon Christ, had indeed been God's gift without measure unto Him. With the Holy Spirit, the Father had given all things into the hand of Christ, His Son. His climactic declaration concerning the Christ was a repetition and confirmation of Christ's words to Nicodemus in verse 16. "He that believeth on the Son hath everlasting life: and he that believeth not the Son shall not see life; but the wrath of God abideth on him" (v. 36).

JOHN CAST INTO PRISON (*Matthew* 14:3-5; *Mark* 6:17-20; *Luke* 3:19, 20)

Climax of John's Ministry. Shortly after this magnificent declaration concerning the seniority and divine sonship of the Christ whom he had introduced, John returned to his preaching and condemnation of sin. He had denounced all sinners and called the Pharisees and Sadducees a generation of vipers (Matthew 3:7). Now this rugged preacher who feared not the person of men denounced King Herod, the Roman governor of Galilee and Perea (Mark 6:17). Sin is sin, even in high places, and John the Baptist said so. Whereupon the wicked Herodias prevailed upon her husband to throw John into prison (Matthew 14:3). This ended the public ministry of John the Baptist.

Personal Influence over Herod. But there are two other events on record in connection with the life of John. The first of these had to do with his personal contact with Herod after he was put in prison. It seemed there was some measure of conscience left in this wicked king, for the Word says he feared John for he knew he was a holy and just man. Herod evidently had many conversations with John and heard gladly many things from him. However, as with Jezebel over Ahab, the wicked Herodias dominated his life. So Herod left him to languish in prison.

The other event in John's life prior to his murder occurred later when Jesus was preaching in Galilee. Jesus was conscious of His relationship with John and was considerate of him. When He heard the Pharisees were comparing John unfavorably with Him, He feared that His ministry would reflect upon John and therefore determined to leave Judea and return to Galilee (John 4:1, 3). The arrest of John came just at this time. Jesus proceeded with His plans to go into Galilee (Matthew 4:12).

CONVERSATION WITH SAMARITAN WOMAN (*John* 4:5-39)

Through Samaria. As usual, Christ's plans were directed by His Father. He was impressed to go through Samaria. It was customary for the Pharisees to detour around Samaria in order to avoid contact with these despised people. But Christ was not a Pharisee, neither were the Samaritans despised by Him. He came to save all men and He was now busy seeking to save some.

Contrast with Nicodemus. We come now to the story of Christ's conversation with the Samaritan woman. This is in contrast with His discourse with Nicodemus. He was a ruler of the Jews and a high level Pharisee; she was a despised Samaritan woman of questionable character. Conversation with these two remotely removed individuals was equally important to Him and had the same objective, the salvation of their souls.

Jesus Begins the Conversation. Jesus and His party doubtless planned for their noon rest by a well of water. Jesus sat on the side of the well to rest after His wearisome journey while the disciples went to the nearby village to buy food. Rebekah of old came to a well in God's providence where she contacted God's messenger through whom she was later introduced to her bridegroom. Now another woman came providentially to another well to find a messenger of God through whom she would receive eternal life. As with Nicodemus, so now the Lord began immediately to explain to her the way of salvation. He used a very natural point of contact and incidentally gave beautiful proof of His real humanity. Like the rest of us, He had become tired by His long exertion. He asked the

Samaritan woman for a drink of water. There was no means attached to these wells by which an individual could draw water. Each person must provide his own bucket, and that is why He, as a stranger, was dependent upon one who lived nearby to come with a bucket with which to draw water. This provided Him with an opportunity to express real humility and friendliness with the neighborhood woman who then chanced to come to the well to draw water.

Prepares Her Heart. Then Jesus began to open the well of her nature in preparation for His teaching concerning the living water. The woman was impressed with His condescension and was ready for His direct statement, "If thou knewest the gift of God, and who it is that saith to thee, Give me to drink; thou wouldest have asked of him, and he would have given thee living water" (v. 10). He had frankly asked her for a gift to induce her to ask of Him a gift in return. Immediately He said the gift would be a person in the form of Him who now spoke to her. He is the source of living water. Her next question was what He wanted her to ask. "Whence then hast thou that living water?" (v. 11). His beautiful description of that water which He would give follows in verses 13, 14. He said it would satisfy completely and finally and would be constantly within a person, springing up into everlasting life. Although she confused the water about which Jesus spoke with the water which she came to draw, she nevertheless asked Him to give her that water. Her respect for Him was indicated by the title "Sir" with which she now addressed Him.

Completes That Preparation. But Jesus had to dig deeper into her life to prepare her for His gift of living water. He tactfully inquired into her private life and caused her to expose and confess her wicked past. Now she balanced the confession of her sin with the confession of her faith in Him as a prophet (v. 19). This led her to a discussion of religion as she knew it. This in turn enabled Jesus to tell her of religion "in spirit and in truth." In so telling, He told the world not only that His Father is a Spirit, but also that He is seeking people to worship Him in spirit and in truth. And now came the climax of the conversation. Of her own accord the woman confessed her faith in the coming Messiah which is called Christ. Jesus immediately announced that He was that Messiah.

Another Figure of Speech. In another beautiful figure of speech Jesus described the new birth by which one enters into the kingdom of heaven. As the wind symbolizes the work of the Holy Spirit, so water likewise is a symbol of the eternal flowing of divine life in those who accept Him as the Messiah.

True to spiritual nature, as with Andrew and Philip, when they first found the Lord, this woman also went into the city and invited others to come out and see this Man whom she had found to be the Christ.

Pattern for Soul Winning. It is good here to notice how Christ's method in winning this soul to himself was a perfect pattern for any soul winner to follow.

1. First of all, He used a happenstance of life: He sat on the well.
2. Then He humbled himself. "Give me to drink."
3. He awakened her curiosity. "If thou knewest."
4. He worked toward the goal of the revelation of himself.
5. He used a point of contact: the water.
6. He introduced what would be an advantage to her. "Never thirst again."
7. He described the greatness of this advantage.
8. He then brought personal conviction and—
9. Built her faith in Him.
10. He avoided controversy.
11. At last He revealed himself as the Messiah.
12. She went to testify.

The results of this personal work were the conversion of the woman herself and of the whole town, thus sowing the seed for the revival which followed under the ministry of Philip as recorded in Acts 8.

Still another figure. In the meantime the disciples returned from the village with food for their noonday lunch. This again was a contact for Christ to use, for His disciples needed His teaching as well as did the Samaritan woman. To them He said, "I have meat to eat that ye know not of" (v. 32). Then came His declaration that the conversation in which He had just engaged with its happy results was indeed the very food of His life. His Father had sent Him to perform that task and He was happy in performing it.

Disciples Must Follow. Jesus then introduced what He would develop and emphasize to the end of His ministry. The work which His Father had given Him to perform was the very work that He would give His disciples to continue. He was instructing them in the very best method of pedagogy; namely, performing in their presence the things which they themselves should perform. As He had encouraged the woman by telling her the advantages of the living water, so He now encouraged His disciples by promising them wages and fruit unto life eternal if they would work in the great harvest field. He instructed them to lift up their eyes and look on the fields which were already ripe to harvest. He spoke too of the succession of workers, for one would sow and another would reap. This is a continuing message to all succeeding generations of those who follow Him.

Many More Converted. The harvest which Jesus began to reap in the salvation of a single Samaritan woman expanded immediately to include many people of the Samaritan village. Following the testimony of the woman, they came themselves to hear Him. When they besought Him to tarry with them, He did so for two days. In so doing He extended and completed His harvest of this village, for many more believed, saying, "This is indeed the Christ, the Saviour of the world" (vv. 41, 42).

PALESTINE
IN THE
TIME OF CHRIST

PHOENICIA

SIDON

SYRIA

MEDITERRANEAN

TYRE

MT. HERMON
CAESAREA PHILIPPI

GALILEE
CHORAZIN
CAPERNAUM
BETHSAIDA

SEA

CANA
TIBERIAS

SEA
OF
GALILEE

GERGESA

NAZARETH

NAIN

GADARA

BETHABARA

SAMARIA

DECAPOLIS

SAMARIA

SYCHAR
MT. GERIZIM

JOPPA

RIVER JORDAN

PERAEA

EMMAUS
JERICHO
JERUSALEM
BETHANY
BETHLEHEM

JUDEA

WILDERNESS OF JUDEA

DEAD

SEA

N A B A T A E A

A R A B I A

62

STUDY QUESTIONS—UNIT ONE

LESSON 1

1. Give the general contents of each of the four units of this course.
2. What two qualities did Christ and the Father share before the foundation of the world?
3. Who was the divine Agent in the creation of the world?
4. List four theophanies of Christ in Old Testament times.

LESSON 2

1. What was the first prophecy concerning Christ?
2. What would you consider the most important type of Christ given in the Old Testament? Why do you consider it so?
3. What feature of the Jewish Messianic expectation was it impossible for Christ to fulfill at His first advent?

LESSON 3

1. Into what three religious sects were the Jews divided when Jesus came?
2. Give three characteristics of the world scene when Jesus came.
3. List all the purposes of Christ's coming that are given in the text.

LESSON 4

1. What is the chief difference between the two genealogies of Jesus?
2. Cite five times in which angels took part in the life of Jesus.
3. What is meant by "The Virgin Birth"?
4. What was the first miracle in connection with the birth of Christ?

LESSON 5

1. List five classes of people related to the birth of Jesus.
2. What is meant by the incarnation of Christ?
3. What two aged people greeted the Baby Christ upon His presentation in the temple?

LESSON 6

1. What do you think inspired the Wise Men to seek Christ at His birth?
2. Who told them where to find Him? And how?
3. Give two reasons why Joseph took the Child into Egypt.

LESSON 7

1. What does the Bible tell us about the early childhood of Jesus?
2. What was revealed about Christ when He was twelve years old?
3. What does the Bible tell us about the later childhood and youth of Jesus?
4. List four textbooks studied by Christ in His education.

LESSON 8

1. Give seven words used in the Bible to describe the ministry of John the Baptist.
2. What were the two great parts of his message?
3. Why was Jesus baptized in water?
4. What three things did Satan tempt Jesus to do?

LESSON 9

1. In what two special capacities did John the Baptist introduce Jesus?
2. Who were Jesus' first five disciples?
3. What was the first miracle Jesus performed?

LESSON 10

1. What quality of His Father did Jesus reveal when He cleansed the temple?
2. Quote two outstanding texts found in Jesus' discourse with Nicodemus.
3. List five different facts which Jesus announced to Nicodemus.

LESSON 11

1. How did John compare himself with Jesus?
2. Why was John thrown into prison?
3. Contrast the Samaritan woman with Nicodemus.
4. List at least six steps which Jesus took in bringing this woman to salvation.

UNIT TWO

Lessons 12 through 23

EARLY GALILEAN MINISTRY

LATER GALILEAN MINISTRY

LAST GALILEAN MINISTRY

Lesson 12

ARRIVAL IN GALILEE (*Matthew* 4:12, 17; *Mark* 1:14, 15; *Luke* 4:14, 15; *John* 4:43-45)

The interrupted journey into Galilee is now continued. Within a short time Jesus enters His native province of the North. This area was ruled over by Herod Antipas who later killed John and before whom Jesus Himself stood when on trial in Jerusalem. This province was about thirty miles wide and sixty miles from north to south. Josephus records that there were then about 240 cities and villages in Galilee with a total of well over three million population. The Sea of Galilee on the eastern border of the province was about thirteen miles long and seven miles wide. It lay 682 feet below sea level.

The Gennesaret plain is located on the northwest shore. This area contained the cities of Capernaum, Bethsaida, and Chorazin, important points on the great caravan route from the eastern countries into Egypt. This contact with foreign travelers gave the people of Galilee a cosmopolitan spirit and viewpoint. They were largely men of the lower and middle classes, tradesmen and laborers, "common people" who heard Jesus gladly. They were not directly under the influence of the priestly and religious class which characterized and dominated Jerusalem and Judea. Galilee proved to be a very fertile ground for the ministry of our Lord.

Christ was conscious of the fact that this was His home province where He had been reared and was known as a fellow laborer. This accounts for the comment in John 4:44, "Jesus himself testified, that a prophet hath no honor in his own country." Although aware of this fact, He also knew and here practiced the great principle of the gospel that one's first spiritual obligation is to his own people. He later was to tell His disciples (Luke 24:47) that they should begin their worldwide ministry at Jerusalem. However, there were many Galileans whose only knowledge and contact with Christ was when they saw Him at the feast in Jerusalem. They had there witnessed the many miracles He did (John 2:23), and some were doubtless among those who there learned to believe on His name. So, when they learned that the new prophet had now come back to Galilee, they received Him. It could have been that many of those who had known Him formerly were now moved by curiosity to come and see what their former neighbor from Nazareth had become.

Another comment concerning the entry of Christ upon His Galilean ministry was that He "returned in the power of the Spirit into Galilee" (Luke 4:14). The Spirit whom John had seen descend upon Jesus in the form of a dove, not only rested upon but remained upon Him (John 1:32, 33). Now, many months later, following His temptation in the wilderness and His early ministry at Jerusalem and in Judea, Jesus was still moving under the anointing of the Holy Spirit. As John said, "God giveth not the Spirit by measure unto him." These words referred to the duration as well as the quantity of that enduement. As Peter later said (Acts 10:38), the anointing with the Holy Ghost and power resulted in His going about and doing good. Upon His arrival in Galilee He immediately began to preach and to say, "The kingdom of God is at hand: repent ye, and believe the gospel." It is specifically recorded that He taught in their synagogues, being glorified of all, "and there went out a fame of him through all the region round about." This indicates a general initial acceptance of His ministry even before the specific miracles and sermons were recorded.

Second Miracle at Cana (*John* 4:46-54)

This incident is told as if it were selected at random from His ministry in the various synagogues and wherever He had proclaimed the kingdom of God and called for the repentance of the people. This event records the appearance of the miracle ministry begun at this very point many months before and practiced in the province of Judea. Cana was the home of Nathanael, and it could have been in Nathanael's home this incident took place.

The Holy Spirit appears to be taking pains to indicate to us that Christ's ministry from the very beginning extended to and included the Gentiles. There is an early and constant emphasis on Christ's love for and ministry to, everybody, including the Gentiles. Foreigners worshiped at His cradle in Bethlehem, and as a baby He was taken to Egypt. John the Baptist proclaimed that He was to bear away the sin of the world and Christ confirmed that God loved the entire world and gave His Son to die for "whosoever believeth in him." John made the sweeping statement that "he that believeth on the Son hath everlasting life" (John 3:36).

Most of the 4th chapter of John is taken up with the account of the conversion of the Samaritan woman, and now at the beginning of His ministry in Galilee we have an extended account of His helping another Gentile. The Roman overlords of the country were noblemen. This "certain nobleman" was resident at Capernaum, a seat of the government of Galilee and the place where the Galileans paid their taxes. Tradition tells us that this nobleman was Chuza, Herod's steward, whose wife Johanna was among the women who ministered unto Christ of their substance (Luke 8:2, 3). The village of Cana is about twenty miles from Capernaum. This nobleman traveled that distance for he had heard that Jesus could be found at Cana. He besought Him that He would come down and heal his son who was at the point of death. Christ's immediate response was characteristic: "Except ye see signs and wonders, ye will not believe" (v. 48). This was not only to distinguish between mere miracle seekers and those who would be sincere believers; it also was a test of the nobleman's faith. Later through His ministry Christ would make similar tests of persons who sought Him.

The incident is worthy of record because this man, like the Syrophenician woman later, passed the test. He not only refused to be discouraged or offended but he pressed his claim, expressing his faith that Christ's coming would save his child. When the Lord told him to go home for his son was living, he immediately accepted His word at its face value and returned to his home. He had faith that acted, and of course it was rewarded by the healing of his son. It might be noticed also that here is a record of gradual healing. True, this was exceptional, for the usual practice was that instant healing followed His touch or His word of authority. But this record is for the encouragement of those whose faith would be tested by a delaying of their healing. Note also that this healing resulted in the man's conversion to Christ along with the conversion of other members of his household. The sincerity of his wife's conversion has been indicated in the paragraph above. It is specifically recorded that this is the second Galilean miracle. However, it is merely the beginning of many marvelous acts of power which later attended Christ's ministry in His native province of Galilee.

PREACHES AT NAZARETH (*Luke* 4:16-30)

In the story we now study, Jesus referred to the things which He had done in Capernaum (Luke 4:23). This evidently referred to deeds of healing, the fame of which had been carried to Nazareth and was already known there before Jesus returned to preach at His hometown. We are often reminded that there were many things which happened in the life of Christ which are not recorded in detail. John himself said (John 21:25) that the full story, if written, would fill the world with the books that should be written.

It was not enough that Christ should go to His home province but He must return to His hometown and the very synagogue He had attended as a child. The little phrase "as his custom was" reveals that our Lord was a habitual churchgoer. He had evidently acquired a certain position in His local church which made it not unusual for Him to stand to read the Scriptures. But this was no ordinary occasion. Much had happened since He had worshiped here. He had been baptized and introduced to His public ministry, far to the south. He had not only gone through the fires of Satan's temptation but He had been proclaimed by John the Baptist as the Son of God and the great Saviour of the world. He had likewise exercised this authority both in cleansing the temple at Jerusalem and in preaching, baptizing, and performing miracles throughout Judea. A certain portion of Scripture was already being fulfilled in His life and ministry. As Jesus stood to read in the synagogue He turned immediately to that passage which is found in Isaiah 61. The Spirit which rested on Christ was the very Spirit who was in Isaiah as he penned those words in the first place. "The Spirit of Christ which was in them" (1 Peter 1:11).

This passage (Luke 4:18, 19) constitutes a preview of Christ's entire ministry. To His own fellow townsmen this premiere was given. How fitting that we as well as they should have a condensed statement of the whole life and ministry of Christ at the very beginning of that ministry. The first declaration was that it was the Holy Ghost himself who was resting upon Christ and was constituting the wisdom and power with which He functioned. Preaching was to constitute the greatest part of His ministry for it is mentioned three times in this preview: He was to preach the gospel, to preach deliverance, and preach the acceptable year of the Lord. He was likewise to heal, to restore sight, and to set at liberty. The objects and recipients of His ministry were to be the poor, the broken-hearted, the captives, the blind, and the bruised. This was to be the acceptable year of the Lord. National deliverance was not included in His program. He was not yet to be the type of Messiah they anticipated. This could easily have been observed, but His listeners shared with their fellow Jews the belief that their Christ would set them free from their foreign oppressors and exalt them over all the nations of the world. It should be noted that Jesus did not quote all of Isaiah's message. The "day of vengeance of our God" (Isaiah 61:2) was deliberately omitted from the reading, for this was not yet the "day of vengeance." However, all the rest was then and there fulfilled, and He quietly announced that fact. This was virtually a proclamation that He was the true Messiah and was about to fulfill the functions described by Isaiah.

The announcement at first stunned His listeners. "The eyes of all of them that were in the synagogue were fastened on him." He doubtless elaborated on the features of His ministry and described the acceptable service which He was to render. They "wondered at the gracious words which proceeded out of his mouth." But then it dawned on them that this after all was Joseph's son. Had He not lived among them for thirty years and shared their lot in an inconspicuous way? They began to think other and more critical thoughts without expressing them. But Jesus read those thoughts and mentioned them publicly. He knew that in their minds they were challenging Him to repeat in Nazareth the miracles He had recently performed in Capernaum. There was evidently sarcasm in their proverb, "Physician, heal thyself."

Jesus knew their exact attitude toward Him and proceeded immediately to meet them on their own ground. As He had forthrightly put His finger on Nicodemus' need sometime before in Jerusalem, so once more he went to the heart of the matter and declared that they were children of their fathers in unbelief. God had to leave the many widows and lepers of Israel in times past to find a Gentile widow and a Gentile leper with faith to be blessed and healed. Instead of acknowledging the truth of His diagnosis and admitting their unbelief and need, they rose up against Him in great wrath. This of course was no surprise to Him for He knew what was in man and realized that rejection hardens and infuriates. But He brought their decision to a climax just the same, and we have the record of His action and their reaction. His time had not yet come for destruction at Jewish hands, so He quietly passed through the midst of them and went His way. This was Satan's second attempt to destroy Him, but His divine Protector-Father again delivered Him.

Lesson 13

Upon this rejection in His hometown, it is recorded that Jesus left Nazareth and came and dwelt in Capernaum. This means that He moved His residence from Nazareth and made Capernaum His new home and headquarters. There is tragedy and pathos in this statement. It is tragic for people to be left behind by the Redeemer, and this early instance in the life of Christ demonstrates that such a tragedy is possible. In Matthew 23 it is recorded that at the end of His earthly ministry He left the Pharisees and the whole Jewish nation. "Behold, your house is left unto you desolate" (Matthew 23:38). When judgment comes it begins at the house of God (1 Peter 4:17). And so we should not be surprised that His first act of rejection came to His own little city of Nazareth. This is a characteristic of the Christ of which we will be wise to take serious note.

This move of Christ's was foreseen by Isaiah. Matthew stated specifically that His move to Capernaum was in fulfillment of Isaiah's prophecy (Isaiah 9:1, 2), "The land of Zabulon, and the land of Nephthalim, by the way of the sea, beyond Jordan, Galilee of the Gentiles; the people which sat in darkness saw great light; and to them which sat in the region and shadow of death light is sprung up." This metropolis of the northern tribes is described as being in great darkness and as having the good fortune that the Light of the world was sent to dwell there. That the region is called "of the Gentiles" is a comment upon the extent to which the Jewish quality of the population had been penetrated by foreigners. The Roman nobleman from Capernaum had already witnessed a mighty healing in his home, and he was but the beginning of the reaping of a Gentile harvest in this area.

73

MIRACULOUS DRAUGHT OF FISHES (*Luke* 5:1-9)

This was not Christ's first visit to Capernaum, even in His capacity as Messiah. Many months before, following His first miracle at Cana of Galilee, He and His mother and His brethren and disciples went down to Capernaum and "continued there not many days" (John 2:12). As seen in Lesson 12 it would appear that He had gone down to Capernaum following the second miracle at Cana and had performed the miracles which He referred to in His sermon at Nazareth. Small wonder then that when He came to Capernaum again the people pressed upon Him to hear His words.

He was evidently a lover of the sea for He was standing by the lake as the people crowded upon Him. It was natural also that He would be there, possibly visiting Simon and Andrew, disciples who had begun to follow Him at Jordan and had been with Him in His Judean ministry and on His return trip through Samaria. They had temporarily gone back to their fishing in Galilee and at that moment were on the shore, washing their nets. He felt free to enter into Simon's ship and request him to move it a little from the land that He might more easily teach the people.

When He finished speaking, He suggested to Simon that they push the ship out into deeper water and attempt to take in some fish. Simon protested that they had been trying all night to catch fish but without success. However, he had learned the authority and power of this Man of Nazareth and agreed to obey Him regardless. He had no sooner done so than they enclosed a great number of fishes, enough to break their net. In God's providence their partners, James and John, were near at hand, so they beckoned to them for help. There were almost enough fish to sink both boats. This is a case of God's abundant provision in response to obedience and in answer to prayer, "Exceeding abundantly above all that we ask or think" (Ephesians 3:20). This was overwhelming confirmation to Peter of the divine power of the new Teacher, and he fell at His feet, confessing his own sinfulness and the lordship of this Christ. The miraculous draught of fishes at the beginning of Christ's ministry was a demonstration and illustration of abundant results in the great enterprise of fishing for souls.

CALLS FISHERMEN (*Matthew* 4:18-22; *Mark* 1:16-20; *Luke* 5:10, 11)

It was on this appropriate occasion that Jesus confirmed His call of these disciples. Their probationary period of following Him was now climaxed by this personal miracle. It provided the assurance that this was indeed the Christ and that He deserved complete and final consecration of their lives to His service. This was also an appropriate situation both for Christ and His disciples in which to make this final decision. As with the woman at the well, to whom He presented the spiritual reality in terms of satisfying water, so now He spoke of Christian service in terms of catching fish. He Himself was the Master along this line as He had so forcefully demonstrated. The literal fish, however, were but symbols of the great multitude of men who needed catching and bringing to shore. Jesus said to Simon, "Fear not; from henceforth thou shalt catch men." Matthew used the expression, "Follow me, and I will make you fishers of men." It would take years of teaching and particularly of following Christ until they could graduate from His school. Peter's first experience on the Day of Pentecost was a graphic demonstration as to how well he had learned his lesson. All four fishermen were now ready to leave their ships, their father, and the old profession to follow Christ.

Casts Out Demons at Capernaum (*Mark* 1:23-28; *Luke* 4:33-37)

Christ respected the religious institutions of His day. He not only taught the people when on the seashore but He taught them also in the synagogue on the sabbath day. They were astonished at His doctrine for His word was with power. They noticed that He taught them as one that had authority and not as the scribes. At Nazareth gracious words proceeded out of His mouth, and now they observed that His word was with power and authority.

On one occasion as they were in the synagogue, a man with an unclean spirit interrupted the service and cried out with a loud voice. Here we have an introduction to the clear teaching of the Scripture concerning the reality of demons. Their presence and activity in foreign lands today is reported by many missionaries. In any country where wicked people give themselves over to demon power the demons move in quickly and possess such persons. Although their activity in and through human beings usually takes the form of pronounced sinfulness, yet they can lie dormant for a while and even go to church.

Here Christ encountered an individual who was possessed of an unclean spirit among the worshipers in the Jewish synagogue. The man disturbed the service with a loud cry, saying, "Let us alone; what have we to do with thee, thou Jesus of Nazareth?" The demon proceeded immediately to identify this Jesus of Nazareth as the Holy One of God. Here was a recognition and confession on the part of the demonic world that Jesus is indeed the Messiah. As James declares (2:19), the demons also believe and tremble. They likewise recognize His power over them, for they expressed the fear that He had come to destroy them. But fear and respect by demons is not pleasing to Christ, and He rebuked the devil and commanded him to come out of the man. He demonstrated the authority which the evil spirit recognized. This was a witness to the assembled people of the unusual character and ministry of the new preacher. They were all amazed and declared, "What thing is this? what new doctrine is this? for with authority commandeth he even the unclean spirits, and they do obey him." "And immediately his fame spread abroad throughout all the region round about Galilee."

HEALS PETER'S WIFE'S MOTHER (*Matthew* 8:14, 15; *Mark* 1:29-31; *Luke* 4:38, 39)

After the church service Jesus and His four committed disciples went to the home of Simon and Andrew. Simon's wife's mother had come in to help in their entertainment; but unfortunately she had become ill with a great fever, possibly that very morning. When the men came into the home they were immediately advised of her illness. They recognized Christ's power over sickness, for had not the nobleman's son been healed in that very city of Capernaum? So they asked Him to intervene on her behalf. He responded and rebuked the fever and took her by the hand and lifted her up. She was healed instantly and went about her task of ministering to the household and guests.

HEALS MANY (*Matthew* 8:16, 17; *Mark* 1:32-34; *Luke* 4:40, 41)

The presence of this great Healer very naturally attracted many sick people of the city. They waited until the sun was setting, which ended the sabbath, and then they swarmed in upon Him. They were very sick, for the Scripture says they had to be brought to Him. He was moved with compassion when He saw them and laid His hands upon every one of them and healed them. There is no respect of persons with our Lord and no limitation or exhaustion of His power. The deliverance of the demoniac at the church service that morning must have inspired faith for the deliverance of others similarly afflicted. Many who were possessed with demons were brought to Him, and He cast out the spirits with His word. Once more they cried out, "Thou art Christ the Son of God," another testimony concerning His Messiahship.

Matthew specifically identifies this healing ministry of Christ with the prediction of Isaiah some seven hundred years previously. In his well-known fifty-third chapter describing the great atonement work of the Cross, Isaiah had said, "Himself took over infirmities, and bare our sicknesses." This definitely designates divine healing as being part of the Atonement. Through the great healing power that was inherent in Him and by virtue of the authority over the power of the devil which He would purchase by His death on the cross, Jesus here proceeded to exercise that Blood-bought right and to destroy the work of the devil. Here is sound scriptural basis for saying that healing is in the atonement of our Lord.

RISES EARLY TO PRAY (*Mark* 1:35-38; *Luke* 4:42, 43)

Here we are introduced to the private devotional life of our Lord. More than that, we have the secret of His wisdom and power. He maintained His filial relationship with His Father by these trysting hours spent alone with Him. Also, as the great pattern-setter for us His followers, He was revealing what could be the secret of divine wisdom and power for us as well. It is the simple secret of prayer. To avoid the rush and the many contacts of the day, He arose a great while before dawn. He sought a solitary place where He could be alone with His Father. The content and substance of His prayer is not revealed. Our only guide to this knowledge is the impulse of our own hearts as we too get alone with God.

At this very beginning of the disciples' walk with Him we see Simon emerging as their leader. "Simon and they that were with him followed after him." Luke states that the people also sought Him and requested Him to abide with them. Jesus' response was that He must press on into the next towns for unto them also was He sent. His face was set on a thorough coverage of His field and the complete consummation of every phase of the work to which His Father had sent Him.

Lesson 14

Tours Galilee (*Matthew* 4:23-25; *Mark* 1:39; *Luke* 4:44)

With this handful of committed disciples Jesus began a tour of all parts of Galilee. It was natural that He used the synagogues as a forum. He preached and taught, casting out devils and healing all manner of sickness and disease among the people. His fame extended not only through Galilee but through the northern country of Syria as well. In this new area "they brought unto him all sick people that were taken with divers diseases and torments, and those which were possessed with devils and those which were lunatic, and those that had the palsy." It is reported simply that "he healed them." Multitudes swarmed on Him from all Galilee and as far south as Jerusalem and Judea and across the river Jordan.

Heals Leper (*Matthew* 8:2-4; *Mark* 1:40-45; *Luke* 5:12-17)

One of the most loathsome and infectious diseases of the East was leprosy. It was natural that Jesus soon would come in touch with this plague. A man who was suffering in the advanced stages of leprosy came to Him, fell on his knees, and besought Him for healing. He put his request into a challenge, "If thou wilt, thou canst make me clean." Here was faith in the Lord's ability but an open question as to His willingness. The Lord accepted the challenge. He proved His willingness and compassion by actually touching the leper and commanding that he be clean. It was not necessary that He touch the loathsome sore, for He had simply spoken the word of authority on previous occasions and demons and diseases had obeyed Him. He went the full length, however, and identified Himself with the need of mankind. He stooped all the way down actually to touch the leper. Immediately the leprosy departed from the man and he was cleansed.

There comes to light here a provision of Old Testament times

78

and an expectation for the healing of leprosy even then. In the 14th chapter of Leviticus a statute was laid down providing the ritual for the returning of a leper to normal life after he had been healed. This revealed that healing was in the great plan of God for the deliverance of mankind. That not one leper in all Israel availed himself of this divine healing, and only Naaman the Syrian was healed in those days, does not reflect upon the validity of God's plan and provision. On this occasion Jesus reverted to that Levitical procedure by instructing the healed leper to show himself to the priest and offer the gift which Moses had commanded.

We can assume that he obeyed the Lord. In addition, however, he went out and blazed the matter abroad, publishing everywhere what the Lord had done for him. This resulted in an increase of the crowds which pressed upon Jesus so that He could no longer enter into a city but was forced to remain outside in desert places. The people came to Him even there from every quarter and were healed of their diseases. In the midst of this ministry, however, it is recorded that He withdrew Himself still further into the wilderness and prayed. He was then visited by a committee of religious leaders and doctors of the law from every town of Galilee and Judea and from Jerusalem. This did not hinder the ministry of the Lord for still "the power of the Lord was present to heal them."

HEALS PALSIED MAN (*Matthew* 9:1-8; *Mark* 2:1-12)

Eventually He was able to return to Capernaum. But immediately the city became aware of His presence. We can assume that He was once more in Simon Peter's home. They crowded in upon Him and quickly there was not even room near the door on the outside. As he preached to them, there was a disturbance. It was not a demoniac this time but a quartet of men who had devised an ingenious plan to bring their palsied friend and place him at Jesus' feet. They bypassed the crowd outside and climbed up and out on the flat Oriental roof of the home. They actually broke up the tile to make an opening large enough to let down the bed on which lay the man who was sick of the palsy. Jesus immediately interpreted this act of theirs as an expression of faith and responded by announcing to the sick of the palsy that his sins were forgiven.

This might have been a surprise to the man and his four friends, but it was more of a shock to the scribes and Pharisees who were sitting there. Everyone seemed to realize that only God could forgive sins, and here was a man quietly assuming a prerogative of deity. Of course, He had already been introduced by John the Baptist as the Redeemer Messiah. The demons in the synagogue had called Him the Holy One of Israel, and He had abundantly demonstrated divine power by the healings which He performed, and by turning the water into wine, and by the miraculous draught of fishes. He himself could have been the one to be surprised by their reaction to His calm procedure in the path of divine activity. However, He was running head-on against the unbelief of His time and He immediately challenged them. As with the congregation in the synagogue at Nazareth, He read their thoughts and announced them openly. He compared the healing which they expected with the forgiving of sins which they did not expect. He asked which was easier to perform. Then He tied the two together and said that His healing power should be accepted as authority for His forgiving power. With this He spoke the word of healing to the man, who responded and took up his bed and went home. This was a graphic demonstration of the double power of the Christ who was in their midst. The people were amazed and glorified God, saying they had never seen it on this fashion before.

CALLS MATTHEW (*Matthew* 9:9; *Mark* 2:13-15; *Luke* 5:27-29)

Jesus now proceeded to ignore and violate the social caste system of His time. The Jews who lowered themselves to become tax collectors for the hated Romans were themselves hated doubly for what was considered their perfidy and treason. They had sold their social standing and patriotic rating for the money they received in payment for their service. But loathed and despised as they were, they still had precious souls and were dear to the heart of the Master. He went His way, evidently on the Capernaum road, and saw Levi the publican, also called Matthew, sitting at the place for the payment of the custom tax. As Jesus passed by, He simply said to Matthew, "Follow me." This was a terse invitation to join His disciples. Matthew recognized it as such and accepted it immediately.

EATS WITH SINNERS (*Matthew* 9:10-13; *Mark* 2:15-17; *Luke* 5:29-32)

Matthew not only left his unpopular calling to follow Jesus but made a great feast in his own home to which he invited Christ and His disciples and a number of other tax gatherers and sinners. This was in honor of the Christ whom he was now to follow. It provided him the proper occasion for announcing his conversion to this Christ and his abandonment of his old profession and circle of friends. The Lord and His disciples responded to this invitation and sat down to eat with Levi Matthew and his many friends.

There was not the privacy to which we are accustomed on occasions like this. Many scribes and Pharisees saw Jesus and His disciples eating with the publicans and sinners. They immediately questioned the disciples as to why and how this could be. Their Messiah was to be a ruler and a leader of the Jews. As such He would certainly maintain the right social position and not associate with those who were disreputable. But here this Man was having no regard for such social prejudice and snobbery. He did not hesitate to express disapproval of the attitude of the Jewish elite. As a matter of fact He used the occasion for announcing His position concerning this matter: "They that are whole need not a physician; but they that are sick. I came not to call the righteous, but sinners to repentance." An immortal announcement is this, precious and sweet to the ears of all people of lowly or disreputable estate.

This announcement carried with it a scriptural rebuke to His critics. He told them to go and learn the true meaning of Hosea's proclamation, "I will have mercy, and not sacrifice" (6:6). This had been among the pronouncements of their prophets for hundreds of years, and yet it had not impressed them. As a matter of fact they had not learned what Hosea really meant by his statement. Jesus knew its meaning and was now acting upon the principle which Hosea had declared. The heart quality of mercy for those who needed mercy was more preferable to the Lord by far than the temple sacrifices. This principle projects into the religious life of all generations. The heart attitude of kindness toward fellow men is worth far more than external religious observances and standards.

CONCERNING FASTING (*Matthew* 9:14, 15; *Mark* 2:18-20; *Luke* 5:33-35)

The disciples of John who had not followed Jesus and had apparently closed their minds to His teachings and leadership now came to argue with the Lord. They and the Pharisees (not too complimentary an association) had a practice of observing religious fasts quite often. With it was the ceremony of making prayers (Luke 5:33). Christ and His followers had no such practice. The disciples of John felt that this was a breach and a reflection upon them. Either they and the Pharisees were wrong or Jesus and His disciples were wrong, and they asked Jesus to defend the position which He and His disciples took.

Jesus' answer was this illustration. Guests at a wedding party do not fast, for it is an occasion of celebration. But when the Bridegroom is gone the situation would revert to normal and those same people could then consistently fast. In other words, "My disciples are rejoicing in My presence with them, and it is not an occasion for fasting. However, after I have gone they shall fast." This was not only a defense of their practice then, which differed from that of John's disciples and the Pharisees, but it was an announcement that after His ascension into heaven it would be consistent and right that His disciples fast.

PARABLES OF THE GARMENT AND BOTTLES (*Matthew* 9:16, 17; *Mark* 2:21, 22; *Luke* 5:36-39)

It was probably on this same occasion that Jesus spoke this double parable to the people. He said it is not customary to patch an old garment with a piece of new cloth, for the patch would be very noticeable and also the sewing together would not hold. The tear would therefore be made worse in the long run. The other part of the parable was concerning putting new wine into old bottles (wineskins). The old wineskins had become hard and stiff. The fermentation of new wine required room for expansion. Thus the new wine would burst the old wineskins and the wine would be spilled and lost. The moral was simply: Put new wine into new bottles. Evidently the teaching is one and the same. What is that teaching? The old custom of the Jews regarding their attitude toward publicans and sinners, for instance, as well as their rigid custom of fasting and "making prayers" was now old and should be discarded. The new wine of the Kingdom which Jesus brought had life and flexibility in it and deserved new bottles. His gospel was admittedly out of harmony with their religious practices but must be given its own setting and clothing. He was saying, "Don't try to force Me and My teaching into your old hardened traditional ways for there is inevitable conflict between the two."

Lesson 15

HEALS IMPOTENT MAN AT JERUSALEM (*John* 5:1-15)

At this point Jesus went south for some additional ministry in Jerusalem and Judea. He took advantage of the fact there was a feast of the Jews in Jerusalem at that time, and traveled down to take part in that feast. The story of this visit to Jerusalem begins at the pool of Bethesda, near the sheep market. Jesus evidently was attracted by the great multitude of impotent folk who were gathered around that pool.

A strange thing happened here periodically. An angel went down at certain seasons to the pool and stirred its water. This evidently gave healing virtue to the water sufficient to deliver the first person who stepped in after the visit of the angel. Could God have been preparing the people at Jerusalem for the visit of Christ, His great "Angel" who would come at the appointed time and bring healing to those who touched Him?

Upon Christ's arrival at the pool of Bethesda He found a certain man who had had an infirmity for thirty-eight years. Jesus asked him, "Wilt thou be made whole?" Here is at least an implication that healing is part of integrated health. In other words, the human being consists of body, soul, and spirit, and if the physical part is impaired then the man is not whole. It takes physical health to round out a perfect man. The man explained that he had no one to help him into the water, but he no longer needed such help. The great "Angel" had himself arrived and He told the man to pick up his bed and walk. The man obeyed and was made whole immediately.

It so happened that this took place on the Sabbath Day, and the Jews saw the man walking and carrying his pallet. It happened also that carrying a burden on the Sabbath was against Jewish law (not Bible law). This provided another collision of Christ with the crusted

83

religious life of His day. It was a foolish bondage which needed to be broken and discarded. Again He connected a healing with an introduction of a new phase of His ministry. He had told the Pharisees at Capernaum that His power to heal was a proof of His power to forgive sins. Now it justified the breaking of the Jewish custom concerning the Sabbath. Of course it was done deliberately. In response to a question of the Jews the healed man informed them that it was Christ who had healed and instructed him to take up his bed and walk.

Jesus Witnesses Concerning Himself (*John* 5:16-47)

This healing on the sabbath brought Jesus face-to-face with His persecutors. They actually sought to slay Him because He had done these things on the Sabbath Day. Directly to His accusers He made the following declaration: "It is not I who am performing these miracles alone, but my Father is working with me." Instead of placating the Jews and mitigating their opposition, He deliberately aggravated it. They knew immediately that He was making God His Father and even making himself equal with God. This to them was the height of blasphemy, and they sought the more to kill Him.

Again Jesus declared His cooperation with His Father in the works that He was doing. This not only was a claim of deity but it provides a revelation to all mankind of the real secret of Christ's success in His teaching and miracle working. "The Son can do nothing of himself, but what he seeth the Father do: for what things soever he doeth, these also doeth the Son likewise." Here is a declaration that Jesus was in constant contact with His Father, He had spiritual vision to see what His Father was doing and He was simply repeating on earth what He saw His Father doing in heaven. He claimed also that greater works than these would follow. These greater works would even include raising the dead, which happened on three distinct occasions in the ministry of Christ. To add still further fuel to the fire, He now told these Pharisees that the hour would come when all that were in the graves would hear His voice and come forth. He would then also be the Judge of all men, for the Father had committed all judgment unto Him. But in all humility He declared, "I can of mine own self do nothing" (v. 30).

And now He calls four witnesses in support of His declaration. John the Baptist is the first. Christ reminded the Jews that they had been willing for a season to rejoice in the light of John the

Baptist. The works which His Father had given Him to perform also bore witness that the Father had sent Him. He reminded them also that the Father himself had borne witness to Him, doubtless referring to the voice from heaven at the time of His baptism. Then the Scriptures were cited as testifying of Him. But He put their conclusion and attitude into these words: "ye will not come to me, that ye might have life." He then predicted that the time would come when another person would come in his own name and they would receive such a person. This possibly referred to the Antichrist with whom they would make a covenant for seven years (Daniel 9:27). He then reminded them that Moses himself would testify against them at the last day, for Moses had written concerning Christ (Deuteronomy 18:15), but they had rejected Moses' writings.

CONCERNING THE SABBATH (*Matthew* 12:1-9; *Mark* 2:23-28; *Luke* 6:1-5)

After this conflict and denunciation of the Pharisees it appears that Jesus returned to Galilee. He had definitely declared and revealed himself as God's Son doing works in the name of His Father, confirmed and supported by many witnesses. He leveled charges against the rebellious Jewish leaders and turned away and left them.

But the Pharisees were everywhere. On the very next Sabbath Jesus was walking through the cornfields, and His disciples were with Him. They were hungry and, as the Mosaic law provided, they plucked some ears of corn in the field through which they passed (Deuteronomy 23:25). The Pharisees, however, had taken this humane provision of the Israelitish code and had added to it their own crusty tradition. It was still all right to pluck the corn but they were not to do it on the Sabbath Day! Jesus recognized this as foolish and acted accordingly. It seems that the Sabbath Day had become the god of the Jewish people. That which was ordained of the Lord as a blessing originally had been so augmented and loaded down with tedious details that it was no more a delight but a burden, which Peter later declared they were not able to bear (Acts 15:10). Jesus was opposed to such foolish burdens and the substitution of this legalistic religion for the religion of the heart and He struck at it.

The Pharisees came on to the attack as He expected. "Why do ye that which is not lawful to do on the sabbath days?" Again Jesus unsheathed the trusted sword of the Scriptures. "Have ye not read what David did, when he was an hungered, and they that were with him; how he entered into the house of God, and did eat the shew-bread, which was not lawful for him to eat?" He reminded them also that the priests in the temple did many things on the Sabbath Day which were not lawful to others and yet were blameless. Again He quoted Hosea 6:6 and said, "If ye had known what this meaneth, I will have mercy, and not sacrifice, ye would not have condemned the guiltless." And here was His summary: "The sabbath was made for man, and not man for the sabbath." In other words, the Sabbath was an institution intended for the blessing of man. Men were not made to conform to this great overlord, the deified sabbath institution. Get things in their correct relative positions. Subordinate the Sabbath to man and not man to the Sabbath. And then came an announcement which to them was shocking: "The Son of man is lord also of the sabbath day." Here was another claim to deity. It was He who had instituted the Sabbath Day in the first place, and it was His prerogative to observe it correctly or to modify and set it aside at His will.

HEALS MAN WITH WITHERED HAND (*Matthew* 12:9-14; *Mark* 3:1-6; *Luke* 6:6-11)

Again He entered into the synagogue and taught, and since it was the Sabbath Day the stage was set for another conflict. On this occasion there was a man in the audience who had a withered hand. They were expecting Him to heal this man and reminded Him of the possibility in the question, "Is it lawful to heal on the sabbath days?" They knew how He would answer this question. They were hoping He would put His disagreement into deeds by once more healing on the Sabbath Day. He did not disappoint them.

He invited the man with the withered hand to "rise up, and stand forth in the midst. And he arose and stood forth." Jesus then turned to the audience and asked them: "Is it lawful to do good on the sabbath days, or to do evil? to save life, or to kill?" By these words He was describing healing as a good thing and a saving of life, which it actually was. He wanted them to see the inconsistency and inhumanity of their position which opposed His doing good and saving life on a Sabbath Day. He continued His argument, "What man shall there be among you, that shall have one sheep, and if it fall into a pit on the sabbath day, will he not lay hold on it, and lift it out? How much then is a man better than a sheep?" For this reason He concluded, "It is lawful to do well on the sabbath days." At this point His anger arose for He was provoked with the hardness of their hearts and the impossibility of the position they were taking. He then commanded the man to stretch forth his hand, and when he stretched it out it was restored whole as the other. This was a further declaration of war between them. The Pharisees then became confederate with the Herodians in their plans to take and destroy the Lord. They too were filled with madness.

Lesson 16

HEALS MULTITUDES (*Matthew* 12:15-21; *Mark* 3:7-12; *Luke* 6:17-19)

Further ministry to this kind of an audience would be useless, so Jesus withdrew himself with His disciples to the sea. He sought an open area where many people could come near Him. It was well that He did, for immediately the plain was filled with a great multitude, not only from Galilee but also from Judea and beyond Jordan, and even as far as Tyre and Sidon on the Mediterranean Sea. They crowded Him so closely that He requested His disciples to prepare a small ship for Him in which He could push a little distance from the land. Here He could address the people without their pressing upon Him too closely. The sick people were anxious to touch Him for there went virtue out of Him and healed them all. Those who had unclean spirits also sought deliverance and were set free. "Unclean spirits when they saw him, fell down before him, and cried, saying, thou art the Son of God." Matthew cites this experience as being the fulfillment of the prophecy found in Isaiah 42:1-4 and interprets the last clause of this prophecy as, "In his name shall the Gentiles trust." Here again mention is made of the ministry of Christ to those who were not of Jewish nationality. He concludes His ministry here by instructing those who were delivered not to proclaim that He was the Messiah. He realized the tense political situation and knew that such a proclamation could precipitate a rebellion against the Romans and thus interfere with His continued ministry of salvation and deliverance.

NAMES TWELVE APOSTLES (*Matthew* 10:2-4; *Mark* 3:13-19; *Luke* 6:12-16)

Jesus had now had sufficient experience with His disciples to know whom He should recognize in a special way. It was an important decision. Upon these twelve men would rest the entire responsibility for carrying on redemption's program after He had paid its price on the Cross. He therefore went into a mountain to pray and continued all night in prayer to God. One matter which He doubtless discussed with His Father was the choice of Judas Iscariot who should betray Him. But it was written in the Holy Scriptures that one of His own who would eat of His bread would lift up his heel against Him (Psalm 41:9; 55:12-14). John tells (6:64, 71) that Jesus knew from the beginning who should betray Him. Thus He deliberately chose Judas the night when He chose all the others.

Jesus now gave the title of "apostle" (a sent-one) to the twelve disciples whom He called by name. They are usually listed in groups of four. Simon, whom He named Peter, "a stone," is always mentioned first, and Judas Iscariot always last. Peter and his brother Andrew, the sons of Jonas, and James and John the sons of Zebedee, constitute the first group. James and John He surnamed Boanerges, which is "the sons of thunder." These all appear to have come from Bethsaida on the northwestern shore of the Sea of Galilee. The name Philip always appears first in the second group. Nathanael, also called Bartholomew, and Matthew and Thomas complete these four. Finally, to complete the list there were: James the less, and Judas, his brother who also is called Lebbaeus and Thaddeus, the sons of Alphaeus; Simon the Canaanite who had been one of the Zealots, a band of nationalist rebels against Rome; and Judas Iscariot who also betrayed Him.

The purpose in calling these apostles is cited as twofold: first that they might be with Him, and second that He might send them forth. How essential it is to be and live with Christ, to learn and absorb of Him before one goes forth to serve Him. The disciples were sent forth to preach and to have power over sicknesses and devils. This is the very ministry which Jesus was performing, and it is easy to see that He was choosing those upon whom His mantle would fall and who would carry on His ministry. After choosing the twelve apostles He went with them into a house.

SERMON ON THE MOUNT (*Matthew* 5, 6, 7; *Luke* 6:20-49)

Immediately the multitudes swarmed on Him again, and this time He went up into a mountain. When He had sat down, His disciples gathered around Him. It has been said that the words which follow on this occasion constitute the great ordination sermon of the twelve apostles. The Scripture, however, says that He "taught them."

First came the beautiful beatitudes which are considered the *magna charta* of the kingdom of God. These foundational utterances of the New Testament doctrine correspond to the Ten Commandments of the Old Testament. How different, however, from the "Thou shalt" and "Thou shalt not" of the former covenant. Here are the keys into the blessed realm where men reach the ultimate in righteousness and heart satisfaction and arrive at the place where God's blessing rests upon them. The qualities cited here are the very antithesis of what are generally considered desirable and legitimate pursuits in life. As Jesus declared later, "that which is highly esteemed among men is abomination in the sight of God" (Luke 16:15). Fundamentally also, "a man's life consisteth not in the abundance of the things which he possesseth" (Luke 12:15). Humility, meekness, mercifulness, purity of heart, loving and making peace, and being willing to be persecuted for righteousness' sake—these are listed by Christ as the highest objectives for human living.

Attaining and living in this blessed state results in a person's holding an unusual relationship to the world around him. His condition of heart and outlook on life is so entirely different to that of all others that it not only makes him hated of men and separated from their company but it imposes a responsibility upon him as a child of the Kingdom. In God's sight these adjusted people are in reality the salt of the earth and the light of the world. He says they are the preserving element in the world that is about to decay and a light to the world that is sunk in darkness. He therefore enjoins upon these His followers that they exert this preserving influence and let their light shine brightly before men. Their objectives in living should be to provoke their fellowmen to glorify their Father in heaven.

He is conscious of the fact that He is talking to those whose standard of living has been the Old Testament law. He proceeds then to relate His gospel to the teachings of Moses. He does not hesitate to say, "Ye have heard that it was said . . . but I say unto you." He had previously declared Himself to be the Lord of the Sabbath, and now He says plainly and boldly that His Word is superior to that of the Old Testament law. He further declares that unless people have a greater righteousness than that manifested by the scribes and Pharisees they will not qualify as citizens of the kingdom of heaven. His emphasis was upon quality and attitude of the heart rather than the outward action and deeds. It was not just killing that was wrong; the very anger itself which caused the killing was the sin He condemned. It was not just the act of adultery that was wrong; it was looking on a woman with impure intentions which constituted adultery already in the heart. It was not sufficient merely to love one's neighbor and hate one's enemy. Jesus taught that one should do good to them that hated him. He cited His Father as an example of generous treatment of good and evil alike and commanded, "Be ye therefore perfect even as your Father in heaven is perfect."

He rebuked the exterior righteousness which was just for public display and then gave a model prayer to be prayed in secret. He gave assurance that we would not ask, seek, or knock in vain. He emphasized the importance of Christian forgiveness of one's enemies and made our own forgiveness dependent upon it. Our first concern should be the kingdom of God, and Jesus obligated His Father to provide material blessings if we put His Kingdom first. He laid down what is known as the Golden Rule, which sets one's own welfare as the standard by which one should treat his fellowmen. He took time to warn of and denounce false prophets. He concluded His discourse with the pronouncement that His sayings were the true foundation upon which, if a man built, he would endure and survive all the storms of life.

HEALS CENTURION'S SERVANT (*Matthew* 8:5-13; *Luke* 7:1-10)

At the conclusion of this priceless presentation of truth to His disciples, Jesus returned to the plain and again entered into Capernaum. A certain centurion evidently was awaiting Him. He came to request Jesus to heal his servant who was seriously ill with the palsy. On a previous occasion a fellow centurion in the same city had asked the Lord to heal his son, and this doubtless inspired faith in his fellow officer. This Roman was already an admirer of the Jewish faith, for he had built a synagogue for the local Jews. This won him favor among the Jewish elders who interceded with Christ on his behalf. The faith and humility of this Gentile "stranger" was also very marked. The Jews reported to Christ that he was worthy of the healing requested; but he himself sent his servants to assure the Lord that he was not worthy that He should enter under his roof. He spoke of his own authority over his soldiers and servants and expressed belief that Christ had similar authority over disease and demons.

This remarkable expression of faith amazed the Master. He declared that He had not found its like anywhere in Israel. He then added that there will be many such coming from the east and west from the Gentile world who would share the kingdom of heaven with Abraham, Isaac, Jacob, and all the prophets. The converse of this blessedness would also be found in the fact that many Jews who had been the "children of the kingdom" would be cast into outer darkness. He then pronounced the word of healing which had been requested, and when the messengers returned they found the centurion's servant was healed.

RAISES WIDOW'S SON (*Luke* 7:11-17)

Jesus moved on in His itinerary to a city called Nain, about eighteen miles from Capernaum. His disciples and many other people followed Him. As He approached the city there came out a large funeral procession taking the only son of a widow to his burial. The woman's tears moved Christ to compassion. He came near and touched the burial bed, and its bearers stood still. He then spake the word of authority which restored life to the son, and he sat up and began to speak. Very naturally this created a great respect and fear in the hearts of the people who immediately exclaimed, "A great prophet is risen up among us."

Lesson 17

JOHN THE BAPTIST SENDS DISCIPLES TO JESUS (*Matthew* 11:2-6;
Luke 7:18-23)

The narrative returns now to the story of John the Baptist. Just
before Christ returned to Galilee, Herod had thrust John into prison
at the instigation of his wicked wife, Herodias. In addition to his
private conferences with Herod, John evidently was allowed contact
with his disciples. But his imprisonment chafed him, and in his
solitude he brooded and allowed doubts to come into his mind. He
actually questioned whether or not the Man whom he had proclaimed as the Lamb of God was in reality the Messiah. Evidently
he too had been affected by the popular opinion that the Messiah
would lead the Jews in throwing off the Roman yoke. And now this
Jesus was doing nothing in that direction. In addition, He was allowing His great forerunner to languish under the Roman heel.
John's doubt went so far that he called two of his disciples and sent
them to Jesus with the blunt question, "Art thou he that should
come?"

To strengthen John's faith Jesus simply called the attention of the
messengers to the many healings which were being performed. He
told them to return and tell John what things they had seen and
heard. He then cited in essence the fulfillment of Isaiah 61 which
He had proclaimed in the synagogue in Nazareth. He even called
attention to the fact that the poor were having the gospel preached
to them. Then followed the gentle exhortation: "Blessed is he, whosoever shall not be offended in me." In other words, "You will be
especially happy, John, if you will not be disappointed in Me."

Jesus did not send to John the words of praise which He was
about to utter, for He wanted John's faith to rest squarely upon His
own true fulfillment of prophecy. But He used the occasion to an-

nounce publicly His great estimation and appreciation of His fore-runner. He confirmed that John the Baptist had fulfilled Malachi's prophecy (Malachi 3:1) and was the messenger who had been sent before His face. In addition, He declared that John was no ordinary prophet but was much more. He said that none born had ever been greater than he. John was also the Elijah whom Malachi had said would come (Malachi 4:5, 6), as the angel Gabriel also had announced to Zacharias before John's birth (Luke 1:17). In comparison with this high attainment on earth, Jesus declared that membership in the kingdom of heaven was even greater. Membership in that Kingdom was now available and they who pressed in might obtain it.

JESUS CONDEMNS THAT GENERATION (*Matthew 11:16-19; Luke* 7:31-35)

The discussion concerning John the Baptist reminded Jesus of the treatment which John and He had received of that generation. He compared His ministry to that of John, since both had been rejected by the people to whom they ministered. He said they were like the children who played in the open marketplace. They called to their playmates saying, "We have played music for you, but you have not danced. We have also pretended that we were mourners at a funeral, but you have not wept." These were the two ministries to which their "fellows" had been indifferent. John is the one who had mourned, for his life and message were austere. Christ had been normal in His eating and drinking and had been a friend of men. It had been impossible to please that generation for both He and John were being rejected.

SINFUL WOMAN ANOINTS HIS FEET (*Luke* 7:36-50)

Regardless of the attitude of the people around Him, Jesus went on being a friend of His fellowmen. He even responded to the invitation of a Pharisee to eat with him. There is no respect of persons with the Lord, and He will always respond to those who reach out toward Him. He would not let others dictate who His friends ought to be and with whom He should mingle. Although responding to the invitation of the Pharisee, at the same time He was open to the approach of ordinary sinners.

A certain sinful woman of the city heard that Jesus was eating in a Pharisee's house and she pressed her way in to seek forgiveness for her sins. She wept bitterly at Jesus' feet and used her hair to wipe away the tears which had fallen upon His feet. She kissed His feet and anointed them with the precious ointment which she had brought for the purpose. Simon, the Pharisee, resented the intrusion and his pride led him to be critical in his heart. He thought it was an indication that Jesus had no discernment and therefore was not a prophet after all. Jesus read Simon's thoughts and asked permission to tell him a story. Whereupon Jesus spoke another of His immortal parables.

It was simply that a certain man had two people who were in debt to him. One owed him ten times as much as the other. This man freely canceled both debts. Jesus asked the Pharisee, "Which of the two former debtors would have the greater love for the man who had forgiven them?" Simon answered, "The one to whom he forgave most." Jesus then made the application. He turned to the woman and said to Simon, "This woman is a great sinner but she has expressed her gratitude most profusely. Your attitude toward Me has revealed very little love on your part. Her many sins are freely forgiven." But even the wisdom of Christ's words did not impress His host and those who were with him for they criticized Jesus for assuming the position of one who could forgive sins. Thus they rejected His deity as well as the fact that He was a prophet. But He quietly assured the woman that her faith had saved her and sent her forth in peace.

PREACHES THROUGHOUT EVERY CITY AND VILLAGE (*Luke* 8:1-3)

In a single sentence Luke gives a remarkable summary of Christ's Galilean ministry: "He went throughout every city and village." This is a statement concerning the thoroughness of our Lord in performing the task to which He had been assigned by His heavenly Father. There was not a city or a village which He did not visit, nor a part of these cities and villages which He did not reach. "Into the highways and hedges" He went, seeking to bring people to His Father's banquet. He not only preached but He pictured the glad tidings of the kingdom of God. He healed the deaf to illustrate His power to enable people to hear the deeper truths of His kingdom. He healed the dumb to prove that He had power to enable people to testify concerning His glory. He healed withered hands to show that He had power to enable people to work for Him, and impotent men to show that He had power to enable men to walk in His paths.

He raised the dead, proving that He could raise those who were dead in trespasses and sins. By physical acts He demonstrated His miraculous power to give spiritual life and vigor to those who would receive it.

"And the twelve were with him." This is the most effective style of teaching. By graphic illustration and demonstration truths are impressed. These twelve disciples were to receive His mantle when He was taken up and were to perpetuate His ministry. He therefore must deeply impress them with His works of power and teach them how to do likewise. There were others in the company whom His Father had raised up to minister to Him and His disciples with their material means.

THE UNPARDONABLE SIN (*Matthew* 12:22-32; *Mark* 3:20-30; *Luke* 11:15-23)

Jesus had just delivered one who was possessed with the devil when the multitude came together again. Their reaction to Him was mixed. Some said, "Is not this the Son of David?" Others who considered themselves His friends felt that He had become irrational and was "beside himself." There were others who were not nearly so kind. The scribes and Pharisees who had come down from Jerusalem said bluntly, "He hath Beelzebub," which is the devil. They said, "This accounts for his power over demons."

Strange argument this, as Jesus quickly pointed out: Why would Satan cast out Satan? He would be opposing himself and destroying his own kingdom if he did so. "By the way," He said, "by whom do your children cast them out?" The fact that Jesus cast out demons proved He was their enemy. The fact that the Pharisees' children could not or did not cast them out proved their friendship with the devils or their impotency in their presence. Jesus said that these children of the Pharisees would be the judges in the argument. He testified, "I with the finger of God cast out devils." If they said that His power was the power of the devil when it was really the power of the Holy Spirit, then they were committing blasphemy against the Holy Ghost. All other sins and blasphemies would be forgiven, but not this one which they were committing. Here is Christ's own definition of the blasphemy against the Holy Ghost: deliberately and knowingly attributing the works of the Holy Spirit to the devil.

Their speaking such evil things, He said, was a proof that their hearts were evil, "for out of the abundance of the heart the mouth speaketh." Their words proved they were veritable vipers, and He denounced them as such. He went on to make the general observation that all words, even idle words, were on record in heaven and would serve as a basis of the judgment which men would receive at the last day.

Jesus then commented upon the necessity of being indwelt by the Spirit of the Lord rather than merely being vacated by an unclean spirit. Positive holiness is necessary rather than a mere negative experience. If a heart which is vacated by an evil spirit by the power of God is not immediately filled by the Holy Spirit, there is grave danger of a relapse into evil wherein the last state is worse than the first.

A WOMAN'S BLESSING (*Luke* 11:27, 28; *Matthew* 12:46-50)

An admiring woman in the company lifted up her voice and cried out, "Blessed indeed is your mother." With all respect for His mother, Jesus replied, "It is even more blessed to hear God's Word and keep it." A little later His own mother and His brethren came to see Him but could not get near Him because of the crowd. Someone told Him they were standing without and wanted to see Him. Again He placed His mother and His brethren below those who heard the Word of God and obeyed it. He said, "They who do the latter are my real brother and sister and mother."

THE SIGN OF JONAS (*Matthew* 12:38-42; *Luke* 11:29-32)

Again the scribes and Pharisees pressed in with a comment. They asked Him to show them a sign. How foolish, in the light of the many signs and wonders which He had been performing all around them. He knew their insincerity but He took the opportunity to predict His resurrection as the great climactic sign of His career. As Jonah was delivered from the whale after three days and three nights of imprisonment in its belly, so the Lord would be delivered from the heart of the earth after imprisonment for three days and three nights therein. The Ninevites were impressed with that great sign in the case of Jonah, and repented. Would the people of His generation do the same? The queen of Sheba, likewise, had come from afar to hear the wisdom of Solomon, and a greater than Solomon was now among them. How would they compare in the judgment with the men of Nineveh and the queen of Sheba?

Lesson 18

PARABLES BY THE SEA (*Matthew* 13:1-53; *Mark* 4:1-34; *Luke* 8:4-15)

Our Lord had now reached a point in His ministry where His teaching should take a distinct turn. The magnificent Sermon on the Mount had been a presentation of eternal truth in a plain, direct form which everyone could easily understand. The Pharisees, however, and many others in His audience rejected His teaching. But He had much more to say and He chose to clothe His sayings in beautiful parables. When the disciples asked the reason for this, He answered, "Because it is given unto you to know the mysteries of the kingdom of heaven, but to them it is not given." Isaiah's prediction that there would be many who, hearing, would not hear was now about to be fulfilled. Christ would speak truth in their hearing, but they would not understand or perceive. Therefore, His truth would be conveyed in a form which would elude the understanding of those who had ears to hear and eyes to see in that and all succeeding generations. So priceless were these truths, Jesus said, that many prophets and righteous men had desired to see and hear them.

The first of these parables of the Kingdom was of a sower who went forth to sow. This is in reality a parable of the soils, for it was the same seed sown in different soils. The wayside, the stony places, the thorns, and the good ground were the different types of soil in which the seed was sown and which produced different reactions and growth. So would it be where the gospel seed was to be sown.

The enemy of the gospel program was introduced in the second parable. A man sowed good seed in his field, but an enemy came and sowed tares, or weeds. When they both came up the difference was detected, and the servants said, "Sir, what shall we do?" The

98

owner of the field instructed them to let both grow together till the harvest when it would be more easy to separate the tares from the wheat. This was a picturesque representation of the future history of the Church. The children of the Kingdom would be imitated by those who were in reality children of the wicked one. The true identification of each must be left to the Great Judge who at the end would command His angels to divide them. This does not refer to hypocrites in the Church but to pseudo-Christians in the whole world, for the "field is the world." It should be noticed too that this story foretells that hypocrites and unbelievers will be cast into a furnace of fire.

The remarkable growth of the Kingdom is represented by the parable of the mustard seed. The tiny seed became a great tree but, lo, the birds of the air came and lodged in its branches. The organized Church would become a great institution, but birds of evil would be attracted to find lodging in its fold. The expanding action of yeast is also used by the Lord as an illustration of rapid expansion of His kingdom.

The great value of the heavenly Kingdom is represented by the parables of the treasure hidden in the field and of the pearl of great price. The field, of course, is again the whole world, and the Church is hidden within its population. The man is Christ who bought the whole world in order to gain this treasure and this priceless pearl. This is His estimation of the value of His Church.

Finally, the story of the end of the age is given us in the parable of the net cast into the sea. As a net catches both good and bad fish, which are separated as the haul is pulled ashore, so at the time of the end angels will separate the wicked from the just and cast the wicked into a furnace of fire. This is the second reference to the furnace of fire which awaits the wicked at the last great judgment.

JESUS STILLS THE STORM (*Matthew* 8:23-27; *Mark* 4:35-41; *Luke* 8:22-25)

Christ's first miracle had been over nature, turning water into wine. Later He had manifested power over demons, disease, and death, and now He turns again to another miracle over the power of nature. He was in a ship on the Sea of Galilee, and His disciples were with Him. He was weary from His intense activity and lay asleep in the stern of the boat. His Father allowed a great tempest to arise that threatened to engulf the ship. Even those of His disciples who were seasoned seamen were alarmed and sensed the jeopardy that had overtaken them. They naturally turned to the Master. Instinctively they realized that He was their hope of salvation. He rebuked the winds and the waves and they ceased their raging immediately. He then turned and asked His disciples, "Why are ye so fearful? how is it that ye have no faith?" This was a magnificent, literal, physical demonstration of the power of our Christ. When we are in the same boat with Him we are safe. He can conquer all of life's disturbances and speak peace to our troubled hearts. His question to them comes down to us, "Why are ye so fearful and of such little faith?"

DELIVERS THE GADARENE DEMONIAC (*Matthew* 8:28-34; *Mark* 5:1-20; *Luke* 8:26-39)

The purpose of the journey across the lake was not only that the glory of the Lord should be manifested in the stilling of the storm, but to bring them on a mission of mercy and deliverance. Immediately upon His coming to land there met Him a man who was devil possessed. Men would call him insane for he wore no clothes and lived among the tombs. He had been captured and bound with chains of iron, but he always broke them and was driven by the devil into the wilderness. Men had ceased to try to tame him, but God ordained that he should be the first one to meet Christ as He arrived in the country of the Gadarenes. He ran and fell down before Jesus and, like demons on previous occasions, he cried out, "What have I to do with thee, Jesus, thou Son of God most high?" Whereupon Jesus demonstrated His power as the Son of God by commanding the demons to come out of him. They tarried only long enough to request permission of the Master to enter into a herd of swine which was feeding nearby. This was a testimony to Christ's power and authority which the demons respected. He gave them permission to enter the swine, whereupon two thousand of them (note how many demons were in this man) ran over a cliff and perished in the sea.

The deliverance of this demoniac occasioned a financial loss to the owners of the swine, against which they protested. Again men were considering material possessions worth more than the welfare of a human being. But this was contrary to the estimation of Christ. The people of the community then actually asked Jesus to leave their country for they preferred their possessions to the deliverance of their fellowman. The man himself, however, was profoundly grateful and Jesus sent him home to tell how great things the Lord had done for him.

HEALS WOMAN AND JAIRUS' DAUGHTER (*Matthew* 9:18-26; *Mark* 5:21-43; *Luke* 8:40-56)

Acceding to the request of the people of Gadara, Jesus left their shores and returned to the other side of the Sea of Galilee. While He was still at the seaside many people gathered around Him. Immediately He was approached by Jairus, a ruler of the synagogue, who fell at His feet with a request that Jesus should go and heal his daughter who was critically ill. As Jesus turned to go with him the crowds still thronged Him. Suddenly Jesus stopped and asked, "Who touched me?" A certain woman came trembling and fell at His feet, confessing that she was the one who had touched Him. Her secret was now revealed. She had been suffering from a hemorrhage for twelve years. She had exhausted every human resource as well as all her finances in seeking healing, "and was nothing better, but rather grew worse." She had come to Christ for the healing which she so sorely needed, pressing through the throng to touch the hem of His garment. The great loving Deliverer of mankind had responded instinctively, and virtue flowed from Him to the distressed woman bringing complete healing to her. Here was a remarkable demonstration of the healing that comes to those who reach out in faith to touch Him.

As Jesus spoke words of comfort to the believing woman, a messenger came to Jairus informing him that his daughter had just died and suggesting that it was useless now for Christ to come. When Jairus was at this point of despair and under pressure not to press his request further, Jesus stepped in with the word, "Be not afraid, only believe." How anxious He is that we should have faith in the darkest hour.

It was in this incident that He made His first distinction between His disciples and allowed only Peter, James, and John to follow Him. This must not be taken as evidence of partiality but recognized as an expression of His discernment of the quality of faith in these disciples. Coming to the house, He brushed aside the professional mourners and ignored their insistence that it was too late. He went into the room where the body of the girl was lying, taking with Him the father and mother and the disciples who had accompanied Him.

He took the girl by the hand and said simply, "I say unto thee, arise." She immediately arose and walked, and Jesus instructed them to give her something to eat. This of course augmented His fame throughout the whole region.

HEALS TWO BLIND MEN AND A DUMB DEMONIAC (*Matthew* 9:27-34)

As Jesus left Jairus' house two blind men followed Him. Addressing Him as the Son of David, they begged Him to have mercy on them. Faith was the key to all of these divine healings, and so He asked them, "Believe ye that I am able to do this?" Upon their affirmative response, He touched their eyes and said, "According to your faith be it unto you." Immediately their eyes were opened. When they went away they told everywhere what He had done, in spite of the fact that Jesus had requested that they should not do so. He was mindful of the political agitation which it might provoke, and He wanted as much time as possible to complete His spiritual ministry before His crucifixion.

The next incident reveals faith on the part of the individuals who brought their needy friend to Christ. This was a dumb man who was also possessed with a devil. Christ responded to the plea of those who brought him, cast out the devil, and restored the man's speech. The multitudes were impressed with His miraculous power, but again the Pharisees committed the unpardonable sin by saying that He cast out devils through the prince of the devils.

Jesus then went to other cities and villages teaching, preaching, and healing (Matthew 9:35-38). His great heart was moved with compassion by the multitudes around Him who fainted under the weight of their sin and sickness. He here issued His great call for prayer that God would send more laborers into His harvest field.

REJECTION AT NAZARETH (*Matthew* 13:54-58; *Mark* 6:1-6)

Once more Jesus determined to go to His own hometown to give them a final opportunity to accept Him. They did allow Him to speak in the synagogue and expressed great wonder at the wisdom of His words and deeds. But again they reminded themselves that He had been a carpenter among them and that His mother and brothers and sisters were still with them. They allowed this fact to reduce their faith in Him to such a low point that He could do no mighty works there, only healing a few sick people. "He marvelled because of their unbelief."

SENDS OUT TWELVE DISCIPLES (*Matthew* 10:1-42; 11:1; *Mark* 6:7-13; *Luke* 9:1-12, 49-53)

The time had now arrived for Christ to plan for His succession. Although He had not as yet told His disciples that He would eventually leave to them the task of preaching the gospel, yet He knew it in His heart and began to train those who were to carry on after His departure. The instructions given to the twelve disciples as He sent them out on their first trial ministry serve also as instructions to all succeeding disciples. They were to go two by two. They were invested with power over unclean spirits and to heal all manner of sickness and disease. They were instructed concerning their personal attire and the equipment they were to take with them. They were told also how to greet the people to whose home they came and the message which they were to preach. He also told them how to react if they should be rejected in any home or city. He said a blessing would rest on those who received them and a curse upon those who rejected them. The record concludes with a comment that the disciples went out and preached that men should repent; they cast out many devils, and anointed many sick people and healed them.

HEROD KILLS JOHN (*Matthew* 14:3-12; *Mark* 6:14-29)

Herod had trifled with his opportunity for salvation during his private conversations with John the Baptist, and now the decision day arrived. It was Herod's birthday on which he made a supper for his lords and captains. Like Belshazzar's feast of old, it proved to be his ruin. The daughter of his wicked wife Herodias danced before the dissolute party, and Herod offered to give her whatever she would ask. She hurriedly consulted with her mother and then asked for the head of John the Baptist. Herod had sworn to grant her request and he considered his oath to be more important than the life of a righteous prophet of God. So John was executed, culminating a life and ministry which was unique among men. Jesus remarked later, "Likewise shall also the Son of man suffer of them" (Matthew 17:12).

Lesson 19

FEEDS FIVE THOUSAND (*Matthew* 14:13-23; *Mark* 6:30-46; *Luke* 9:10-17; *John* 6:1-15)

When Jesus heard of the tragic death of John He sought the solitude of a desert place. However, the people saw Him departing and followed Him in throngs. When Jesus saw them He was moved with compassion and healed their sick. Toward sundown the disciples suggested that He send the multitude away to secure food and lodging for the night. But Jesus replied, "Give ye them to eat." They replied, "We have no more but five loaves and two fishes . . . but what are they among so many?" Thus the stage was set for that miracle which is recorded in all four Gospels.

Jesus first instructed that the people be seated in groups of fifty. He then took the food, returned thanks, and gave it to the disciples to set before the multitude. Like the servants at the wedding in Cana of Galilee, the disciples obeyed the Master, and the silent miracle occurred in their hands. As they distributed to the multitude the food was multiplied, and five thousand men, beside women and children, were fed so abundantly that there were "twelve baskets full" of fragments left over. The Jehovah who had caused the barrel of meal and the cruse of oil not to fail the widow of Zarephath, and who had multiplied the oil of the widow of the prophet in Elisha's day to meet the need of her emergency, had now performed a similar miracle through the great Prophet, His Son. The creative miracle prompted by the loving heart of the divine Host impressed the recipients that He was indeed the Messiah who should come. But their perverted conception of what Messiah would do found expression in their coming to take Him by force and make Him their King. This He avoided and went up into a mountain apart to pray.

WALKS ON THE SEA (*Matthew* 14:24-33; *Mark* 6:47-52; *John* 6:16-21)

At His instruction His disciples had taken ship to go to the other side before Him. When it became dark a strong wind arose and the waves were tossing high. All night they toiled in rowing. Toward morning Jesus came to them, walking on the sea, another miraculous demonstration of His deity. He was near to the boat, thus making himself available to them, but "would have passed by them." Later He manifested the same characteristic when, in talking to the two disciples on the way to Emmaus after His resurrection, "He made as though he would have gone further." The disciples in the boat did not recognize Him at first, and the supposed apparition only added to their fear. But when He spoke they recognized Him. Impulsive Peter revealed his developing faith in the Master by suggesting that he be invited also to walk upon the water. Jesus said, "Come." Peter's faith was rewarded for he too walked upon the water. But, like a child who falls so easily, his infant faith failed, and he began to sink. The strong faithful Master stretched forth His hand and lifted Peter up. It must be recorded that Peter walked again in faith and came with Christ into the ship. As soon as they came into the vessel the wind ceased. Instead of being overwhelmingly convinced, they were "sore amazed in themselves beyond measure" for they had already forgotten the miracle of the loaves and their hearts were hardened.

HEALS AT GENNESARET (*Matthew* 14:34-36; *Mark* 6:53-56)

A familiar scene was here reenacted. When it became known that Jesus had arrived, the people ran throughout the whole region to bring the sick, even in beds, to where He was. He responded and then went into their villages and cities and the country round about and healed the sick everywhere. All who touched the hem of His garment were made perfectly whole.

DISCOURSE CONCERNING THE BREAD OF LIFE (*John* 6:22-71)

The five thousand men, beside women and children, who had been left on the other side of the sea, "also took shipping, and came to Capernaum, seeking for Jesus." When they found Him, Jesus immediately engaged them in serious conversation. As with Nicodemus, He came immediately to the point. They had displayed their mistaken concept of the Messiah by wanting to make Him king, and Jesus told them plainly now that their motive in following Him was to eat again of the bread that He might create for them. He encouraged them to seek rather for the food which would endure unto everlasting life. Although Jesus offered to give them this spiritual food, they asked how they might earn it by the "works of the law." It was difficult for them merely to believe. In the face of the wonderful miracle of the multiplying of the loaves and fishes which they had seen and of which they had partaken, they again asked Him for a sign. They followed in the steps of the Pharisees and scribes in ignoring the signs which He had already shown them and unbelievingly asked for more.

Here was Christ's opportunity to present himself as the Bread from heaven. In contrast to the manna which His Father had given them through Moses, God was now offering them Bread which would satisfy their hunger completely. Partaking of this Bread would give them everlasting life and assure them of resurrection at the last day. Incidentally, He here gave His personal testimony that His purpose in coming to the earth was to do the will of His Father. He said that He lived by partaking of His Father, and He was inviting His hearers to live by partaking of Him, the true Bread.

The Jews then murmured at Him and many even of His disciples turned back and walked no more with Him. He asked the twelve if they also would go away, and Peter spoke on their behalf, "Lord, to whom shall we go? thou hast the words of eternal life. And we believe and are sure that thou art that Christ, the Son of the living God." Christ then gave His first intimation that He would later be betrayed by one of their number.

REBUKES TRADITION OF ELDERS (*Matthew* 15:1-20; *Mark* 7:1-23)

Shortly thereafter a delegation of Pharisees and scribes from Jerusalem came to interview Jesus. They had another charge to make against Him. In addition to making Himself equal to God and breaking their Sabbath, they now asked Him why His disciples did not observe the tradition of their elders. His reply was a question similar to theirs except that their failure concerned the commandment of God himself. He pressed the argument to the conclusion that this revealed their insincerity and hypocrisy.

He then used this opportunity to teach concerning the source of human wickedness. All kinds of evil, he said, including evil thoughts, foolishness, covetousness, pride, blasphemy, thefts, adultery, and murder, are based in the human heart. This conception is the foundation of His teaching concerning true holiness.

HEALS SYROPHOENICIAN WOMAN'S DAUGHTER (*Matthew* 15:21-28; *Mark* 7:24-30)

Jesus was prompted now to make an excursion into strictly Gentile country. He went to the area of Tyre and Sidon and there entered into a home, possibly seeking for some rest. But His presence soon became known. A certain woman whose daughter had an unclean spirit came and fell at His feet and besought Him for deliverance for her. Here follows another example of outstanding Gentile faith. To bring out the full beauty of this woman's faith, the Lord at first did not even answer her. The disciples then requested Him to send her away. But she did not go. Jesus then declared that His ministry was primarily to the house of Israel. At this the woman merely worshiped Him, pleading, "Lord, help me." Jesus declared that it was not proper to take that which belonged to His children and give it to Gentile dogs. Thus the full limit of discouragement was placed in her way. She surmounted all these difficulties, however, and took the place of a dog as she claimed the right of a dog to eat the crumbs which fall from the children's table. Jesus then responded to her need, declaring that her faith was great. She returned home in faith to find her daughter completely delivered.

HEALS THE DEAF MUTE AND MULTITUDES (*Matthew* 15:29-31; *Mark* 7:31-37)

Jesus then returned to the Sea of Galilee, this time to the Decapolis which lay southeastward of the sea. Here a deaf man with an impediment in his speech was brought to Him for healing. Jesus took him aside, laid His hand upon him, and put His finger into the man's ears. He touched his tongue and sighing, said, "Be opened." And immediately the man was completely delivered. Although He requested the people not to, they publicized this healing greatly, saying, "He hath done all things well." Great multitudes then came to Him, bringing those who were lame, blind, dumb, and maimed, and He healed them all. "And they glorified the God of Israel."

HEROD FEARS (*Matthew* 14:1, 2; *Mark* 6:14-16; *Luke* 9:7-9)

When Herod heard of the fame of Jesus, his conscience smote him. Immediately he said, "This is John the Baptist; he is risen from the dead." This was his explanation for the mighty works which were manifested through the Lord Jesus. Others of the people said, "This is Elias which was to come." Still others said, "One of the old prophets has risen again." Thus the idea of the resurrection from the dead seemed to be current in Israel. Herod expressed a desire to see Jesus.

Lesson 20

FEEDS FOUR THOUSAND (*Matthew* 15:32-39; *Mark* 8:1-9)

Returning to the presence of Jesus, we find Him still surrounded by great multitudes, many of whom He had just healed. They had now been together for three days without food, and Jesus was concerned about them. Again the disciples protested that there was not enough food to meet the need. They only had seven loaves and a few small fishes. In spite of the fact that His previous feeding of the five thousand had caused the people to press their mistaken conceptions of the Messianic kingdom, and many had become His followers merely to eat of the food that He provided, He proceeded once more to "set a table in the wilderness" for the people. This time His guests were four thousand men, besides the women and the children, and seven baskets of broken pieces of food were left over. Afterward He took ship again and sailed this time to the town of Magdala on the western shore.

PHARISEES DEMAND A SIGN (*Matthew* 16:1-4; *Mark* 8:10-13; *Luke* 12:54-57)

Here the Pharisees and Sadducees once more desired Him to show them a sign from heaven. Jesus reminded them that they were well able to read the daily weather signs in the skies and wondered that they were not able to read the "signs of the times." He rebuked them for constantly ignoring the miracle signs with which He had surrounded them and continually asking for additional ones. He said there was one more sign which would be shown them, the sign of the prophet Jonas—His own resurrection after having been three days in the heart of the earth. Then He again took ship and crossed the sea.

109

BEWARE OF LEAVEN (*Matthew* 16:5-12; *Mark* 8:14-21; *Luke* 12:1)

The recent presence of the Pharisees and the Sadducees reminded Jesus of their great sin. In crossing the sea the last time the disciples had forgotten to take more than one loaf of bread with them. So when Jesus warned them to "beware of the leaven of the Pharisees and of the Sadducees" they connected His remark with their failure to take bread. He corrected their mistake, commenting also that they had very little faith in His ability to supply their physical needs even though they had recently witnessed the miracles of the feeding of the five thousand and of the four thousand. He then said plainly that it was not bread He was talking about but the leaven of hypocrisy which permeated the doctrine of the Pharisees and the Sadducees.

HEALS BLIND MAN (*Mark* 8:22-26)

Jesus came now to Bethsaida, and they brought a blind man for Him to touch and heal. At this time He took the blind man by the hand and led him out of the town to perform the healing. He put His hands upon him and asked if he could now see. The blind man replied, "I see men as trees, walking." Once more the Lord put His hands upon him and asked him to look up. This time he "saw every man clearly." This is the only recorded instance in which complete deliverance did not come instantly. It serves as an encouragement to others whose healing is delayed. But perfect deliverance did come.

PETER'S CONFESSION (*Matthew* 16:13-20; *Mark* 8:27-30; *Luke* 9:18-21)

Caesarea Philippi lay about thirty miles north of the Sea of Galilee on the northern edge of Jewish territory. When Jesus visited this area He engaged His disciples in a conversation concerning who men thought that He was. His coming to earth was to reveal himself as the Messiah and the Son of God. The disciples revealed that the populace did not yet accept Him in this capacity, saying instead that He was John the Baptist, or Elijah, or Jeremiah, or one of the other prophets returned to life again. Then Jesus put them on record as to who they thought that He was. Peter again was their spokesman and declared, "Thou art the Christ, the Son of the living God." Jesus commented, "Blessed art thou, Simon Barjona: for flesh and blood hath not revealed it unto thee, but my Father which is in heaven." Then He referred to the name Peter, which He had given

Simon upon His first meeting with him on the banks of Jordan. As explained then (John 1:42), the word "Peter" or "Cephas" meant a stone (*Petros,* a little rock). This gave occasion for a play upon the word "rock" and Jesus said, "Upon this rock [*Petra,* a larger rock] I will build my church." This is a reference to the great declaration of faith in Christ as the Son of God as the foundation stone upon which the Lord has built His Church. John so considered it when he remarked later, "Every spirit that confesseth that Jesus Christ is come in the flesh is of God" (1 John 4:2). The strength of this Church which Jesus was to build, He said, would resist the attack of hell itself.

Peter's initiative in making this great declaration, and the fact that His Father had chosen Peter to whom to reveal it, led Jesus to give to Peter the special privilege of "the keys of the kingdom of heaven." This doubtless refers to the honor which was Peter's of opening the kingdom to the Jews on the Day of Pentecost and to the Gentiles at the house of Cornelius. The authority which the Lord here gave Peter to bind and to loose on earth and have it confirmed in heaven was later to be shared with all the other apostles and the whole Church (Matthew 18:18; John 20:23; 1 Corinthians 5:4, 5, 13).

FORETELLS HIS DEATH (*Matthew* 16:21-23; *Mark* 8:31-33; *Luke* 9:22)

Following this revelation of His Messiahship, the Lord hastened to remind the disciples that this did not mean He would immediately assume rulership of the world but that the plan of God called first for the redemption of the world by His sacrifice and death. Although Peter had been chosen by the Father to make the great declaration which was the foundation of the Church, and Jesus had given him the honor of having the keys of the kingdom, yet this same Peter not only had a wrong conception of the Messiahship but was bold enough to suggest that the Lord himself was mistaken. "Be it far from thee, Lord: this shall not be unto thee." Jesus recognized this statement as being inspired by Satan and rebuked Peter sharply because of it. He explained that Peter was judging after the standards of men rather than those of God. It is so human to do this, and Peter had already revealed how very human he was.

THE VALUE OF A SOUL (*Matthew* 16:24-27; *Mark* 8:34-38; *Luke* 9:23-26)

This was the right occasion for Jesus to declare that His life was the correct pattern for men to follow. It was a universal law ("If any man") for all disciples of His to deny themselves and take up their respective crosses and follow Him. If any one would shrink from that procedure, as Peter had suggested that He do, it would result in the loss of his life; but whoever would deliberately lay down his life, as Jesus was about to do, would thereby insure his keeping it. Here follows the immortal challenge, "What shall it profit a man, if he shall gain the whole world, and lose his own soul? Or what shall a man give in exchange for his soul?" Jesus faithfully warned that if anyone would not listen to these words of His and follow them, He would be ashamed of him at His second coming when He would reward every man according to his works.

Lesson 21

PART 6—LAST GALILEAN MINISTRY

THE TRANSFIGURATION (*Matthew* 16:28 *to* 17:9; *Mark* 9:1-10; *Luke* 9:27-36)

The heavenly Father had planned to give reassurance and confirmation to His Son concerning the path of suffering which lay before Him. Jesus chose three of His disciples to share that experience with Him. He announced that some of those who were standing there would get a foretaste of the kingdom of God along with Him. Six days later this was fulfilled when Christ took Peter (who particularly needed this revelation), James, and John and led them up into a high mountain.

Christ's primary purpose in going up to this mountain apart was that He might engage in prayer. It was when He prayed that "his countenance was altered, and his raiment was white and glistering." "His face did shine as the sun, and his raiment was white as the light." At this moment Moses and Elias appeared and talked with Jesus. The subject of their conversation was the death which Jesus should die at Jerusalem. This confirmation helped Jesus as He approached that tragic day.

The disciples whom Jesus had planned to share this experience with Him had fallen asleep! But they awakened in time to see His glory and also to see the two men who were there with Jesus. It was only as Moses and Elias were departing to return to heaven that Peter awakened sufficiently to suggest that they be allowed to make three tabernacles, or booths, for the use of Jesus and His heavenly guests. Peter really did not know what to say, for they all were frightened.

At this time a cloud descended upon them and enveloped them, increasing their fear. Out of this cloud, however, there came a reassuring word, "This is my beloved Son, in whom I am well pleased; hear ye him." When the disciples heard this voice they fell on their faces and were "sore afraid." But Jesus came and touched them and said, "Arise, and be not afraid." As they came down from the mountain Jesus instructed them to tell no man what things they had seen until He was risen from the dead. Although He had told them plainly, following Peter's declaration that He was indeed the Son of God, that He was to be killed and would rise again after three days, yet they questioned one with another what the rising from the dead should mean.

The appearance of Elias on the Mount of Transfiguration reminded the disciples of Malachi's prediction that Elijah would be sent before the coming of the great and terrible day of the Lord (Malachi 4:5). They asked Jesus why this should be. Jesus replied that it would truly come to pass and that Elijah would surely come and restore all things. Jesus then reminded the disciples that the angel Gabriel had told the father of John the Baptist, before the birth of the prophet, that he would come "in the spirit and power of Elias" (Luke 1:17). This, said Jesus, had already happened in the coming of John the Baptist.

HEALS LUNATIC SON (*Matthew* 17:14-21; *Mark* 9:14-29; *Luke* 9:37-42)

When they arrived on the plain the very next day Jesus found the other disciples surrounded by a great multitude of people. Upon His arrival they immediately turned their attention to Him. It was apparent that the purpose of their coming together was to see another miracle. A certain man had brought his lunatic boy to the disciples for healing, but they could not cure him. Jesus invited them to bring the lad to Him. He asked the father concerning the need of his child, and was told that an evil spirit possessed him, often casting him into the fire and into the water to destroy him. The father expressed some faith in Christ: "If thou canst do anything, have compassion upon us, and help us." Whereupon Jesus pronounced the eternal principle, "All things are possible to him that believeth." The father then asked the Lord to help his unbelief, whereupon Jesus delivered the boy.

When the defeated disciples came into the house they asked Jesus the reason for their inability to cast out the evil spirit. Jesus again emphasized the need for faith, saying that real faith, though small, would enable them to do anything. He added, however, that this particular kind of problem could be solved only by prayer and fasting.

AGAIN FORETELLS HIS DEATH (*Matthew* 17:22, 23; *Mark* 9:30-32; *Luke* 9:43-45)

Jesus began another tour through Galilee. He correctly sensed that His disciples did not understand concerning what was shortly to befall Him, although He had told them plainly. So once more He explained: "Let these sayings sink down into your ears, for the Son of man shall be betrayed into the hands of men: and they shall kill him, and the third day he shall be raised again." In spite of the clearness of this declaration it is recorded that they did not understand Him and were afraid to ask Him.

COIN IN FISH'S MOUTH (*Matthew* 17:24-27)

Upon their return to Capernaum the tax collector came to Peter and inquired concerning whether or not Jesus paid taxes. Peter assured him that He did and came to report the matter to the Lord. Before He spoke, however, Jesus posed a problem for him: Is it the custom for kings to tax their own children or their subjects? When Peter replied, "Their subjects," Jesus said, "Then are the children free." By this He meant that He and His disciples were the children of the great King of all the earth and should therefore be free from taxation. But, He recognized, they were living in Caesar's realm and had an obligation to him. Therefore He instructed Peter to go to the sea and cast in a hook. He assured him that the first fish he would catch would have a coin in its mouth. This would be sufficient to pay the tax for himself and for Peter too.

Lesson 22

SERMON ON A CHILD (*Matthew* 18:1-7, 10; *Mark* 9:33-37, 42; *Luke* 9:46-48)

While they were at Capernaum Jesus gently reprimanded the disciples for a conversation which they had had among themselves on the road. He asked them to tell Him about it, but they hesitated for they had been arguing together who should be the greatest. Jesus then took a child of the house where He was staying and, holding him in His arms, said, "The way to be the greatest in the kingdom of God is to become as a little child. Also, there is a special protection given to those who believe on Me as a little child, for in heaven each such childlike believer has an angel appointed by My Father. And to cause such a believer to stumble is so serious an offence that it would be preferable to the offender to have a millstone hanged about his neck and to be drowned in the depths of the sea."

DISCIPLINE IN THE CHURCH (*Matthew* 18:15-20)

"And if one of these brethren in the kingdom shall trespass against another, the one who is wronged should go and talk the matter over with the one who has sinned against him. It is to be hoped that reconciliation can be made and thus settle the matter. But if the wrongdoer will not admit his sin, then the brother shall take two or three of his brethren with him in an effort to make peace between them. If the offending brother still refuses to repent, the whole church should be informed of his attitude and should unite in an effort to win him back. If they fail there is no alternative but to cut him off as a brother."

In this connection Jesus spoke further of the united power of believers. Any two of them could agree in prayer, He said, and He promised that His Father would respond to their petition. Also,

116

even two or three gathered together in His name could be assured that He would be there personally in their midst.

A PARABLE OF FORGIVENESS (*Matthew* 18:21-35; *Luke* 17:3, 4)

An occasion arose shortly for Jesus to teach the importance of Christians forgiving one another. Peter came to Jesus with a question. "How oft shall my brother sin against me, and I forgive him?" Peter suggested that seven times might be enough. Jesus replied, "No, not seven times, but seventy times seven." He then told a story to emphasize His answer.

A certain king discovered that one of his servants owed him "ten thousand talents" (about ten million dollars). He was about to take the customary action in the matter and sell the man, his wife, his children, and all that he had in an effort to recover something of the debt. The servant, however, fell down before him and worshiped him, pleading that mercy might be extended to him. He promised to pay all that he owed if he were given time in which to do so. The king forgave the man and canceled the entire debt. But then this liberated servant went out and found a man who owed him about 20 dollars and demanded roughly that he pay the debt. The same scene was enacted as that in which this forgiven man had been the debtor a few days before. The man who owed 20 dollars pled for mercy, but the forgiven servant would not forgive his fellow-servant. Instead he actually cast him into prison till he should pay the debt.

The story of what had happened came to the ears of the king, and he called the first servant into his presence again. He was exceedingly angry with the servant, canceled his forgiveness, and delivered the man to the tormentors. Now the shocking conclusion to this story, in the words of Jesus, was: "So likewise shall my heavenly Father do also unto you, if ye from your hearts forgive not every one his brother their trepasses." How solemn is this declaration and how urgent is the requirement that we shall forgive freely and fully our brethren in the Lord.

REBUKES SECTARIANISM (*Mark* 9:38-41; *Luke* 9:49, 50)

Again Jesus taught His disciples concerning their attitude toward their fellow servants. This time it was John who came to Him. The disciples had found one who was casting out devils in Christ's name and they had forbidden him to do so because he was not following

them. Jesus rebuked this attitude and assured John, and us all, that
"He that is not against us is with us." Everything from performing
miracles to giving a cup of water in His name because one belongs
to Christ is sure to have a reward.

WARNS OF HELL (*Matthew* 18:8,9; *Mark* 9:43-50)

The seriousness of the possibility of a millstone being hanged
around one's neck and his being cast into the sea, and the certainty
that our heavenly Father will not forgive those who do not forgive
their fellowmen which will result in their being delivered to the
tormentors, led Jesus to comment at length about the reality of hell.
He stated that it would be far better to have one's hand and foot
cut off and one's eye plucked out if these members caused us to sin
than to miss heaven entirely. Then He gave a faithful, plain description of the unquenchable fire of hell and a warning that existence there would never be extinguished. "Where their worm dieth
not, and the fire is not quenched."

Lesson 23

COST OF DISCIPLESHIP (*Matthew* 8:19-22; *Luke* 9:57-62)

As they walked along Jesus found opportunity to emphasize the cost of being one of His disciples. To one man who volunteered to follow Him Jesus said, "Even the animals and birds have their holes and nests, but I have nowhere to lay My head." Another requested that he might be allowed first to go home and attend the funeral of his father. To this man Jesus said, "Let those who themselves are dead in their sins take care of such matters: it is urgent that you go now and preach the kingdom of God." To a third man who requested permission to pay a farewell visit to his home Jesus said, "If a man starts following me and then looks back, it proves that he is not fit for the kingdom of God."

SENDS SEVENTY FORTH (*Luke* 10:1-12)

The need for training His successors was evidently upon the mind of the Lord for He now chose seventy other disciples and sent them forth to gain experience in gospel ministry. As with the twelve on a previous occasion, He sent them two by two and gave them instructions about their clothing and other equipment. He told them what to say when they first entered a home. They were also told not to go from house to house but remain in the first home into which they came, partaking of its hospitality. They were to heal the sick and proclaim the arrival of the kingdom of God. He warned them that they would be as lambs among wolves. If they should be rejected, they should make it very clear that since their hearers had rejected their opportunity of salvation, their guilt was greater than that of Sodom. The need for their going was urgent for Jesus said, "The harvest truly is great, but the laborers are few." They were to pray as they went that "the Lord of the harvest . . . would send forth laborers into his harvest."

UPBRAIDS CERTAIN CITIES AND REBUKES HEROD (*Matthew* 11:20-24; *Luke* 10:13-16; 13:31-33)

Christ's reference to Sodom (Luke 10:12) led Him to compare the fate of some of the cities in which He had ministered with that of Sodom and Tyre and Sidon. Chorazin, Bethsaida, and Capernaum all came under His denunciation. He declared that the ancient cities would have repented in sackcloth and ashes if they had had the opportunity for salvation which had been accorded these cities on the shores of Galilee.

Jesus also took the attitude toward Herod which His forerunner, John the Baptist, had taken. He sent a message to "that fox" to the effect that Herod could not kill Him for it was ordained that He should perish at Jeruslem.

RETURN OF THE SEVENTY (*Luke* 10:17-24; *Matthew* 11:25-30)

In due time the seventy disciples whom Christ had sent forth on a preaching mission returned to report. With joy they told the Lord that even the demons had been subject to them through His name. He told them not to rejoice in that fact but rather that they were among His disciples and that their names were written in heaven. Jesus also commented that Satan was a defeated foe and that He had indeed given His disciples power over all power of the devil.

This fact caused Jesus to rejoice in His own spirit and thank His Father that these spiritual verities had been hidden from the wise and prudent of the earth but had been revealed to babes such as His disciples. All such mysteries and such power had been given unto Him, and He in turn had revealed them to those whom He had chosen. Turning to His disciples He said, "You are indeed fortunate to see the things that you now see, for many prophets and kings before you have desired to see and hear them but have not been able."

Not forgetting the multitudes that were around Him, Jesus turned and issued the immortal proclamation, "All that labor and are heavy laden are invited to come unto me, and I will give them rest. In addition, if they will take my yoke and learn of me, they will find a still deeper rest in their souls."

HIS BROTHERS DERIDE HIM (*John* 7:1-9)

When it was time for the Feast of Tabernacles, Jesus' brothers suggested that He attend in order to further what they thought were His political ambitions. It was thus revealed that His own brothers did not yet believe on Him as the great Messiah. Jesus replied that they should go on to the feast for they were free to come and go as they chose. They were in perfect harmony with the populace. But as for himself, His times were controlled by His Father, and this restrained Him from going to the feast immediately. He also indicated that He was out of harmony with the world around Him; as a matter of fact, the world hated Him because He had testified that its works were evil.

Within a short time, however, He left Galilee, crossed the river Jordan, and approached the border of Judea. Here as formerly the multitudes followed Him, and He taught them again and healed them.

HEALS TEN LEPERS (*Luke* 17:11-19)

On this journey which had Jerusalem as its objective, Jesus passed through a certain village where He was accosted by ten lepers. In conformity with the restraint placed upon people having this loathsome disease, the lepers stood at a distance from Him. But they lifted up their voices and cried out, asking Him to have mercy upon them. They were not close enough for Him to touch them the way He had touched and healed a leper in the first part of His ministry, so He merely called to them, instructing them to follow the directions which Moses had given to be observed by those who were healed of leprosy. Here is another intimation that divine healing of leprosy was possible in the Old Testament economy. Jesus had commented in His first sermon at Nazareth that the lepers in Israel had not availed themselves of this provision and that Naaman, the Gentile Syrian, was the only one of that generation who had been healed of this disease by the power of the Lord. But now all ten of these leprous men started off in obedience to the command of the Lord to show themselves as healed men to the priests. This action on their part showed their faith. Although they were all healed only one turned back to give thanks to the Lord for his healing. This one was not a Jew, and Jesus commented upon this fact. He then spoke reassuringly to the healed Samaritan, "Arise, go thy way: thy faith hath made thee whole."

PARABLE OF GOOD SAMARITAN (*Luke* 10:25-37)

Jesus perhaps had the experience of this grateful Samaritan in mind when He encountered a certain lawyer who sought to test Him. This lawyer asked Jesus what he should do to inherit eternal life. Jesus required the man to give his own opinion in the matter. The lawyer then quoted the words of Moses concerning loving God supremely and loving one's neighbor as one's self. Jesus then said, in substance, "What further do you think is needed by way of answer to your question?" He of course knew but He wanted to draw the lawyer out. The man then asked for a technical definition as to who one's neighbor was. He doubtless wanted to quibble in the matter and give no more compliance to the law than that which was necessary.

Without becoming technical Jesus told him a sweet and wonderful story. It concerned the man who went down from Jerusalem to Jericho and fell among thieves. Both a priest and a Levite in turn passed him by. (It was kind of the Lord not to speak of a lawyer.) Later a Samaritan came by and had great mercy on the wounded man, doing everything possible for his comfort and restoration. Jesus then let the lawyer himself tell who he thought was neighbor to him that fell among thieves. The answer was so obvious that when it came Jesus simply remarked, "Go, and do thou likewise." This then was not only the academic answer to the lawyer's question; it was personal instruction to him to practice being a neighbor wherever he went.

STUDY QUESTIONS—UNIT TWO

LESSON 12

1. What was the second miracle which Jesus performed in Cana of Galilee?
2. From what Old Testament book did Jesus read when He stood up to preach in His home church at Nazareth?
3. What were the results of this, His first sermon at Nazareth?

LESSON 13

1. What miracle on the shore of Lake Galilee was the occasion of the permanent call of Peter, Andrew, James, and John?
2. What disturbance occurred in the service when Jesus taught in the synagogue at Capernaum?
3. When Jesus healed so many people at Capernaum what prediction by Isaiah did Matthew say was being fulfilled?

LESSON 14

1. Mention two special miracles which Jesus performed when He began a tour of Galilee.
2. How did Jesus break social custom when He called Matthew to be His disciple?
3. What was Jesus' response when they accused Him of eating with publicans and sinners?

LESSON 15

1. What miracle did Christ perform at the pool of Bethesda at Jerusalem?
2. Name the four witneses which Jesus cited in defense of His claim to be the Son of God.
3. What attitude did the Lord take toward the Sabbath which so enraged the Jews?

LESSON 16

1. Name the twelve apostles.

2. What are the first twelve verses of the Sermon on the Mount usually called?
3. What attitude did the Lord take toward the Old Testament law?

LESSON 17

1. What proof did Jesus send to John the Baptist that He was indeed the Messiah?
2. What did Jesus say is the unpardonable sin?
3. What was the "sign of the prophet Jonas"?

LESSON 18

1. Name four of the parables which Jesus told as recorded in Matthew 13.
2. What was the attitude of the citizens of Gadara toward Jesus when He cast the legion of demons out of the possessed man?
3. What miracle did Jesus perform in the home of Jairus, a ruler of the Jews?
4. Describe the death of John the Baptist.

LESSON 19

1. What did the five thousand men do when Jesus multiplied the loaves and fishes to feed them?
2. What spiritual truth did Jesus illustrate by giving bread to the multitude?
3. Why did Jesus hesitate to heal the daughter of the Syrophonician woman?

LESSON 20

1. What was the leaven of the Pharisees and the Sadducees?
2. What was the Rock upon which Jesus said He would build His church?
3. After Peter's confession that Jesus was the Son of God, what surprise announcement did Jesus make?

LESSON 21

1. Describe the transfiguration of Jesus.
2. What was the subject of conversation between Jesus and Moses and Elijah?
3. How did Jesus get the money with which to pay the taxes for himself and Peter?

LESSON 22

1. What example of humility did Jesus use to show how one could enter into the kingdom of heaven?
2. What procedure did Jesus say should be followed in the church when one brother transgressed against another?
3. What punishment did Jesus say our heavenly Father would mete out to those who will not forgive their brethren?
4. How did Jesus describe hell?

LESSON 23

1. With what did Jesus compare the fate of Capernaum, Bethsaida, and Chorazin?
2. What did Jesus tell the seventy disciples whom He sent out on a preaching mission was more wonderful than their ability to cast out devils?
3. What spiritual lesson did Jesus teach by the parable of the Good Samaritan?

UNIT THREE

Lessons 24 through 35

JERUSALEM AND PEREAN MINISTRY

LAST JOURNEY TO JERUSALEM

LAST PUBLIC MINISTRY

Lesson 24

ATTENDS FEAST AT JERUSALEM (*John* 7:10 *to* 8:1)

Our Lord's journey now brought Him to Jerusalem in time for at least a part of the Feast of Tabernacles (a seven-day festival). The people were disturbed about Him, some being for Him and some against. Upon arriving He went immediately into the temple and began to teach. The Jews were impressed with His learning, especially since He had not been educated in their rabbinical schools. (Incidentally, here is a perfect definition of formal and informal education: "How knoweth this man letters?" informal education: "having never learned?" formal education.)

Jesus explained, "My teaching is really not mine, but his that sent me." As He said later, "The words that I speak unto you I speak not of myself" (John 14:10). "For I have not spoken of myself; but the Father which sent me, he gave me a commandment, what I should say, and what I should speak" (John 12:49). He went on to say, "If a person will obey my words, he will realize that it is the Father that is speaking through me." He then added an eternal principle: "He that speaketh of himself seeketh his own glory: he that seeketh his glory that sent him, the same is true, and no un-righteousness is in him" (John 7:18). An argument ensued among the Jews which culminated in the Pharisees sending officers to arrest Jesus. These men, however, were so impressed with the beauty and truth of His words that they returned without arresting Him.

Each morning of the Feast of Tabernacles a priest went from the temple to the pool of Siloam, where he filled a golden vase with water and carried it to the temple amid joyful cries of the people. He poured it out at the side of the altar of burnt offering. The rabbis connected this ceremony with the latter rain and the pouring out

129

of the gift of the Holy Spirit as predicted by the prophets (Isaiah
44:3; Joel 2:28, 29). On the last day of the feast Jesus publicly declared the true spiritual significance of this ceremony: "If any man
thirst let him come unto me, and drink" (John 7:37). Conscious of
the fact that His crucifixion was near at hand, He promised also,
"He that believeth on me . . . out of his inmost parts shall flow
rivers of living water." This was a reference to the Holy Spirit
indwelling believers and flowing out through them to the thirsty
people of succeeding generations.

FORGIVES ADULTEROUS WOMAN (*John* 8:2-11)

Jesus continued His ministry in the temple after the feast was
past. One morning the scribes and Pharisees conspired to trap Him
in His talk. They brought to Him a woman who had been arrested
for adultery. They cited that Moses commanded that such should
be stoned, and asked Him what they should do. Would He contra-
dict Moses or would He act with a severity which they felt was
contrary to His nature? Jesus did not answer immediately but stooped
down and with His finger wrote on the ground. Perhaps He delayed
so as to be sure that He had His Father's answer. When they insisted
that He reply, He said to them, "He that is without sin among you,
let him first cast a stone at her." How devastating a reply! It is the
classic answer to people who are quick to accuse their neighbor.
Again Jesus stooped down and wrote on the ground, and one by
one the woman's accusers shamefacedly went away. Only the woman
was left standing before Jesus. He asked, "Hath no man condemned
thee?" And He neither condemned nor condoned her, His answer
was simply, "Go, and sin no more."

DISCOURSE CONCERNING HIMSELF (*John* 8:12-30)

All the real issues of life focus upon Jesus Christ. He turned then
to encourage His listeners to believe in Him so that, in believing,
they might have life in His name (John 20:31). He had recently
declared that He is the divine Water sent to slake the thirst of the
world. He now declared, "I am the light of the world." When the
Pharisees accused Him of boasting, He reminded them that it was
not He alone who made this claim, but the Father who was with
Him confirmed it. He cited their law to the effect that the testimony
of two men can settle a case. Thus He declared that He and the
Father are two distinct personalities. This is in direct opposition to

the teaching of Unitarians who exalt either the Father or the Son as the one Person in the Godhead. Jesus climaxed His claim concerning Himself by saying, "If ye believe not that *I am* [the great Jehovistic title of Exodus 3:14] he, ye shall die in your sins." He then gave them an intimation of His approaching crucifixion, "When ye have lifted up the Son of man, then ye shall know that I am." And many believed on Him then.

Concerning Freedom (*John* 8:31-59)

Jesus began immediately to instruct those who had just believed on Him. He told them they would have to continue in His Word to become His disciples indeed. There was much truth ahead that they would come to know, and this truth would make them free. But immediately they stumbled at His teaching. They resented the implication that they were not already free. Jesus then declared the eternal truth, "Whosoever committeth sin is the servant of sin." He told them frankly that He was the one, the only one, who could make them free indeed. They contended that they had no need because they were Abraham's seed. Jesus pointed out that their deeds and attitude were not those which Abraham would do or take and that, therefore, they were not real children of Abraham. In reality, they revealed that their true father was the devil, for it was his lust that they were indulging. The devil is a murderer, and they were seeking to conceal their sin, thus acting a lie. He then challenged them to convict Him of sin and thus justify their antagonism to Him. They then showed their unbelief by asking, "Art thou greater than our father Abraham?" He replied simply, "Before Abraham was, *I am*." Here again He used the Jehovistic title. This time they picked up stones to cast at Him, but He quietly went through their midst out of the temple.

Mary and Martha (*Luke* 10:38-42)

About two miles east of Jerusalem was the village of Bethany, the home of Martha and Mary and Lazarus. Martha welcomed Jesus into their home. As Martha was preparing a meal to entertain her Guest, her sister Mary forgot to help her, so interested was she in the words of Jesus. Martha did not appreciate being left alone with the "much serving," and even gently chided the Lord himself, accusing Him of not caring that Mary had left her alone to serve. "Bid her therefore that she help me." Ignoring Martha's criticism of Him, Jesus called attention to her being so troubled about many "things." "A simple meal would have been sufficient, and your sister, Mary, has shown the better judgment by evaluating My words greater than the material things about which you are so concerned." He refused to take away that "good part" from Mary who sat at His feet and heard His word.

Lesson 25

MAN BORN BLIND (*John* 9:1-41)

While itinerating one day Christ saw a man who was blind from birth. This provoked a question from His disciples. "Master, who did sin, this man, or his parents, that he was born blind?" Here was either preexistence or the transmission of sins to succeeding generations. Jesus rejected both theories and offered a new one: "He is blind that the works of God shoud be made manifest in him." This was His introduction to the miracle which He was about to perform. But He first declared that His works were in reality the works of Him that sent Him. And He added, "I must work the works of Him that sent me, while it is day: the night cometh, when no man can work." A little while before this He had declared, "I am the light of the world." He now modified this statement, saying, "As long as I am in the world, I am the light of the world." He had previously stated at the Feast of Tabernacles that He could slake the thirst of the world and that after His going the Holy Spirit would provide rivers of living water through believers. Now He implied that the Light of the world, which He now was, would be projected through believers long after He had withdrawn from the world. This was clearly stated in the Sermon on the Mount, "Ye are the light of the world."

Jesus then turned to the work which His Father had given Him to do. He anointed the eyes of the blind man with clay and told him to go wash in the pool of Siloam. The man expressed his faith by going, and he came back with his eyesight restored. It is interesting to note the progress of faith which this healed man showed. In answer to his neighbor's questions, he said to them, "A *man* that is called Jesus anointed mine eyes, . . . and I received sight." They then brought the healed man to the Pharisees who also interrogated

him. The Pharisees could not appreciate the miracle because Jesus
had performed it on the Sabbath Day. He had violated their law
concerning the Sabbath, which to them outweighed the beneficent
miracle of restoring sight to the blind man. In their query of the
man born blind, they asked what he thought of Jesus. This time he
said, "He is a *prophet.*" They retorted, "He is a sinner." The man
replied valiantly, "One thing I know, that, whereas I was blind,
now I see." They reviled him and cast him out of the synagogue.

Jesus, hearing of the result of the man's encounter with the Pharisees, sought him out and asked him plainly, "Dost thou believe on
the Son of God?" To the man's question, "Who is he, Lord, that I
might believe on him?" Jesus replied simply, "It is he that talketh
with thee." The man replied, "Lord, I believe," and worshiped
Him. This was the climax of the development of his faith in his
Healer and Saviour. Jesus then announced, "I have a dual purpose
in coming into this world: to give sight to the physically blind and
to condemn those who wilfully are spiritually blind." To the Pharisees He then said, "Your sin remaineth."

THE SHEEPFOLD (*John* 10:1-42)

The pool of Siloam, at which the blind man had washed and
received his sight, was in Jerusalem. It was therefore evidently in
this environment that Jesus made His great declaration concerning
the sheepfold. The Bible calls it a parable since it clothed some
beautiful spiritual thoughts in simple common language. He spoke
of the shepherd and the sheep, the sheepfold and the door. He
referred also to hirelings and strangers, thieves and robbers. And
then He explained, "I am the good shepherd" (vv. 2, 11). "My sheep
are they that hear my voice and follow me" (v. 27). He said He is
the door of the sheepfold (vv. 7, 9). He promised to lead His sheep
in and out to find pasture, always going before them. There would
be thieves and robbers, who would try to get into the sheepfold,
who would not acknowledge Him as the door. Their purpose would
be to steal, to kill, and to destroy. Strangers, hirelings, would
attempt to lead the sheep, but the sheep would not follow. The
hirelings would abandon the sheep in an hour of peril, but He the
Good Shepherd would give His very life *for* the sheep. Further,
He would give His life *to* the sheep that they might have life more
abundantly (v. 10).

The Jews surrounded Jesus as He taught and asked Him to tell them plainly if He was the Christ. He replied, "I have already told you, but you have not believed. Your lack of faith proves that you are not my sheep. They who are really my sheep hear my voice and follow me, and I give them eternal life. No man will be able to pluck them out of my Father's hand or out of my hand, for I and my Father are one." This was His insistent, truthful witness concerning himself. The Jews then proved His estimation of them by taking up stones to kill Him. Jesus reminded them of the good works which He had shown them from His Father. They declared plainly that they considered Him a blasphemer because He made himself the Son of God. He asked them, "How can you say that he whom the Father hath sanctified and sent into the world is blaspheming because he saith, 'I am the Son of God'?" But they would not believe and sought again to take Him. This time He went away beyond the river Jordan to the district called Perea.

REBUKES PHARISEES AND LAWYERS (*Luke* 11:37-54)

Beyond Jordan in Perea Jesus continued His ministry. Again a Pharisee invited Him for a meal. And again a conflict ensued. The Pharisee "marvelled" that Jesus had not gone through their ceremony of a ritualistic washing of hands before sitting down to eat. Immediately the Lord called his attention to the greater necessity of cleansing one's heart. He cited how foolish it is to cleanse oneself outwardly and to leave one's heart full of wickedness. He said a woeful fate awaits those who observe outward religious ceremony, even tithing, but who ignore the love of God which is far more important. He said the outward performance is proper, but by no means should the inward operation and condition be omitted or ignored.

Some lawyers who were present immediately said, "Master, thus saying thou reproachest us also." Christ agreed and called attention to the special sins of which the lawyers were guilty. They made grievous laws for the people to observe but they themselves would not conform to them. He then revealed that it was within the wisdom of His Father to send prophets and apostles to that sinful generation, and that these wicked children of those who had killed the prophets would add to the wickedness of their fathers by following in their footsteps. Accumulated judgment would fall upon that generation for the blood of righteous men from Abel until the present time.

He then noted the particular sin of the lawyers in refusing to go God's way and not allowing others to do so either.

THE RICH FOOL (*Luke* 12:13-21)

It was probably on this occasion that a certain person of the group that surrounded the Master sought to gain His assistance in a personal quarrel with his brother. It appears that their father had died, and the brother of this man had seized upon the whole inheritance. The man asked the Lord to instruct his brother to divide the inheritance with him. The Lord refused to be drawn into this personal quarrel, avowing that He had not been made a judge or a divider in such a matter, and He used the occasion to issue a general warning. Both of these contending brothers had betrayed the covetousness of their hearts. Jesus therefore warned all people to "beware of covetousness: for a man's life consisteth not in the abundance of the things which he possesseth." How profound and revolutionary is this teaching and how counter to the usual standards of life.

To emphasize and illustrate His teaching, Jesus told the story of a certain rich man. He had reaped an abundant harvest, more than he had room to store away, and was in the act of building greater barns when his soul was called into judgment. "Then whose shall those things be, which thou hast provided?" The answer is apparent. It is far better to be rich toward God than to lay up treasure on earth.

Lesson 26

The Importunate Friend (*Luke* 11:5-13)

Jesus turned then to teach the immortal lesson of importunate prayer. He told the story of a person who went at midnight to a friend's house to borrow three loaves of bread. He explained that he had received unexpected company and needed the bread to serve them. The man within resented the intrusion at that hour of the night and refused to get up and give the man what he asked. But the man on the outside continued to call and request assistance until the friend within finally arose and gave him what he asked, simply to get rid of him and his disturbance. Jesus said, "This is a picture of what a person may sometimes encounter when he comes to God in prayer. Not that God the Father is indifferent to the need and request of His children, but He deliberately delays His response in order to test the earnestness and faith of the individual who is asking."

Three degrees of prayer are here taught: ask, seek, and knock. It is purely incidental that the letters with which these three words begin form the word *ask.* Jesus taught that one should persist through all three stages and degrees of prayer when desiring from the heavenly Father the Holy Spirit or other good things. He assures us, however, that the heavenly Father is far more willing to give good gifts to His children than earthly parents are to give to their children. David said (Psalm 103:13), "Like as a father," and now Jesus adds, "how much more." Here is beautiful consolation and encouragement to those who come to God in prayer.

Watching for the Wedding (*Luke* 12:35-38)

In speaking to His disciples concerning their privilege in prayer, Christ's thoughts turned to the hour of His second coming. We will find in His story of the unjust judge, who finally avenged the widow because of her continual coming, that He concluded that story with the phrase (Luke 18:8), "When the Son of man cometh, shall he find faith on the earth?"

The way to be ready for His coming is to keep one's loins girded and one's light burning. This refers to faithful witness unto the end and a constant readiness to leave this world. He said also that His disciples should look for His coming and be ready to welcome Him at any moment. And now He makes an amazing offer and prediction. He will even "gird himself, and make them to sit down to meat, and will come forth and serve them." We can imagine ourselves as embarassed as Peter when the Lord girded Himself to wash the disciples' feet, or as John the Baptist when Jesus requested to be baptized by him. He will still be "this same Jesus," and His disciples will ever be the fortunate recipients of His love and mercy. Blessed indeed are the servants who are watching for His return.

REPENT OR PERISH (*Luke* 13:1-5)

Something happened then that gave Jesus occasion to declare another immortal truth. Certain people told Him that Pilate had killed some Galileans and had actually mingled their blood with the sacrifices that were being offered in the temple. Jesus then indicated that these were not unusual sinners who had suffered such a fate. Another current event of that time was the falling of a tower at the pool of Siloam, which had killed eighteen persons. Were these also very wicked sinners? Jesus answered for them and for men of all times that people who lose their lives in such accidents are not necessarily unusually wicked, but simply are made an example so that men may see that death awaits all people who will not repent.

PARABLE OF BARREN FIG TREE (*Luke* 13:6-9)

Our Lord's thoughts then turned to the nation as a whole that sometimes in the Scriptures is likened unto a fig tree. He told the story of a man who planted a fig tree in his vineyard and naturally expected it to bear fruit. For three years, however, the tree did not bear, and he commanded the vineyard keeper to cut it down. The keeper requested that one more year be given in which he would give special treatment to the tree in the hope that it would still bear. If it then did not bear he would agree that it be cut down. This was a picture of God's infinite patience with His people, the

Jews, in spite of their not living and serving as He had planned they should. He would probably still give them a little further opportunity. This was fulfilled in the forty years extension of judgment which should have fallen upon them immediately upon their crucifixion of God's Son.

WOMAN LOOSED FROM INFIRMITY (*Luke* 13:10-17)

Again He taught in a synagogue on a Sabbath Day. In the audience was a woman who was so stooped that she was "bowed together" and could not lift up herself. She had been like this for eighteen years. When Jesus saw her He was moved with compassion for her and called her to Him. He laid His hands on her, spoke the word of authority to loose her from her infirmity, and immediately she lifted herself up and glorified God. The people naturally rejoiced at this wonderful healing, but the ruler of the synagogue was angry. Was it not the Sabbath Day? He announced to the people that healing was all right on the other six days of the week but not on the Sabbath. Why? Jesus pointed out that the position of the ruler of the synagogue was untenable for the simple reason that any one of that audience would not hestitate to loose his animal from its stall and lead him away to water on the Sabbath Day. Healing and being healed was no harder work than that. He said this daughter of Abraham, "whom Satan hath bound," ought to be loosed from her bondage even on the Sabbath Day. Incidentally, Jesus here called attention to the fact that it was Satan who had bound her. This identifies the origin and author of sickness. Peter said later (Acts 10:38) that Jesus "went about doing good, and healing all that were oppressed of the devil."

HEALING OF MAN WITH DROPSY (*Luke* 14:1-6)

The contention about the Sabbath Day would not subside. The Pharisees made traps to provoke Jesus to heal on the Sabbath Day. A chief Pharisee invited Him to dinner on the Sabbath and also invited a certain man who had dropsy. They rightly expected that Jesus would heal the man. Before doing so, however, Jesus asked the lawyers and Pharisees who were present if it would be lawful for Him to heal the man. They preferred to make no comment. But Jesus was not so politically minded. He healed the man and then asked His critics, "Are there any of you who would not extend a kindness even to your animals if one fell into a pit on a Sabbath Day?" Of course they could not answer Him.

Lesson 27

THE AMBITIOUS GUEST (*Luke* 14:7-15)

The dinner at the Pharisee's home also provided Jesus with an opportunity to teach another lesson. He had noticed how, when the guests arrived, they did not wait to be seated by their host but went immediately to the place of honor. He reminded them of the possibility of their being asked to vacate the seat they had chosen for one that was less honorable. He said it would be much wiser had they taken the lower place first and then been invited to come up higher. He cited the eternal principle, "Whosoever exalteth himself shall be abased; and he that humbleth himself shall be exalted."

To His host also Jesus had a word of exhortation. He condemned the common practice of inviting one's friends and rich neighbors to a feast for the purpose of being invited by them in turn. It would be far more unselfish and noble to invite people to a feast who would not be able to return the invitation. He promised, however, that such an action would be compensated at the "resurrection of the just." Someone present at the dinner called out the true observation, "Blessed is he that shall eat bread in the kingdom of God." That indeed is the highest honor!

THE GREAT SUPPER (*Luke* 14:16-24)

To the person who had remarked about the value of eating bread in the kingdom of God, Jesus addressed the following parable. It concerned a certain man who made a great supper and issued invitations to many people. When the time arrived, the servant whom the host sent to call the invited guests met with many excuses. Some were too busy with material and domestic matters to accept the invitation. When this was reported to the host, he was angry and sent his servants to invite the poor and the crippled. This was exactly what Jesus had just instructed His own host at the dinner which

they were then attending. In the story Jesus told, the servant actually brought in many people of this description but still there was
room at the feast. The climax of the story shows the servant being
sent out again into the highways and hedges to constrain people to
come in, for the giver of the supper was anxious that his house be
filled. This parable illustrates God's great desire that people of the
world should accept His bounty, but it also shows God's anger at
those who reject His invitation.

THE UNFINISHED TOWER (*Luke* 14:25-33)

To those who would follow Him Jesus announced plainly that
their estimation of Him and His teaching should be higher than
their evaluation of sacred family ties and even of their own individual
lives. Christ taught that anything that comes between a man and
his spiritual welfare is in reality an enemy and as such should be
hated. If turning one's back on things that hinder constitutes a cross
to a would-be disciple, then he should take up that cross and follow
Christ regardless. As a matter of fact, one should forsake all he has
in order to follow Christ.

He warned His listeners that they should carefully count the cost
as they contemplated following Him. He gave two illustrations. Who
would undertake to build a tower and not have sufficient money to
finish it? Would the unfinished structure not mock the man who
had foolishly begun it? Would it not be wise of a king to make peace
with an enemy who came against him with double the force that he
himself had, rather than to suffer certain defeat at the hand of his
enemy? For these reasons, Jesus said, anyone who contemplated
becoming His disciple should carefully consider the full extent of
what was involved before he turned to follow Him.

THE LOST SHEEP AND THE LOST COIN (*Matthew* 18:11-14; *Luke* 15:1-10)

Again the Pharisees criticized Jesus for mingling with "sinners"
and eating with them. (They had not yet perceived that He considered the Pharisees the greatest sinners in His audience.) But Jesus
defended His mingling with needy men by telling the following
stories.

A man could have one hundred sheep, ninety-nine of which were
safe within the fold, and yet not be satisfied until he found the one
sheep that was lost. And when he found that sheep he would actually

call his friends and neighbors together to rejoice with him. Jesus then declared that in heaven there is great joy when one sinner repents.

Likewise, a woman could own ten pieces of silver and lose one and be greatly disturbed at its loss. She would light a candle, sweep the house, and seek diligently till she found the coin. She too would call her friends and neighbors to rejoice with her in having found the piece that was lost. Again the Lord declared there is joy in the presence of the angels of God in heaven over one sinner that repents.

THE PRODIGAL SON (*Luke* 15:11-32)

The most famous, and possibly the most effective, of the stories which Jesus told to illustrate the value of a lost soul is the one known as the Prodigal Son. This brings the matter into the human domestic realm which is so close to us all. The story concerns a father and his two sons. The younger of the two tired of the parental roof and asked his father for his share in the estate, in advance of his falling heir to it. His motive was clear. He rebelled against his father's control and wanted to launch out on his own. The father graciously acceded to his request and bade farewell to his erring son. As the father doubtless warned him, it was not long until he was fleeced of all his wealth and was reduced to being a menial servant. In his destitute and desperate condition he repented of his foolishness and rebellion and determined to return home and humble himself by asking to become a servant in his father's house.

But the father had not lost his love for the wayward boy. When he arrived, his father would not consider employing him as a servant but restored him to the full status of a son. He even made a great feast to celebrate his return. This part of the story was to illustrate the heavenly Father's love for all wayward men.

But this story provided the Lord opportunity to illustrate the attitude of His critics. The wayward son had an elder brother who had remained faithfully at home. But he had no love for his younger brother and did not regret his absence. As a matter of fact, he seemed to resent his return. He would not attend the celebration feast and angrily rebuked his father for showing such attention to the son who had returned. The father patiently explained that all that he had belonged to the older son and it was proper that he should join his father in rejoicing at his brother's return. It would therefore be far more fitting for these Pharisees to rejoice when sinners repented than to despise them and criticize the Man who loved them.

THE UNJUST STEWARD (*Luke* 16:1-17)

Our Lord had much more to teach His own disciples. He now told them a story to illustrate the best possible use of earthly goods.

There was a steward whom a rich man had engaged to supervise his goods. The rich man became suspicious that this supervisor was wasting his master's possessions. When it became apparent that the steward was about to lose his position, he began to prepare for the future. He used his position while he still had it to give great discounts to his lord's debtors. He figured that by so doing he would make friends who would receive him into their homes when he lost his job. The Lord commended the steward's foresight (but not his action) and that in the use of money the people of this world are wiser than His own people.

What Jesus meant by this statement became clear as He went on to instruct his disciples about the proper use of money. He warned them that the time would come when they too would have to give account of their earthly stewardship, and they had better begin to plan for that day. They should use the money which had been entrusted to them by God to make friends who would receive them into the everlasting habitations of heaven. This could be done by investing and spending money in such a way that it would be converted into spiritual values which would be to their credit when they arrived at the judgment bar of God. He had told them before, in the Sermon on the Mount, that they should not lay up for themselves treasures on earth but rather lay up treasures in heaven. This was a truth which He was illustrating by His story of the unjust steward. He reminded the disciples that all they had in this life belonged to another (namely, God). They should supervise that treasure in a way which would bring glory to God and which, incidentally, would provide for themselves the true riches of eternity. He warned them against loving "mammon" for mammon's sake but encouraged them to use mammon for God's sake. He concluded the story by saying that man's standard of values is often the exact reverse of God's standard. His followers should live according to God's standards.

Lesson 28

THE RICH MAN AND LAZARUS (*Luke* 16:19-31)

Here follows a story which evidently was not a mere parable for the leading character was named. Lazarus was a beggar who was so helpless that he was carried and laid at the gate of the rich man that he might beg for the scraps which came from the rich man's table. Lazarus died and was carried by the angels to the place in Paradise where Abraham was. Eventually the rich man also died. His soul went into hell where he was in torment. The Lord said that this rich man was able to talk to Abraham. He requested Abraham to send Lazarus to give him the relief which a drop of water on his tongue could afford. But Abraham cited the justice of the situation. He reminded the rich man that he had lived for the good things when he was on earth and had received them. On the other hand, Lazarus had stored up treasure in heaven and now was enjoying his comforts. But in addition, Abraham said, God had made it impossible that there should be transfer across the great gulf which was fixed between them. Then the rich man replied, "Well, at least send him back to my father's house to warn my five brothers of this place of torment which surely awaits them also." But Abraham reminded him that his brothers had the faithful witness of Moses and the prophets. The rich man seemed to think that a person returning from the dead would have greater influence over his brothers than the prophets of old. But Abraham reminded him that if people do not listen to God's Word they will not listen to anything, even to one who has risen from the dead.

This true story is the voice of one who himself has risen from the dead and who knows all about the afterlife. He tells us that laying up treasures not on earth but in heaven will yield eternal dividends.

Also that all men have abundant warning from God in His wonderful Word concerning these eternal verities.

A WORD TO HIS DISCIPLES (*Luke* 17:1-10)

The ignoring of Lazarus by the rich man led Jesus to comment that this would be the lot of His children. However, He warned that if anyone should offend one of His little ones it would be better for him that he be cast into the sea with a millstone about his neck. Verily, "The Lord God of recompenses shall surely requite" (Jeremiah 51:56).

The apostles responded by requesting that the Lord would strengthen their faith. He assured them that this was an appropriate request because faith is exceedingly powerful. Faith as small as a grain of mustard seed would give them power with which to pluck up a tree and command that it be planted in the sea.

On the other hand, they should not become elated by the use of this power but should remember that it is God's power entrusted to them as His servants. To illustrate this Jesus spoke of a hired man on the farm who finished his work in the field and returned to the farmhouse. Jesus asked if it was customary that such a servant be invited to come in and sit down at the table with the owner for whom he worked. Christ said it would rather be expected that the servant would prepare the meal and serve it to his master. Would such service deserve unusual thanks or would it rather be considered in the routine of duty? "So likewise ye, when ye shall have done all those things which are commanded you, say, We are unprofitable servants: we have done that which was our duty to do."

THE UNJUST JUDGE (*Luke* 18:1-8)

On a previous occasion Jesus had illustrated the value and necessity of importunate prayer. He had told the story of the friend who came at midnight to ask for bread and who received the bread only after refusing to go away without it (Luke 11:5-13). Now Jesus told the parable of a hardhearted judge who feared neither God nor man. A widow in that city appealed to him to defend her against a person who was taking advantage of her. But the judge was not interested and ignored her. However, she kept on coming to him, and finally he granted her request in order to get rid of her. Again we see the effectiveness of importunity. How much more will not

God hearken to the cry of His own children who cry day and night unto Him, though sometimes He delays to answer them?

Jesus here made a pathetic comment, as if in meditation. His mind ran forward to the hour of His return to this earth. Passing over the glory of that hour with its great vindication of the Saviour who had been crucified, and all the joy that would be His in that victory. He asked the plaintive question, "When the Son of man cometh, shall he find faith on the earth?" The importunity of this widow was an example of persistent faith. Now He seemed to yearn that there be people on the earth when He returned who would be exercising that kind of faith. Perhaps His return would be in response to that faith. How often do His latter-day children pray, "Even so, come, Lord Jesus."

LAZARUS RAISED FROM THE DEAD (*John* 11:1-46)

Shortly before He left Jerusalem for His Perean ministry Jesus had been entertained in the home of Mary and Martha. These devoted sisters had a brother call Lazarus, who became sick when Jesus was away beyond Jordan. The sisters sent a messenger to Jesus asking Him to come and heal Lazarus. Jesus then commented to His disciples that this sickness was for the glory of God, that the Son of God might be glorified thereby. He then tarried two days before responding to the call of the sisters.

When He started to go to them the disciples reminded Him that the Jews had tried to stone Him when He was there the last time. The Lord used a beautiful figure of speech in His response. He said, "If any man travels in the light of the day he does not stumble because the sun shines on his path. It is only in the night that a man stumbles." This meant, "The great Light of Life is shining upon My pathway, and therefore I will not stumble or make a mistake in My walking." When He started on His journey, Thomas, who later acquired a reputation for doubting, manifested the beautiful spirit of being willing to die with his Lord. He said, "Let us also go, that we may die with him."

When Jesus arrived at Bethany He found that Lazarus was dead and had lain in the grave for four days already. There was still great mourning in the house of Mary and Martha. The news of Christ's coming went before Him and Martha came to meet Him. (This eagerness on her part to meet Christ can be taken to counter her reputation for being cumbered with many things. Her expressions of faith and confidence on this occasion reveal her true spiritual quality.) Martha informed Jesus of the death of her brother, and in turn Jesus told her that her brother would rise again. Martha's mind went forward to the resurrection at the last day, and she declared her faith in that resurrection. But Jesus brought her back to the present. He said, "*I am* the resurrection and the life." She had told the Lord that if He had been there her brother would not have died. This was faith in the past. Also she showed her faith in the great resurrection. This was faith in the future. Jesus was calling for her faith at the present when He said, "I am." Her response was to declare unreservedly, "I believe that thou art the Christ, the Son of God."

Mary then joined them, and they went together to the tomb. Jesus entered into their sorrow and wept. When they arrived at the cave in which Lazarus was buried, upon which a stone was laid, Jesus immediately gave orders that they should take away the stone. Martha reminded Him that Lazarus had been dead for four days. But Jesus reminded her of what He had just told her, that if she would believe she would see the glory of God.

When the stone was rolled away Jesus prayed, "Father, I thank thee that thou hast heard me. And I knew that thou hearest me always; but because of the people which stand by I said it, that they may believe that thou hast sent me." His Father and He had already planned the raising of Lazarus, but Christ was anxious that the people should recognize the Father's part in this great miracle. He then cried with a loud voice, "Lazarus, come forth." This was the voice that at the end of the world is to summon all the dead to come forth (John 5:28). But here the call was to one man only. Lazarus' response to that call is proof that all the world will respond when they hear Christ's voice. This miracle resulted in the conversion of many who saw it, but there were those who would not believe and who went away to report to the Pharisees what Jesus had done.

PHARISEES PLOT TO KILL HIM (*John* 11:47-57)

Raising Lazarus from the dead was the climax of Christ's miracles. The Pharisees recognized it as such and consulted together what they should now do. They realized that His power was such that the whole populace could shortly turn to Him. This they did not want for, they said, it would mean that the Romans would come and take away their place and nation. Thus it was evident that their own position of leadership was more important to them than the arrival of the Messiah.

A strange thing then happened. The high priest remarked that it would be better for one man to die for the people than that the whole nation should perish. This was a clear statement of the substitutionary nature of the death of Christ, although Caiaphas did not realize it. The Scripture says that "he prophesied that Jesus should die for that nation; and not for that nation only, but that also he should gather together in one the children of God that were scattered abroad." The Pharisees then decided that they should kill Him at the first opportunity. The Passover which was near at hand would provide them with the chance they sought.

Lesson 29

PART 8—LAST JOURNEY TO JERUSALEM

BEGINNING OF JOURNEY (*Luke* 9:51-56)

When Jesus knew their plot to kill Him, He retired to a village called Ephraim (John 11:54), about fifteen miles from Jerusalem. Jesus also knew that the approaching Passover would be the great climax of His life. As the hour came, "he steadfastly set his face to go to Jerusalem." Nothing could delay or defeat Him in His determination to offer himself for the sins of the world. He sent messengers ahead to make ready for Him. He planned possibly to stay all night in a village of the Samaritans. Evidently the antipathy of the Samaritans to the Jews was as great as that of the Jews to the Samaritans. When the people of this village learned that the Lord was on His way to Jerusalem they would not receive Him or His messengers. This provoked James and John (the sons of thunder), and they asked the Lord's permission to call down fire from heaven to consume the people even as Elijah of old had done. Here was an exhibition of faith but also of carnal temper. Jesus restrained them, saying, "Ye know not what manner of spirit ye are of. For the Son of man is not come to destroy men's lives, but to save them."

TEACHING AND JOURNEYING (*Luke* 13:22-30; 17:20, 21)

Jesus and His company quietly turned from this hostile village and went on to another. As He resumed His journey toward Jerusalem, someone asked Him if there were only a few people who would be saved. He answered that many would seek to enter heaven's gate but would not be able. Upon rejection, they would protest that they had seen the Christ and that He had taught in their streets.

149

Jesus said the answer from heaven would be, "You yourselves are workers of iniquity; therefore you must depart from me." It takes more than merely seeing Christ or entertaining Him in one's home to secure an entrance into heaven. As individuals, men must not be workers of iniquity. Jesus then declared that at the last day all the prophets would be in the kingdom of God and even many people from the east and west and north and south, while certain Jews who had been intended of God to share that Kingdom would instead be thrust out. Here is a declaration that the righteous men of the Old Testament will have a part in the kingdom of God along with Gentiles from all over the world. This was also an anticipation of the time when the wall of partition will be broken down and Jews and Gentiles constitute one body in Christ (Ephesians 2:11-18).

Some Pharisees then asked Him when the kingdom of God would come. This was His opportunity to tell them that He, the King of that Kingdom, was already there among them.

PHARISEE AND PUBLICAN (*Luke* 18:9-14)

While talking to the Pharisees Jesus told them the following story. A Pharisee and a publican (a common sinner) were in the temple, praying. The Pharisee, as a matter of fact, was reciting to the Lord all of his own virtues. According to his story, he was a very high-class religious man, faithful in all of his religious practices. On the other hand, the sinner was really praying, asking God to be merciful to him. The pride of the Pharisee stood in sharp contrast to the humility of the sinner. Christ's comment was that the sinner was more justified in the sight of God than the Pharisee, for "every one that exalteth himself shall be abased; and he that humbleth himself shall be exalted." This is a fundamental and eternal principle of the kingdom of God.

TEACHING ON DIVORCE (*Matthew* 19:3-12; *Mark* 10:2-12; *Luke* 16:18)

The Pharisees were not easily routed. Again they came to Jesus and this time asked Him, "Is it lawful for a man to put away his wife for every cause?" His answer referred them to the statement in Genesis 1 that God had made them male and female in the first place and quoted the Scripture portion that a man should "leave his father and mother, and shall cleave unto his wife: and they shall be one flesh" (Genesis 2:24). Jesus remarked, "What therefore God hath joined together, let not man put asunder." This was a statement that one man and one woman should live together as man and wife as long as they both should live. The Pharisees rejoined that Moses had allowed divorce and asked Jesus why that could be. Christ explained that Moses made a concession because of the hardness of their hearts, but He insisted that from the beginning it was not so. Therefore, Jesus said, "Whosoever shall put away his wife, except it be for fornication, and shall marry another, committeth adultery: and whoso marrieth her which is put away doth commit adultery." The consensus of Christ's teaching found in Matthew 5:31, 32 and in the three passages cited above, supported by Paul's teaching in Romans 7:1-3 and 1 Corinthians 7:11, 39, seems to be that one could put away his wife for fornication, and the wife her husband for the same offense.

Conservative evangelical scholarship generally accepts the term *fornication* as meaning "habitual sexual immorality." Jesus did not encourage divorce. However, He recognized that persistent marital unfaithfulness may make divorce necessary and permissible (Matthew 19:9). Neither did Jesus encourage remarriage. The grammatical construction of the text, nevertheless, shows that the exception permitting divorce related to remarrige also.

BLESSES LITTLE CHILDREN (*Matthew* 19:13-15; *Mark* 10:13-16; *Luke* 18:15-17)

It often happens that the individuals who are hurt most in divorce are the little children. At that very time some children were brought to Christ for His blessing. He showed His love for children by placing His hands upon them and blesisng them. He told His disciples not to forbid mothers to bring their children to Him. He then declared that if a person would not humble himself and become as a little child he could not enter into the kingdom of heaven.

Lesson 30

THE RICH YOUNG RULER (*Matthew* 19:16-26; *Mark* 10:17-27; *Luke* 18:18-27)

Then a certain young man came to Jesus with a personal question. "Good Master, what shall I do that I may inherit eternal life?" Before Christ answered his question, He in turn asked the young man why he had called Him good. Did he thereby mean to call Jesus God (for there was none good but God)? Christ was here telling the world that perfect goodness is found only in God. He was also testing this young man as to whether or not he believed in Him as the Son of God. Without waiting for an answer (for He was soon to discover that answer) He asked the young man if he kept the commandments which he already knew. The young ruler replied that he had kept them from his youth. This was morality and legal righteousness. Jesus thereupon taught him and us all that these are not sufficient qualifications for inheriting eternal life. There must be an acceptance of Christ himself and a complete surrender to Him.

In the case of the young man, Jesus said he should demonstrate his faith in Christ by selling his earthly possessions in exchange for treasure in heaven and, most important of all, he should follow Christ. Here was a choice between earthly possessions and the Saviour of his soul. Unfortunately, he turned away from his Saviour and returned to his possessions. Jesus loved this young man, but to change or lower the standard of entrance into the Kingdom would not be a true expression of love for him. Christ used the occasion to call attention to the fact that it is very difficult for people who trust in riches to enter into the kingdom of heaven. As a matter of fact, Jesus said, it is just as difficult for a rich man to enter into the Kingdom as it is for a camel to go through the eye of a needle. No wonder the disciples were amazed when He made this statement and asked Him, "Who then can be saved?" Jesus' reply was that it was impossible for man but He said, "With God all things are possible."

THE APOSTLES' PLACE IN THE KINGDOM (*Matthew* 19:27-30; *Mark* 10:28-31; *Luke* 18:28-30; 22:28-30)

Christ's statement jarred the disciples. Peter expressed their fear. "Behold, we have forsaken all, and followed thee; what shall we have therefore?" Jesus assured them that they had met the test, for they had turned from possessions to follow Christ the Saviour. As a matter of fact, since they were pioneers among the disciples, He had ordained that they should eat and drink at His table in His Kingdom and should sit on twelve thrones, judging the twelve tribes of Israel. He added that not only these twelve disciples, but all those who forsook earthly family and possessions for His name's sake, would be amply repaid in this present time and in the world to come would have everlasting life.

LABORERS IN THE VINEYARD (*Matthew* 20:1-16)

The thought of reward for leaving all to follow Christ led Jesus to tell another story to illustrate the matter. A certain householder went out early in the morning to hire laborers to work in his vineyard. He agreed to give them a certain sum for the day's work. He found that he needed more laborers and so went back to hire others. He did this four successive times through the day. When he asked those whom he hired an hour before sundown why they had been idle all day, they explained that it was because no one had hired them. He then sent them into his vineyard and promised he would give them what was right. At the close of the day all the laborers were paid for their work. To the surprise of those who had worked all day, he gave a full day's wages to all the laborers. Their surprise turned into murmuring and criticism. They protested that they had worked much more than these last and therefore should receive more pay. The lord of the vineyard called their attention to the fact that he had paid them what he had promised. As regards what he had given to those hired at the last, that was strictly his own business. It was lawful for him to do as he chose with his own, and he had a right to be "good" if he wanted to.

The lesson which Christ pointed out was that it made no difference when one was called to work for Him, just so the one called responded. Those who were called first could incur His displeasure

if their attitude toward Him was not right. We can also learn here
the accurate justice of our Lord. It was really not the latecomers'
fault that they had not worked all day, for no man had hired them.
God will judge one's motives and one's opportunities in the overall
appraisal and in the dispensing of eternal reward.

FORETELLS HIS DEATH (*Matthew* 20:17-19; *Mark* 10:32-34; *Luke*
18:31-34)

Again the shadow of the Cross fell across Christ's pathway. He
took the twelve to one side and reminded them faithfully what
awaited Him in Jerusalem. He was to be betrayed by the chief
priests and scribes and delivered over to the Gentiles. They in turn
would mock and scourge Him and put Him to death. But the third
day He would rise again. This, He said, was to be in fulfillment of
what the prophets had spoken concerning Him. Strangely enough
the disciples did not understand what He told them.

WHO WILL BE THE GREATEST? (*Matthew* 20:20-28; *Mark* 10:35-45;
Luke 22:24-27)

In spite of Christ's faithful warning that death awaited Him, John
and James, two of His most intimate disciples, showed that they
did not comprehend His words and, as a matter of fact, were plan-
ning on something which was the very opposite. The Jewish conception of a material Messiah lay deep within them, and they had
attached their own personal fortunes to that prospect. They used
the subtilty of getting their mother to be their spokesman. They
even used the childlike ruse of asking for a blanket promise—trying
to get Jesus to promise them whatsoever they should desire.

When they told Him that they wanted to sit one on either side
of Him in His Kingdom, He told them frankly that they did not
realize what they were asking. They wanted a position of material
power in an earthly kingdom, but His Kingdom was that place of
rulership which He was to purchase with His death upon the Cross.
He asked these disciples if they were able to drink of His cup of
suffering. Without realizing what was really involved, they quickly
responded that they were able. Jesus then predicted that they would
indeed drink of His cup and be baptized with His baptism of suffering. But sitting on either side of Him in His Kingdom, He said,
was not His to give; it would be given to those whom His Father
decided were worthy.

James and John were not alone in this mistaken conception and ambition. When the other ten disciples heard the request which James and John had made, they were angry against the two brothers for having put in their bid first. Jesus then laid down to all twelve of them the fundamental law of the Kingdom which He had come to introduce. It was the exact opposite of the principle underlying human government. Human leaders exercise authority over those whom they rule. In the kingdom of heaven they who serve their fellowmen will be considered the greatest. Jesus cited himself as an example. "The Son of man came not to be ministered unto, but to minister." His service to His fellowmen would be demonstrated by His giving His life for their ransom.

Lesson 31

BLIND BARTIMAEUS (*Matthew* 20:29-34; *Mark* 10:46-52; *Luke* 18:35-43)

On His journey to Jerusalem the Lord chose to go through Jericho. He knew there were two individuals who would welcome Him and be transformed by His contact with them. One of these was blind Bartimaeus, the beggar, and the other was Zacchaeus, the rich publican.

Bartimaeus and another blind man were sitting by the wayside begging when they heard that Jesus was passing by. They cried out loudly, "Have mercy on us, O Lord, thou son of David." The crowd sought to quiet them, but they called the louder, "Have mercy on us, O Lord, thou son of David." Characteristically, Jesus heard the cry of need and stood still. He commanded that the men be brought to Him and then asked them what they wanted Him to do. They asked that they might receive their sight. Jesus had compassion on them and touched their eyes, and immediately they received their sight and followed Jesus in the way. When the people saw it they joined the blind men in giving praise to God.

ZACCHAEUS (*Luke* 19:1-10)

Without respect of persons, Jesus now turned His attention to a rich man whom He also found in the way. Being small of stature, Zacchaeus had run ahead of the crowd and climbed up into a sycamore tree that he might get a better view of the Lord as He passed by. This also gave the Lord a better view of him. He saw that Zacchaeus was a potential disciple, so He called for him to come down and take Him home to be his guest. Zacchaeus quickly and gladly responded, and they went together to Zacchaeus' home. The crowd knew that this man was a hated tax collector and wondered

156

that Jesus would associate with him. Jesus had proven His love for just this type of sinner by making Matthew one of His disciples. Zacchaeus was overwhelmed by the condescension and love of the Lord and immediately surrendered his life to Him. Jesus said, "This day is salvation come to this house," and then gave the beautiful proclamation: "For the Son of man is come to seek and to save that which was lost."

TEN POUNDS (*Luke* 19:11-28)

Jesus was coming ever nearer to Jerusalem, and the people were thinking that He would soon enter into His Kingdom. The Lord therefore told them a story to describe the true character of the kingdom of God.

A certain nobleman went into a far country to receive a kingdom and then to return. (This was a clear prediction that He would have to go into a far country first before setting up His Kingdom here on earth.) Before leaving, this nobleman called his ten servants and delivered unto them ten pieces of silver, telling them to trade with them until he returned. He had no sooner started on his journey, however, than some of those over whom he ruled rebelled against him and even sent a messenger advising him of their rebellion. He went on his journey, however, and received his kingdom before he returned home.

Upon arriving home his first act was to call his servants to him to find out how much each man had gained by trading. They reported different degrees of success. One had even gained ten pounds with the single pound which he had received, and another had gained five. To these faithful servants the nobleman assigned authority over cities in proportion to their success in trading. One servant, however, reported that he had preferred not to trade with the silver which his lord had given him, but instead had kept it laid up in a cloth. This was displeasing to his lord who commanded that the silver should be taken from him and given to the servant who had been the most successful in trading.

In this story Jesus revealed that upon His return to the earth after receiving His Kingdom He will call His servants before Him for an accounting of their stewardship. He will give the true riches (eternal reward) to those who have been the most faithful in improving the opportunities for service which were given them. Jesus then turned to the punishment of those who have rebelled against Him. His enemies will hear these dreadful words, "Bring them hither, and slay them before me."

ANOINTED BY MARY (*Matthew* 26:6-13; *Mark* 14:3-9; *John* 12:1-11)

Jesus had now arrived at Bethany, which was only two miles from Jerusalem and a mile from the summit of Mt. Olivet. Although this was the home village of Mary and Martha and Lazarus, yet He was entertained in the house of Simon the leper. Evidently he was one of the many lepers whom Jesus had healed. Martha, the neighbor, had volunteered to assist in serving at the supper, and Lazarus was one of the guests who sat at the table with Jesus. Mary again showed her spirit of devotion to Christ, this time by anointing His feet with a very costly ointment and wiping them with her hair.

A Pharisee had criticized the Lord on a previous occasion when a woman had wiped His feet with the hairs of her head. But this time it was His own disciples, Judas being the spokesman, who were His critics. They considered that this was a waste of the ointment. Judas suggested that it could have been sold and the money given to the poor. This was a revelation of the greed of his heart, for the Scriture says that he was a thief and, being the treasurer, he wanted access to these additional funds.

Jesus heard their murmuring and replied, "The poor always ye have with you; but me ye have not always." He announced that Mary had kept this treasure for this occasion and was using it as an anointing of Christ's body in preparation for His burial. Here again He disclosed that He was approaching the time of His death. It seems that Mary was the only one of His followers who had understood and received His repeated predictions of His own death. He rewarded her for this devotion by declaring that wherever His gospel was preached throughout the whole world the story of her anointing His body for His burial would be told as a memorial of her.

There was another interesting sidelight in connection with this feast. Many people came to see Lazarus, whom Jesus had raised from the dead. So great was the influence which Lazarus had upon the people, simply by appearing as one raised from the dead, that the Jews sought to put Lazarus also to death. They who have been raised from the dead (trespasses and sins) by the power of the Lord are a powerful testimony for Him by the resurrected life which they live.

Lesson 32

TRIUMPHAL ENTRY (*Matthew* 21:1-9; *Mark* 11:1-10; *Luke* 19:29-40; *John* 12:12-19)

From Bethany Jesus sent two of His disciples into a neighboring village to secure an ass and her colt which He said they would find tied there. It was a young colt upon which a man had never sat. They were simply to advise the owner that the Lord had need of them. Jesus was conscious of the prophecy of Zechariah (9:9), "Rejoice greatly, O daughter of Zion; shout, O daughter of Jerusalem: behold, thy King cometh unto thee: he is just, and having salvation; lowly, and riding upon an ass, and upon a colt the foal of an ass." He realized that the hour had come for its fulfillment.

When they brought the animals to Jesus they put their garments upon the colt and Jesus sat upon it. Others spread their garments in the way, or cut down branches from the trees and strewed them in the road. Thus began the procession into Jerusalem. Unconscious of the prophecy of Zechariah, the multitude began to rejoice greatly and to shout. They cried, "Hosanna; Blessed is he that cometh in the name of the lord." They praised God with a loud voice for all the mighty works that they had seen and they acclaimed Jesus "the King that cometh in the name of the Lord." It looked as if the hour of His ascending the throne of His father David had arrived, and the people thrilled at what they considered was their approaching deliverance from the domination of Rome.

In a recent consultation together the Pharisees had decided among themselves that the acclamation of Christ as King would bring the Romans upon them to take away their place and their nation. Rather than have anything happen to take away "their place," they determined that as soon as possible they would put Jesus to death. So, as the moment approached for His proclamation as King, they feared that it might be too late to dispose of Him. All they could do was to seek to persuade Jesus himself to stop the shouts and praises of the people. But Jesus answered them that if the people held their peace the very stones would immediately cry out for that prophecy must be fulfilled. Incidentally, we notice here that it is instinctive and right that those who worship the Lord should cry out and shout His praises.

WEEPS OVER JERUSALEM (*Luke* 19:41-44)

As the procession passed over the brow of the hill, Jesus beheld His beloved city and burst into tears. He was not weeping for the prospect of suffering and death which lay immediately before Him but for the heinous crime which that city was about to commit, and for the awful punishment which would befall it for that crime. The spiritual blindness of the leaders of Jerusalem was preventing their being conscious of the better way which was possible for them. The way of peace was hidden from them, and they were plunging into war and destruction. "The days shall come upon thee, that thine enemies shall cast a trench about thee, and compass thee round, and keep thee in on every side, and shall lay thee even with the ground, and thy children within thee." This was the occasion of the deep grief of His heart. He loved deeply even His bitterest enemies and was weeping at the tragedy which would befall them.

CLEANSES THE TEMPLE (*Matthew* 21:10-17; *Mark* 11:11, 15-19; *Luke* 19:45-48)

When Jesus arrived in Jerusalem He went into the temple and again cast out those who had made His Father's house a house of merchandise. The wrath which He had showed at the beginning of His ministry for this profane practice was still burning in His heart. He protested that His father's house was a house of prayer for all nations, so He turned and made it just that. The blind and the lame came to Him in the temple and He healed them. The children kept crying, "Hosanna to the son of David." And He taught again in the temple. The Pharisees still protested against the praises of the people; whereupon Jesus reminded them of the Scripture portion, "Out of the mouths of babes and sucklings thou has perfected praise" (see Psalm 8:2). At eventide He went out to Bethany with the twelve.

CURSES FIG TREE (*Matthew* 21:18-22; *Mark* 11:12-14, 20-26)

The following morning Jesus returned from Bethany to Jerusalem and saw a fig tree which even at a distance was full of leaves. Although the regular fig harvesttime had not come yet, the many leaves on this tree indicated that some figs should be there also. However, upon arrival at the tree they found no figs, so Jesus cursed it. The cursing of this fig tree was not just simply its rebuke for having deceived people but it was an apt illustration and symbol of the Jewish nation. Its religious life seemed to be flourishing, but there was no real spiritual fruit in it. This called for the rebuke of the husbandman who had already digged around this tree for three years and who was justified now in commanding that it be cut down (Luke 13:6-9).

Later, as they passed by, they saw the fig tree dried up clear down to its roots. This was a vivid example of the power of Christ over nature. He explained that this was a demonstration of the power of faith. He added that the disciples themselves could have this faith and power. Then He gave the eternal law: "What things soever ye desire, when ye pray, believe that ye receive them, and ye shall have them." There must be purity of heart, however, in praying, for if there is enmity in one's heart against another, Jesus reminded them, the Father in heaven would not forgive their trespasses and certainly would not hear their prayer.

AUTHORITY QUESTIONED (*Matthew* 21:23-27; *Mark* 11:27-33; *Luke* 20:1-8)

The day before (after His triumphal entry into Jerusalem) He had cleansed the temple and rebuked the Pharisees publicly. They naturally awaited with indignation His return to the city and to the temple. Upon seeing Him they immediately asked by whose authority He did these things. His answer was a question in return, "The baptism of John, was it from heaven, or of men?" He had already told them on previous occasions the source of His authority (John 6:37; 10:36, 38), so He took this opportunity to point out to them the inconsistency of their position. If they should say the baptism of John was from heaven, they knew He would immediately ask them why they did not believe him. If they denied John's divine commission they would incur the displeasure of the people, for John was popular. Being good politicians they merely said, "We cannot tell." Jesus replied, "Neither do I tell you [again] by what authority I do these things."

PARABLE OF TWO SONS (*Matthew* 21:28-32)

Having exposed their rejection of John, the popular prophet, Jesus told a story to illustrate their disobedience to the will of God.

He represented His Father as having two sons whom He instructed to go and work in His vineyard. The first one flatly refused, but afterward thought better of his attitude and went in obedience to his father. The other hypocritically pretended to be obedient but did not actually obey. Jesus then asked the Pharisees which of the two did the will of his father. They naturally replied, "The first." Jesus immediately made the application: "There are wicked people, publicans and harlots, who have repented and now seek to do God's will. They are believers in John, whom ye refuse to endorse. And you, who pretend to do God's will, do not respond to John's call to repentance but continue to disobey the will of the Father."

Lesson 33

PARABLE OF HOUSEHOLDER DEMANDING FRUIT (*Matthew* 21:33-46; *Mark* 12:1-12; *Luke* 20:9-19)

Jesus proceeded to illustrate and drive home the wickedness of these Pharisees and the fate that awaited them. He told the story of a certain landlord who had a valuable vineyard which was well kept and equipped, who rented it to certain men before he went on a long journey. He arranged that at harvesttime each year they would pay him a portion of the harvest. To the surprise of this landlord, the people to whom he had rented his vineyard severely treated the messengers whom he sent to receive the portion due him. They even stoned and killed some of the messengers. The landlord then exhibited a rare patience and tolerance. He simply sent more messengers to insist upon his share of the harvest. True to their wicked nature, the tenants treated the second group of messengers the same way as the first. The supreme height of patience and kindness was reached by the landlord when he decided to make one more effort to collect his due portion and sent to them his only son. This height of love was matched by an amazing depth of wickedness and stupidity on the part of the tenants. They actually seized the heir and killed him.

Jesus then asked the Pharisees what they thought should be the proper treatment of such wicked men. Unwittingly they pronounced their own verdict of condemnation. "He will miserably destroy those wicked men and will let out his vineyard unto other husbandmen." To confirm the sentence which they had pronounced on themselves, Jesus then quoted from Psalm 118:22, 23. "The stone which the builders refused is become the head stone of the corner. This is the Lord's doing; it is marvellous in our eyes." In other words, they were rejecting the Heir of the Kingdom, God's beloved Son, who

163

would nevertheless become the head stone of the corner. The kingdom of God would indeed be taken from them and be given to a
nation bringing forth the fruits thereof. Furthermore, it would indeed break their pride and independence to accept Christ (fall upon
this Stone), but in rejecting Him they made it inevitable that this
Stone would fall upon them and grind them to powder.

MARRIAGE OF THE KING'S SON (*Matthew* 22:1-14)

Still contemplating the climax of the age when each would receive
his due, Jesus then told a story which would illustrate another aspect
of that great consummation day. There would indeed be the judgment of those who rejected Him, but He now introduced the fact
that that climax will be as a marriage feast. There will be those who
will have great rejoicing at that day in contrast to those who will
receive God's punishment.

Jesus told of the marriage of the son of a certain king and the
invitations to the wedding which went forth. There were many who
actually refused the invitation, claiming the pressure of business as
an excuse. The king was indignant and sent his armies to destroy
those insolent citizens whom he had intended to honor. After destroying those who rejected his invitation, the king proceeded to
gather others into the wedding, even sending his servants into the
highways and hedges to find them. Another part of the story was
that the king discovered a man among the guests who did not have
on a wedding garment. He commanded him to be expelled from
the room. So there had been two elimination processes. All who
refused the king's invitation were rejected, and also those who pre-
sumed to come to the wedding without proper preparation. Jesus
interpreted the story with the simple statement, "Many are called,
but few are chosen."

ABOUT TRIBUTE MONEY (*Matthew* 22:15-22; *Mark* 12:13-17; *Luke* 20:20-26)

The Pharisees and Herodians then countered with a subtle question. Their plan was to provoke the Lord to say something which
they could interpret as criticism of the governor. They pretended
that they were "just men," to throw Him off guard. They prefaced
their question with complimentary remarks about His being a true
teacher who had no respect of persons.

Their question was, "Is it lawful to give tribute unto Caesar, or not?" Instead of entangling Him they provided Him an opportunity to display His discernment and remarkable wisdom. He denounced them as the hypocrites that they were and then asked to be shown a tribute coin. He called attention to the engraving of Caesar on the coin and then gave His classic answer: "Render therefore unto Caesar the things which are Caesar's; and unto God the things that are God's." This was a simple and yet profound declaration of the right relation between church and state. The Pharisees and all succeeding generations have marveled at His wisdom.

ANSWERS SADDUCEES (*Matthew* 22:23-33; *Mark* 12:18-27; *Luke* 20:27-40)

As the Pharisees and Herodians retired in defeat, the Sadducees took their turn questioning Him. This sect did not believe in a resurrection and naturally attempted to prove their point. They cited an illustration.

First of all, they referred to the Mosaic law that a man should marry the widow of his brother and perpetuate his brother's family. They told of seven brethren who one after the other died, leaving the widow to the successive brothers. They asked the Lord whose wife would she be in the resurrection, since she had been the wife in turn of all seven while here on earth. To them this proved there could be no resurrection. Jesus pointed to their double error: they did not know the Scriptures, nor did they know the power of God. He declared there will be a resurrection, for God said that He is the God of Abraham, Isaac, and Jacob, who are living eternally with Him. However, in the resurrection world there will be neither death nor marriage, the two things that had created the problem of which they spoke. The Sadducees had no reply to His explanation, but certain scribes confessed, "Master, thou hast well said."

THE GREATEST COMMANDMENT (*Matthew* 22:34-40; *Mark* 12:28-34)

The Pharisees now returned to the attack. One of them, a lawyer, asked Jesus a question, hoping that His answer might provide them further opportunity to trap Him. The question was, "Which is the great commandment in the law?" Jesus did not hesitate to answer him. "Thou shalt love the Lord thy God with all thy heart, and with all thy soul, and with all thy mind." His Spirit had dictated that command originally, so He knew it well. Jesus added, "This is the first and great commandment. And the second is like unto it, Thou shalt love thy neighbor as thyself." A certain scribe who was present heard His answer and complimented Him. The scribe then added, "To love him [God] with all the heart, with all the understanding, and with all the soul, and with all the strength, and to love his neighbor as himself, is more than all whole burnt offerings and sacrifices." Here was a spiritual evaluation which was true but very rare in those days. Jesus recognized that the scribe's answer was discreet and said to him, "Thou art not far from the kingdom of God."

HE QUESTIONS THE PHARISEES (*Mastthew* 22:41-46; *Mark* 12:35-37; *Luke* 20:41-44)

Jesus now turned the questioning upon the Pharisees. "What think ye of Christ? whose son is he?" They answered, "The son of David." They were familiar with the great Davidic covenant in which Jehovah had promised that of David's sons He would raise up the Redeemer (2 Samuel 7:12, 13). Jesus then quoted David (Psalm 110:1), "The Lord said unto my Lord, Sit thou on my right hand, till I make thine enemies thy footstool." He asked the Pharisees to explain how the Messiah could be David's son and his Lord at the same time. Without spiritual comprehension, they could not explain. The answer was simply that the Messiah would be David's son after the flesh but would also be the Lord God. This question of Christ's seemed to silence His opponents completely, and from that day onward no man asked Him any more questions. However, He continued preaching to the common people who heard Him gladly.

Lesson 34

PHARISEE RELIGION (*Matthew* 23:1-12; *Mark* 12:38, 39; *Luke* 20:45, 46)

To an audience of all the people Jesus proclaimed: "Beware of the scribes, which love to go in long clothing, and love salutations in the marketplaces, and the chief seats in the synagogues, and the uppermost rooms at feasts." These scribes and Pharisees, He continued, posed as Moses' successors. The commands which they issued were all right, but their personal conduct was evil. "They say and do not" is an accurate definition of hypocrites. The Pharisees did not practice their own preaching. Jesus gave a further definition of hypocrites, "All their works they do for to be seen of men." Their religion was in their "garments," and in their external religious observances.

The essence of Christ's religion is humility and sincerity. He reminded them, "All ye are brethren. Refuse titles of dignity and take the place of a servant. Whosoever shall exalt himself shall be abased, and he that shall humble himself shall be exalted."

DENOUNCES PHARISEES (*Matthew* 23:13-39; *Mark* 12:40; *Luke* 20:47)

In this lengthy passage Jesus wrote deeply upon the record His fierce denunciation of hypocrisy. It is apparent in all of Christ's attitudes and teachings that this is the most abominable of sins. It ranks first in enormity and sinks deepest under the wrath of God.

Jesus pronounced eight distinct woes upon "scribes and Pharisees, hypocrites." He said, "Ye blind guides which strain at a gnat and swallow a camel." He created a hypothetical picture of a person who is so fastidious that he carefully strains out a little gnat which has fallen into his drink, and then utterly ignores and proceeds to swallow a camel, if that were possible. The contrast is ludicrously extreme, and He intended it so. He then cited five distinct sets of

167

"camels and gnats," little matters about which the Pharisees were fastidious, and great horrible sins which they committed without hesitation.

For instance, they made long prayers but also devoured widow's houses. The gold of the temple they considered very sacred, but the temple itself they defiled and defamed. The outside of a cup the Pharisees carefully cleaned, but the inside of their lives was full of extortion and wickedness. Their influence upon others was also a high crime. They shut up the kingdom of heaven and would not let others enter. They compassed land and sea to make proselytes, and then made them twofold more the children of hell than themselves. The climax was in the awful words, "Ye serpents, ye generation of vipers, how can ye escape the damnation of hell?"

Even in the pouring out of His furious denunciation on the Pharisees, Christ broke into a touching lament for the city which He thus condemned. "How often would I have gathered thy children together, . . . and ye would not." And then a distant ray of hope! The time would come when they should say of Him, "Blessed is he that cometh in the name of the Lord."

THE WIDOW'S MITE (*Mark* 12:41-44; *Luke* 21:1-4)

At another time Jesus sat over against the treasury and watched how the people gave their money to the house of God. The rich men gave much, but a certain poor widow cast in two little bits of money, equivalent to one-half cent in value. Whereupon Jesus called His disciples to Him and remarked, "This poor widow has given more than all these rich people, for she in her poverty has given her entire living, whereas they have only given of their abundance."

GREEKS COME TO SEE HIM (*John* 12:20-26)

The Jews had definitely and finally rejected Christ, and as a result He had denounced them and pronounced, "Your house is left unto you desolate" (Matthew 23:38). At this juncture certain Greeks expressed a desire to see Him. This approach by representatives of this intellectual people could hold the possibility of His being accepted by them. This would have meant the turning aside from the appointed path which was soon to lead to His death and the redemption of the world. As such He recognized and rejected it as a temptation of the devil. Christ's response to the Greeks was that the hour had come, not that He should turn aside to earthly approval but that "the Son of man should be glorified." For Him and for all men it is always true that "except a corn of wheat fall into the ground and die, it abideth alone: but if it die, it bringeth forth much fruit." He would not refuse to fall into the ground and die, for in dying He would bring forth much fruit, even the salvation of the world. He now annunciated the eternal truth, "He that loveth his life shall lose it." He also promised if men would follow Him in this pathway of surrender and death they would receive the same exaltation which He would also receive at His Father's right hand.

HIS SOUL TROUBLED (*John* 12:27-36)

Jesus now turned to contemplate the experience which lay directly before Him. He admitted that His soul was troubled. He asked Himself, "Shall I request My Father to save Me from this hour?" He immediately answered His question, "But for this cause came I unto this hour." So, instead of asking His Father for deliverance from Calvary, He rather prayed, "Father, glorify thy name." In this instance there came a voice from heaven in answer, "I have both glorified it, and will glorify it again." Jesus explained to the people who stood by, "This voice came not because of me, but for your sakes." The matter was settled deep in His own heart, but He and His Father were still attempting to persuade these people of His deity.

He then commented upon His approaching death. He declared that His death would be the judgment of the world. That is to say, He would bear the sins of the world. Also at Calvary the power of the devil would be broken. He described the method of His approaching death by the words, "If I be lifted up from the earth," indicating crucifixion. But there was also the glorious promise that His being lifted up would benefit all men. He advised those around Him that there was only a little while left to walk in His light, for He would be taken from them shortly.

LAST APPEAL TO THE JEWS (*John* 12:37-50)

It was evidently a marvel to His disciples that the people did not believe on Him in view of the many miracles which He wrought before them. But Isaiah had prophesied that there would be those who would not believe. Also, their eyes would be blinded and their hearts hardened so that they would not be converted to Him. Isaiah was particularly speaking of Christ, for "he saw his glory, and spake of him." Certain rulers, however, did believe on Him, but it is recorded to their eternal discredit that they loved the praise of men more than the praise of God.

Once more Jesus called aloud, "He that believeth on me, believeth not on me, but on him that sent me." He declared once more, "He that seeth me seeth him that sent me." This was positive identification with God His Father. And then He gave a final warning against rejecting Him. "The word that I have spoken, the same shall judge him in the last day." This was another claim of deity, or rather a revelation of the fact that He is indeed the great eternal judge.

Lesson 35

THE OLIVET DISCOURSE (*Matthew* 24:1-51; *Mark* 13:1-37; *Luke* 21:5-38)

As Jesus was leaving the temple, His disciples pointed out to Him its goodly stones and gifts. Whereupon Jesus revealed to them that the time would come when there would not be one stone left upon another but all would be thrown down. They then went across to the Mount of Olives where Peter and Andrew and John and James asked Him pointedly when that destruction would occur. In their minds that time would be identified with Christ's return to this earth and the end of the age. There was indeed such a similarity between the destruction of Jerusalem at the end of the Israelitish age and the return of Christ at the end of the ecclesiastical age that one description generally would apply to them both. With this in mind, Jesus answered.

The coming of false Christs to deceive the disciples was the first item that Jesus cited as characteristic of the last days. Then would come great international conflict, involving wars and rumors of wars with accompanying famines, pestilences, earthquakes, and fearful sights and great signs from heaven. This universal turmoil would also include great persecution of the saints. But He promised that He would be with them in that persecution, and the Holy Spirit would give them words to speak in testimony and defense. In the midst of it all the gospel would be preached in all the world for a witness unto all nations.

At this point Jesus confirmed the prophecy of Daniel concerning the desecration of the holy place by the Antichrist. He said that this would be a signal for the disciples to leave Jerusalem and flee to the mountains. Looking forward to the immediate prospect of the destruction of Jerusalem (which happened in 70 A.D.), He warned

171

the disciples that when the city was surrounded by armies then they should flee. (Subsequent history tells us that when the city was surrounded by the army of Titus, the Roman general, the Christians who were in Jerusalem remembered the warning of the Lord and fled the city, and not one was lost in its destruction.) Following the revelation of Antichrist there would come the climactic tribulation of all the ages. It would result in the destruction of the lives of all the people of the earth, if it were not providentially shortened. In the midst of this great confusion and tribulation false prophets would arise and perform great miracles. Christ warned against being deceived by these emissaries of Satan. Then would come the great climax of the day of the Lord, the personal, visible appearance of the Son of man himself, coming in the clouds of power and glory.

At this juncture in the Olivet discourse Jesus told them a parable. It concerned the fig tree and all the trees as springtime approached. As their branches were tender and they put forth their leaves it could be clearly seen that summer was near at hand. It would be like that, He said, in determining the nearness of the hour when He would return. The events of the great consummation period would be included in the lifetime of one generation. Jesus said the exact hour, however, no man could know for neither He nor the angels in heaven knew exactly the hour of His return.

He gave an illustration also for the guidance of His disciples as to the days when the Son of Man would be revealed. He cited the days of Noah and Lot as being comparable to the days when He would return. The exceeding wickedness of those former days is described in the Book of Genesis. Jesus added that one characteristic would be the complete absorption of the people in the material, physical things of earthly life, and their utter indifference to the certainty of their punishment. To His disciples He gave the warning of the suddenness of His return.

He gave still another illustration. If the owner of any house was warned that a thief would attempt to break in, he would of course be constantly on guard to prevent it. His disciples, therefore, being faithfully warned, should be constantly watching for His return.

He gave a special warning to His own servants whom He would appoint as rulers over His own great household. They should be careful to give meat in due season. If they were faithful He would make them rulers over all His goods, but if they were not faithful He would reject them and appoint them a portion with the hypocrites. (How terrible that would be He had recently warned the hypocritical Pharisees themselves.) He then added that the extent of the responsibility given to His servants would be the extent of their accountability when He returned.

Finally, He compared His going away and coming again to the case of an earthly householder. This man gave authority to his servants and to every man his work. Jesus said that His disciples, likewise, should be constantly faithful to their assignment for they would not know the exact hour of His return. "Lest coming suddenly he find you sleeping." He enjoined them to be constantly watchful and always praying that they might be accounted worthy to escape all these things that should come to pass and to stand before the Son of man.

TEN VIRGINS (*Matthew* 25:1-13)

Jesus continued His description of the end time. "Then [at that time] shall the kingdom of heaven be likened unto ten virgins." He had just referred to His own coming, and now He told about ten young ladies who went forth to meet a bridegroom who was coming. The application is obvious. These young ladies were variously prepared for the arrival of the bridegroom. The difference was simply that five of them took along a reserve supply of oil for their lamps and the other five took no oil with them. Jesus called the first five virgins wise and the others foolish. The wisdom of the first group was revealed when they were able to go out and meet the bridegroom with their lamps burning. The foolishness of the other five virgins became evident when they attempted to light their lamps and only then realized they should have made advance preparation by bringing a supply of oil. Now it was too late for them to join the procession. When the bridegroom arrived, the five whose lamps were burning went in to the wedding, but the other five were excluded. This story illustrates the necessity of being constantly ready for the coming of the Lord. It also intimates that having an abundance of the oil of the Holy Spirit in one's life is a good way to assure readiness for Christ's return.

PARABLE OF THE TALENTS (*Matthew* 25:14-30)

Jesus had much to reveal concerning His return so He told another story. A certain man traveled into a far country, but before leaving he delivered unto his servants the responsibility of administering his affairs. To one who was especially capable he gave a very large portion, to another a smaller portion, and to still another a rather small assignment. Upon his departure certain servants undertook the discharge of their responsibilities. They administered well and invested wisely with the result that their master's gifts gained considerably. However, the one who had received only a small amount to administer vindicated his lord's lack of trust in him, for he refused or neglected even the small assignment that his lord had given him.

"After a long time," Jesus said (an intimation that His own going away would be for a long time), that lord returned and demanded an accounting from his servants. Those who had been faithful were glad to report the amount of their respective gains. When they reported their respective successes the lord gave them identical reward and compensation, although they had received different amounts in the beginning. "Thou hast been faithful over a few things, I will make thee ruler over many things." It is apparent that faithfulness is what He seeks and what He approves rather than the amount and extent of success which His various disciples gain.

The servant who had refused to obey his lord was also called into account. In spite of his attempt to defend himself by accusing his lord of severity, he made his judgment the worse. Here Jesus interpreted this part of His parable. He said the unprofitable servant would be cast into outer darkness where there was weeping and gnashing of teeth.

LIVING NATIONS JUDGMENT (*Matthew* 25:31-46)

From parable and illustration Jesus then turned to direct prophecy. He said there would be a judgment of all nations when He came. He would be seated upon the throne of His glory, and all nations would be gathered before Him. He would separate them as a shepherd does the sheep from the goats. The basis of this separation would be the attitude which nations had taken toward "these my brethren." Who were these brethren? The prophet Zechariah had predicted (Zechariah 12:9-14) that the Jews who would pierce Him would look upon Him with great remorse for having crucified their brother. This reconciliation between Christ and the Jewish nation would be effected immediately upon His return to the earth. Therefore it doubtless was these Jewish brethren of His to whom He referred when He spoke of the great judgment of the living nations. Those nations who had been kind to the Jews were to be allowed to remain on the earth and enjoy the millennial kingdom which had been prepared from the foundation of the world. On the other hand, the nations who had refused to minister to and succor the Jews were dissolved and their responsible leaders sent off into everlasting fire. Thus the Lord will choose the citizens over whom He will reign.

JEWS PLOT TO KILL HIM (*Matthew* 26:1-5; *Mark* 14:1, 2; *Luke* 22:1, 2)

While Jesus carefully and faithfully warned His disciples concerning the end of the age, the Jews were busy plotting His death. The chief priests and scribes and elders of the people assembled in the palace of the high priest to plan how they might arrest Him without creating a popular uprising in His behalf.

It may have been at that very moment that Judas Iscariot, one of Christ's own disciples, arrived with the nefarious intention of selling his Lord. He asked, "What will ye give me, and I will deliver him unto you?" They quickly agreed that the price would be thirty pieces of silver.

STUDY QUESTIONS—UNIT THREE

LESSON 24

1. What promise concerning the Holy Spirit did Jesus make at the Feast of Tabernacles?
2. What Jehovistic title did Jesus use as His own in His discourse concerning Himself?
3. What was Mary's "good part" which Jesus said would not be taken away from her?

LESSON 25

1. Give two figures of speech which the Lord applied to himself in His parable of the sheepfold.
2. Complete the following quotation: "A man's life consisteth not _____."
3. Tell the parable which Jesus gave to illustrate the worthlessness of riches.

LESSON 26

1. What degrees in prayer did Jesus teach?
2. How will Jesus express His humility at the Marriage Supper of the Lamb?
3. Who did Jesus say is the author of sickness?

LESSON 27

1. What were the lessons taught in the parable of the Great Supper?
2. What was the chief lesson of the parable of the Prodigal Son?
3. In the parable of the Unjust Steward, what did Jesus say is the proper use of money?

LESSON 28

1. What story did Jesus tell to illustrate the torment of hell?
2. How did Jesus conclude His parable of the Unjust Judge?
3. List all the occasions when Jesus raised people from the dead.

LESSON 29

1. Why did Jesus not allow James and John to call down fire on the Samaritan village that would not receive Him?
2. What did Jesus teach by His story of the Pharisee and the publican who went into the temple to pray?
3. State the consensus of Christ's teaching on divorce and remarriage.

LESSON 30

1. Why is it difficult for those who trust in riches to enter into the kingdom of heaven?
2. What place in the Kingdom did Jesus promise to His disciples?
3. Who will be the greatest in the Kingdom?

LESSON 31

1. Name two followers whom Jesus won on His way to Jerusalem through Jericho.
2. Cite three lessons to be learned from the parable of the Pounds.
3. Who was the only one of His followers that believed beforehand that Jesus would be killed and proved it by a beautiful act of devotion?

LESSON 32

1. Christ's triumphal entry into Jerusalem was a fulfillment of which Old Testament prophecy?
2. Why did Jesus burst into tears as He saw the city?
3. What was the national spiritual significance of Christ's cursing the fig tree?

LESSON 33

1. Cite two extremes of attitude shown by the principles in the parable of the Householder demanding fruit.
2. What were the two elimination processes used by the king in the story of the marriage of the king's son?
3. Quote Christ's declaration of the right relation between church and state.
4. What is the greatest commandment?

LESSON 34

1. Give Christ's definition of a hypocrite.
2. What did Jesus mean when He said the Pharisees strained at a gnat and swallowed a camel?
3. What is the meaning of Christ's statement, "Except a corn of wheat fall into the ground and die, it abideth alone: but if it die, it bringeth forth much fruit"?

LESSON 35

1. In what chapter of Matthew does Jesus give the most detailed description of His return to earth?
2. What is the lesson taught by the parable of the Ten Virgins?
3. What Christian virtue is rewarded in the parable of the Talents?
4. Describe the living nations' judgment.

UNIT FOUR

Lessons 36 through 47

FAREWELL MINISTRY

TRIAL AND CRUCIFIXION

RESURRECTION

Lesson 36

PART 10—FAREWELL MINISTRY

PASSOVER PREPARED (*Matthew* 26:17-20; *Luke* 22:7-14; *Mark* 14:1, 12-17)

The feast of unleavened bread was a period of seven days. It was a holy time in which no work was to be done and from which leaven, a type of sin, was to be excluded from the daily diet. The spiritual fulfillment was the period of time in which Jesus celebrated the Last Supper and entered into the shadows and the suffering of Gethsemane and the Crucifixion and emerged triumphantly from the grave on that great resurrection morning. It embraced the feast of the Passover and the sheaf of the firstfruits.

On the first day of this feast of unleavened bread the disciples, under Jesus' direction, prepared for their eating the Passover feast together. When the hour was come, Jesus sat down with the twelve disciples.

PASSOVER OBSERVED (*Matthew* 26:26-29; *Mark* 14:22-25; *Luke* 22:15-20)

Melchizedek, the first high-priestly type of our Lord, brought forth bread and wine when he met Abraham. His great Antitype now brings forth bread and wine to set before the disciples. Jesus interpreted the symbols. "The bread," He said, "represents my body, and the wine stands for my blood, which I will shed for you." He thus defined the essence of the significance of Calvary. His blood would be shed as redemption for all the world, and His life would be provided as spiritual food for those who accept His redemption. The New Covenant which was promised by Isaiah (61:8), Jeremiah (31:31-34; 32:37-42), and Ezekiel (11:19, 20; 36:25-27), would begin, Jesus said, at Calvary. He also included the thought of His return to eat and drink with them again in His Kingdom.

181

WASHES DISCIPLES' FEET (*John* 13:2-20)

At the conclusion of the meal, it seems, Jesus was reminded of the tremendous scope of His mission and power. The Father had given all things into His hands. He had come from God and was about to return to God. And yet, with this background of sublimity and power, Jesus humbled himself to wash His disciples' feet. He laid aside His seamless robe and girded himself with a towel as a servant. With a basin of water He proceeded to wash their feet, wiping them with the towel. When He came to Simon Peter, His impetuous disciple protested. Jesus explained that the significance of His act would be revealed to Peter later. This, however, did not satisfy Peter, and he refused to allow Jesus to wash his feet. The Lord warned him that if he did not humble himself to accept the ministry of his Master it would eliminate him from among His disciples. With this Peter completely surrendered.

After Jesus had finished washing their feet, He took His garments again and sat down to teach them, as He promised Peter that He would. "I have given you an example, that ye should do as I have done to you." He is indeed the Lord and Master, and His disciples must follow His example. Judas would not follow for he was about to lift up his heel against the Lord.

BETRAYER REVEALED (*Matthew* 26:21-25; *Mark* 14:18-21; *Luke* 22:21-23; *John* 13:21-30)

All twelve disciples partook with Christ of the Passover feast. It was during that paschal meal that Jesus made an astounding revelation to His disciples. He remarked that one of them would betray Him. This disturbed the disciples greatly for they could hardly believe that one who had learned to know Him so intimately would actually betray Him. One said, "Is it I?" Then another, "Is it I?" Peter signaled John, who sat closer to Jesus, to ask Him directly who it was. Christ's answer was to take some food and hand it to Judas Iscariot. The Scripture records that at this moment Satan entered into Judas. Jesus then dismissed Judas from their company with the words, "That thou doest, do quickly." He went out immediately, "and it was night."

A NEW COMMANDMENT (*John* 13:31-35)

With the introduction of the New Covenant, which Jesus said the shedding of His blood would represent, there was given a new commandment. This was that they should love one another as He had loved them. What an example and what a measure! His life had exemplified the love which He was now commanding His disciples to manifest each to the other. Obedience to this commandment would prove to all men that they were indeed His disciples.

PREDICTS PETER'S DENIAL (*Matthew* 26:31-35; *Mark* 14:27-31; *Luke* 22:31-34; *John* 13:36-38)

Peter, who had narrowly escaped exclusion from the disciples by his refusal to allow Jesus to wash his feet, needed some further testing. Satan was on hand to test him. But Jesus warned Peter of the coming testing and also assured him that He had prayed for him in advance that his faith would not fail. Along with the other disciples Peter was amazed that one of the twelve should betray his Lord, and now he, Peter, also one of the twelve, was to deny Him. Peter boasted, "I will lay down my life for thy sake," and the other disciples joined him in this pledge of loyalty. Always careful to fulfill the Scriptures, Jesus quoted Zechariah (13:7), "Smite the shepherd, and the sheep shall be scattered." "All of you will desert me when I am being smitten, but Peter will go so far as to deny that he knew me." Whereupon Peter heatedly insisted that he would rather die than deny his Lord.

LAST-MINUTE INSTRUCTIONS (*Luke* 22:35-38)

Jesus had previously sent out His disciples two by two on temporary missions to heal and preach and prepare the way before Him. Now He was shortly to send them on lifetime missions with a similar objective. Just as they had lacked nothing in their previous experience, so He would provide for them again. However, they were to take with them such personal equipment as they had. In the meantime, He said, the Scripture would be fulfilled concerning His death and identification with transgressors.

FINAL WORDS OF COMFORT AND ENCOURAGEMENT (*John* 14:1-31)

His message of comfort was twofold: He would come back to them again, and in the meantime He would provide for them a Comforter who would abide with them forever. The purpose of His going away was to prepare a place for them in His Father's heavenly home. He assured them that He would see them again after He had concluded preparing that place for them. He would personally come for them and take them away with Him that they might be together with Him forever. He was going now to His Father and He told them how they too might come to the Father. They were to accept and follow Him, for He is the Way, the Truth, and the Life. Once more He explained to them that the Father himself dwelt within Him, the Son, and was doing the works and speaking the words through Him. This same vital relationship was to exist between Him and His disciples so that His works would be manifest through them. He promised that they could have communion with Him as He had communion with His Father.

The Comforter, whom He would send, would in reality be the gift of His Father and would be none other than the Holy Ghost, the third person of the blessed Trinity. His mission, when He came, would be to teach them all things and bring to their remembrance whatsoever Christ had spoken unto them. (This is how we today have the record of the very words which Jesus spoke to His disciples when on earth.) Jesus also reminded them that it would be necessary for them to keep the commandments which He had given, particularly the great new commandment that they love one another.

Lesson 37

THE VINE AND THE BRANCHES (*John* 15:1-17)

Jesus again referred to the vital relationship which would exist between Him and His disciples. He was to be like a vine and His disciples like branches in the vine. The Father would care for them both. Their spiritual life would require purging (pruning) from time to time, with the purpose of increasing their spiritual productiveness. He emphasized that the secret of their spiritual success was simply that they abide (rest, remain quietly) in Him. They were to draw from Him the vitality which was His and which would always be present in them. If they would do this they would bear fruit, more fruit, and much fruit, and their Father would be glorified. If they would not do this they would be cast off and thrown into the fire. (The memory of Judas would ever be with them.)

Again He reminded them of the necessity of their keeping His commandments. If they did this and abode constantly in Him, they could ask what they would and it would be done for them. This meant that they would abide in the Father's love and also that the joy which Christ experiences would be realized to the full in them. He reminded them that they had not chosen Him but He had chosen them, and thus the responsibility would be His.

THE DISCIPLES' RELATIONSHIP TO THE WORLD (*John* 15:18 *to* 16:6)

Jesus warned the disciples plainly that a state of enmity existed between them and the world. He cited how He himself had been constantly opposed and attacked by evil and hypocritical men. He was soon to suffer physical abuse and death at their hands. He was to bequeath to His disciples not only the responsibility of the perpetuation of His ministry but also the relationship which He himself had held to the world. "If the world hate you, ye know that it hated

185

me before it hated you." This hatred would result in their being cast out of the synagogue and even being killed by their enemies. He warned them faithfully in advance so that they would not be surprised when it came to pass. Also, He promised they would receive the Comforter, the Spirit of Truth, who would join them in bearing witness to Him.

MINISTRY OF THE HOLY SPIRIT (*John* 16:7-15)

Jesus then explained why it was necessary that He go away and the Comforter come in His stead. His own personal ministry on earth was limited to the individuals with whom He came into contact in His physical body. He assured the disciples that even though He was gone they would not be left alone. The Holy Spirit, who would not be limited by the restrictions of a physical body, would be sent to act as their Comforter, but not theirs alone. The Holy Spirit would be able to go into all the world and perform His appointed task using redeemed beings as agents.

The Spirit's task would be twofold: it would concern the world and it would concern Christians of each succeeding generation. He would reprove and convict the world of sin, of righteousness, and of judgment. The *sin* of which He would convict them would be their unbelief toward Christ. He would explain to the world that there is no true *righteousness* except in Him. He would warn them of the *judgment* which would fall on them as surely as upon Satan, their leader. The task of the Holy Spirit as it concerned believers was to guide them into all truth (He himself is the truth). He would reveal to them the things which were to come to pass in the future. His ministry would be to glorify Christ and take the things which the Father had given Him and show them to the disciples.

DISCIPLES' PERSONAL REACTION TO HIS GOING AWAY (*John* 16:16-33)

And now Jesus returned to the subject which was so tender to Him and to them. "A little while, and ye shall not see me." He immediately assured them, "Again, a little while, and ye shall see me." From our position in history we know that He referred to His crucifixion and resurrection. The disciples, however, in spite of His oft-repeated warning that He was to be crucified, did not seem to realize that it was to be literal and physical. So Jesus once more told them plainly, "I leave the world and go to the Father. This will give you great sorrow for a time, like a woman who is in travail before the birth of her child. Her sorrow is soon forgotten in her joy with the babe in her arms. So you will have sorrow when I am taken away, but within a short time it will be completely overwhelmed by your joy at having me with you again. You must also remember," He continued, "that my Father will be very real and dear to you." He reminded them, "The Father himself loveth you. You may therefore come boldly into the Father's presence and ask and receive that your joy may be full. It is true that in the world you shall have tribulation, but I have overcome the world. The Holy Spirit will be with you always, to teach and to guide, and your Father will always listen to your cry."

THE HIGH-PRIESTLY PRAYER (*John* 17:1-26)

Concluding His words to His disciples, Jesus now lifted up His eyes and spoke to His Father. Here we enter into the Holy of Holies. This is His longest recorded prayer. He prayed many times, at His baptism in Jordan, His transfiguration on the mount, and His agony in Gethsemane, but here we are permitted to listen to Him pray. We can conclude also that this is a sample of His praying at His Father's throne in heaven where He "ever liveth to make intercession for us."

"The hour is come." Jesus used this expression often enough through His life (with His mother in John 2:4 and His brothers in John 7:6) to show that He moved along on God's appointed schedule for Him. This was the greatest "hour" of all. He had asked himself in John 12:27 if He should pray, "Father, save me from this hour" but immediately He had answered His own question, "For this cause came I unto this hour." He faced it courageously.

His high-priestly prayer can be considered in three main divisions. In verses 1 to 5 He prays for himself; in verses 6 to 19 He prays for the disciples then living; in verses 20 to 26 He prays for those who would later believe on Him. For himself He prayed that the Father would glorify His Son. He had prayed these words before (John 12:28), and His Father had answered, "I have both glorified it, and will glorify it again." But Jesus put it on record once more that the world might know that He went down into the valley of Calvary trusting that His Father would glorify Him by raising Him from the dead. Even the chief priests knew of this confidence which He had in God, for on the cross they taunted Him saying, "He trusted in God; let him deliver him now, if he will have him: for he said, I am the Son of God" (Matthew 27:43). Jesus' prayer was not so much for His own glorification but "that thy Son also may glorify thee." The Father's faithfulness would be demonstrated and vindicated when Jesus rose from the dead.

Another purpose in His being glorified by the Father was that He should give eternal life to as many as the Father had given Him. His Father first and the world next—these were His concerns in His high-priestly prayer. His definition of eternal life also exalted His Father as the one true God and as the One who sent Jesus Christ to redeem the world. Jesus then began His report to the Father concerning His work on the earth: "I have finished the work which thou gavest me to do." This was in anticipation of His final cry, "It is finished," which He would utter when He hung on the cross (John 19:30). Then He records His confidence that the Father would restore Him to the glory which He had enjoyed with the Father "before the world was."

CHRIST PRAYS FOR HIS DISCIPLES (*John* 17:6-26)

Jesus now described the men whom the Father had given Him and for whom He was praying. He reported that He had manifested His Father's name unto them and "they have kept thy word." Also, "They have known that all things" which were manifested in Jesus' life had really been from the Father. It was for these men that the Lord was now praying, since they were to be left in the world. "Holy Father, keep through thine own name those whom thou hast given me." The object of this desired preservation was "that they may be one, as we are." Up to that hour He himself had kept them, but now He turned them over to His Father's keeping. The purpose of the keeping was not only that they might be one but that they might have His joy fulfilled in themselves. He was conscious of the fact that they would be hated by the world as He had been, and therefore they would need His Father's protection. He did not ask that they should be taken out of the world, but that they should be preserved from the evil which is in the world. Jesus also prayed that His Father would sanctify His disciples. He himself had been sanctified by His Father and sent into the world (John 10:36). Now He was sending them into the world in like manner. He asked that they too should have His Father's ordination to their mission.

Assuming in faith that His Father would answer His prayer and that His disciples would go into the world as He had gone into the world and would make other disciples for Him, He now turned to pray for those who "shall believe on me through their word." He prayed the same prayer for them that He had prayed for the disciples then living. "That they may be one, even as we are." But here He added that the purpose of this oneness in Him and the Father would be that the world might see and believe. He now expanded the scope of His prayer to ask that His disciples share with Him the glory which He had with the Father before the world was. He asked that the love which He had enjoyed from His Father before the foundation of the world might also rest upon His disciples.

Lesson 38

PART 11—TRIAL AND CRUCIFIXION

GETHSEMANE (*Matthew* 26:30, 36-45; *Mark* 14:26, 32-41; *Luke* 22:39-46; *John* 18:1)

At the conclusion of Christ's high-priestly prayer they sang a hymn together and went out across the brook Cedron, which was at the base of the Mount of Olives. There was a garden here called Gethsemane into which Jesus was accustomed to retire for prayer. He said to His disciples, "Pray that ye enter not into temptation," and then He himself withdrew from them about a stone's throw. He took with Him Peter and the two sons of Zebedee, James and John. To them He said, "My soul is exceeding sorrowful even unto death." He told them to tarry at that point while He went still farther and fell on His face and prayed. Still, more closely, He was facing "the hour." The "cup" which He was about to drink was filled with more suffering than we can possibly understand. Some say that it was merely the human in His nature that shrank from the physical suffering which He was soon to endure. From our knowledge of what Calvary involved, we know He was soon to bear the sins of the whole world and that this would require that His Father turn His face from Him for the moment. Surely great was the suffering of that hour. For this reason He prayed that if it were possible the cup would pass from Him. He hastened to add, however, "Nevertheless, not my will, but thine, be done."

At this moment there appeared an angel from heaven to strengthen Him. Then, in agony, He prayed more earnestly, and His sweat was as it were great drops of blood falling to the ground. He prayed "with strong crying and tears unto him that was able to save him from death, and was heard in that he feared" (Hebrews 5:7). He then turned to His disciples and found them sleeping. He chided Peter with, "Couldest not thou watch one hour?" Already Peter was revealing that "the spirit truly is ready, but the flesh is weak." The Lord then returned and prayed again using the same words. Again He returned to His disciples and once more found them asleep. For the third time He returned to prayer, using the same words. When He came back to His disciples again He told them to sleep on and take their rest.

THE BETRAYAL (*Matthew* 26:45-50; *Mark* 14:42-45; *Luke* 22:47, 48; *John* 18:2, 3)

Shortly after this Jesus awakened them saying, "It is enough, the hour is come; behold, the Son of man is betrayed into the hands of sinners. Rise up, let us go; lo, he that betrayeth me is at hand." Judas knew the place, for he had often gone there with the other disciples. He assumed that Jesus once more would be in His accustomed place to pray. Carrying out the covenant which he had made, Judas now came with a band of men and officers which he had received from the chief priests and Pharisees. The chief priests themselves, and the elders and captains of the temple, were also in the crowd. They came with lanterns, torches, and weapons. Judas had said he would give them a sign: the one whom he should kiss would be Jesus. As he drew near to kiss the Lord, Jesus said, "Friend, wherefore art thou come? betrayest thou the Son of man with a kiss?"

THE ARREST (*Matthew* 26:55, 56; *Mark* 14:46, 48-50; *Luke* 22:52, 53; *John* 18:4-9)

He then said to the people, "Whom seek ye?" They answered Him, "Jesus of Nazareth." He replied, "I am he." He thus identified himself as the One they sought and at the same time was using the great Jehovistic title. Once before He had said, "Before Abraham was, I am." This was why they were crucifying Him, but He still quietly insisted, "I am." At this majestic word "they went backward, and fell to the ground." Upon their recovery Jesus said to them, "If therefore ye seek me, let these go their way." He then said to them, "Be ye come out, as against a thief, with swords and staves? When I was daily with you in the temple, ye stretched forth no hands against me: but this is your hour, and the power of darkness." Then they laid their hands upon Him and took Him.

PETER SMITES MALCHUS (*Matthew* 26:51-54; *Mark* 14:47, 51, 52; *Luke* 22:49-51; *John* 18:10, 11)

At this point Peter drew his sword to attack the mob that had arrested his Lord. At his first blow he smote Malchus, the high priest's servant, and cut off his right ear; whereupon Jesus told Peter to put up his sword into its place. "I shall drink the cup that my Father has given me. If I chose I could pray to my Father, and he would give me twelve legions of angels for my defense, but this would be in violation of the Scripture, and that must never be." He then touched the ear and healed the man. An anonymous young man was also in the group, having only a linen cloth around his body. (Some believe this was Mark, the only writer who records the incident.) The mob sought to take him also, but he left the linen cloth in their hands and fled.

FIRST JEWISH TRIAL (*Luke* 22:54; *John* 18:12-14, 19-23)

When the band and the captain and officers of the Jews seized Jesus, they first bound Him and took Him away to Annas. Annas at this time was an old man, having been high priest previously. Although his son-in-law, Caiaphas, was the high priest at that time, Annas still retained the prestige of the office. Annas asked Jesus concerning His disciples and His doctrine. The Lord, realizing that He was on trial, reminded Annas that His whole story was open to the world, since He taught publicly in the synagogue and in the temple. He suggested that it would be better form in a trial for the judge to call for witnesses from those who had heard Him, for they knew what He had said. This reply of Christ's was resented by one of the officers, who slapped Jesus. Jesus answered Him, "If I have spoken evil, let it be on the record; but if I have spoken well, why do you slap me?"

PETER'S DENIAL (*Matthew* 26:58, 69-75; *Mark* 14:66-72; *Luke* 22:55-62; *John* 18:15-18, 25-27)

When they arrested Jesus and led Him away, Simon Peter and another disciple followed Him. This other disciple, who was presumably John (for it is he who records the incident), went in with Jesus into the palace of the high priest. Peter stood without. Then the other disciple, who was known to the high priest and apparently was given privileges in the palace, went out and told the maid who kept the door that it would be all right to let Peter in. The girl suspected that Peter was one of Christ's disciples and asked him if it were so. Peter protested, "I am not." The night air was cold, and the servants and officers made a fire. Peter stood with them and warmed himself. He evidently had lost faith already for the record states that he sat there "to see the end."

After his first denial, Peter went out into the porch where another maid saw him. She accused him of being with "Jesus of Nazareth." This time Peter used an oath with his denial. Then a cock crowed. An hour later still another person accused Peter of being one of Christ's disciples, citing his Galilean speech as proof. This time Peter cursed and swore and said, "I know not this man." Then for the second time the cock crowed. It was in the very presence of Jesus that Peter denied Him, for upon this third denial the Lord turned and looked on him. This brought to Peter's remembrance the word of the Lord that he would deny Him three times before the cock crowed twice. This brought remorse to Peter's heart. He went out and wept bitterly.

Lesson 39

SECOND JEWISH TRIAL (*Matthew* 26:57, 59-68; *Mark* 14:53-65; *Luke* 22:63-65; *John* 18:24)

At the conclusion of the hearing before Annas, they left Jesus bound and sent Him to Caiaphas, the real high priest. Here the chief priests, elders, and scribes were assembled. This was the Sanhedrin which was qualified by law to conduct an ecclesiastical court. A legal meeting of such a court could not be held before sunrise, but the Jews were eager to prepare their case. First of all, they sought witnesses, and many people came to testify against Jesus. But their testimony did not agree, and thus was of no value. At last two people were found to testify concerning the statement that Jesus made at the beginning of His ministry to the effect that if they would destroy the temple He would build it again in three days. Of course Jesus meant the temple of His own body which would be raised again three days after they destroyed it. However, they took it literally and used it as an accusation against Him. This was not sufficient evidence, however, to justify a sentence of death, and the high priest turned to Christ himself and asked Him why it was that He had no answer. Again Jesus answered nothing.

In desperation the high priest came immediately to the root of their antipathy to Him. Jesus had said He was the Son of God, so the high priest asked Him plainly, "Art thou the Christ, the Son of the blessed?" Jesus had refused to speak when it did not appear so consequential, but now at this crucial question He chose to make a declaration. He knew it would incriminate Him but He had come into the world for this purpose, and once more He wanted it upon the record regardless of the consequences. Jesus answered the high priest, "I am." He added, "Ye shall see the Son of man sitting on the right hand of power, and coming in the clouds of heaven." This last statement was an amplification of His declaration that He is the

194

Son of God. "Let there be no mistake about it, I am indeed the Son of God, but I am also the Son of man. I am to sit on the right hand of the Majesty on high and I will come back again in the clouds of heaven."

This is all His accusers needed to hear. The high priest rent his clothes and declared, "What need we any further witnesses? Ye have heard the blasphemy." Then he asked them for their verdict, and they answered immediately, "He is guilty of death."

At this point this court of the aristocracy of the Jewish nation lost its dignity and degenerated into a brawl. They attacked Jesus physically. They spat in His face. They struck Him, slapped Him, and taunted Him. They blindfolded Him and in derision said, "If you are the Christ, tell us which of us smote you this time."

JUDAS' REMORSE (*Matthew* 27:3-10)

Evidently Judas, who had betrayed Him, was present during Jesus' trial. When He saw that Jesus was condemned, great remorse overtook him. He had doubtless not anticipated this turn of events. He knew His Lord's power and probably expected Him to use it in His own defense. His clever ruse to gain thirty pieces of silver had led to the approaching death of his wonderful Lord. His deep regret prompted him to bring back the thirty pieces of silver to the chief priests and elders with the confession, "I have sinned in that I have betrayed the innocent blood." But they were not impressed with this confession and refused to accept the money. Whereupon Judas threw it down and went and hanged himself. Then the chief priests picked up the silver pieces and, realizing that they could not put it into the treasury because it was the price of blood, decided to buy with it a pauper's field in which to bury strangers. This was a fulfillment of the Scripture found in Zechariah 11:12, 13.

THIRD JEWISH TRIAL (*Matthew* 27:1; *Luke* 22:66-71; *Mark* 15:1)

As soon as the hour arrived when a legal trial could be held, they went into formal session. Again they asked Him, "Art thou the Christ?" He replied, "If I tell you, ye will not believe." He then repeated what He had told them earlier, "Hereafter shall the Son of man sit on the right hand of the power of God." They were not satisfied with this answer and asked again, "Art thou then the Son of God?" He said unto them, "Ye say that I am." In other words, "I have told you that I am and you have repeated it." Then they said, "What need we any further witness? for we ourselves have heard out of his own mouth." Then the whole court arose and led Him to Pilate.

FIRST ROMAN TRIAL (*Matthew* 27:2, 11-14; *Mark* 15:1-5; *Luke* 23:1-5; *John* 18:28-38)

When they arrived at the hall of judgment they would not enter lest they be defiled. This was a demonstration of the superficiality and inconsistency of their religion. They would not cross a certain threshold but they would murder the Son of God. So Pilate went out to them.

Naturally his first remark was, "What accusation bring ye against this man?" It seems the chief priests felt that Pilate should have accepted their sentence of "guilty of death" and merely have ratified it. The Jews were not authorized by Roman law to execute any person. Any sentence of death which they would pass upon their prisoners had to be confirmed by the Roman governor whose soldiers would carry out the execution. They showed their annoyance at Pilate by replying, "If he were not a malefactor, we would not have delivered him up unto thee." Pilate answered, "Take ye him, and judge him according to your law." Then they told him plainly, "We want Him put to death, but it is not lawful for us to do so." Thus, unconsciously, they were fulfilling Christ's own prediction concerning the method of His death (John 12:32).

At this point Pilate called Jesus into the judgment hall with him that he might interview Him privately. His first question was, "Art thou the King of the Jews?" This naturally would interest Pilate for he himself was governor of the Jews and would not brook a rival. Jesus' answer explained that He was indeed a king but that His kingdom was not of this world. It was a spiritual kingdom, and they who were of the truth would hear His voice and belong to His kingdom. This induced Pilate to ask, "What is truth?" He did not wait for an answer but concluded immediately that Jesus was no peril to him. So he went out to the Jews and announced his verdict, "I find in him no fault at all." Whereupon the Jews began to accuse Christ of many things, but to these accusations He answered nothing. Among the accusations was the statement that Jesus had forbidden them to give tribute to Caesar. This was a deliberate misrepresentation, for only a few days before they had asked Him if it was lawful to pay tribute to Caesar, and He had confounded them with His classic reply, "Give to Caesar that which belongs to Caesar and to God that which belongs to God." They felt that such a charge would be of weight before Pilate and therefore did not hesitate to make the false accusation. Again Pilate told them, "I find no fault in this man." Then they became clamorous in their protest, "He stirreth up the people, teaching throughout all Jewry, beginning from Galilee to this place." But still Jesus answered not a word. This caused the governor to marvel greatly.

SECOND ROMAN TRIAL (*Luke* 23:6-12)

The reference to Galilee in the Jews' accusation gave Pilate the thought that he could transfer responsibility in the trial of this Man to Herod, who had jurisdiction over Galilee. It so happened that Herod also had come down to Jerusalem at that time, for a great concourse of people gathered at Jerusalem at the time of the Passover. Pilate therefore sent Jesus to Herod to be tried by him.

When Herod saw the Lord he was glad, for he had heard much concerning Him and had hoped to see some miracle performed by Him. He therefore plied Him with many questions, but Jesus did not answer him at all. It seems that Herod had forgotten all about John the Baptist whom he had beheaded. But not so the Christ. Herod had proved his utter unworthiness of any attention from the Lord, and so Jesus gave him none. The chief priests and scribes again brought their vigorous and serious charges against Christ, but nothing substantial in the way of evidence was presented, and so Herod sent Him back to Pilate. But first Herod and his soldiers ridiculed Christ and mockingly arrayed Him in a gorgeous robe. This mutual contact with Christ by Herod and Pilate strangely enough made them friends again, for up until that time they were enemies.

Lesson 40

BARABBAS RELEASED (*Matthew* 27:15-26; *Mark* 15:6-15; *Luke* 23:13-25; *John* 18:39, 40)

By sending Jesus to Herod, Pilate had not escaped the responsibility of condemning Jesus but had merely made another man share that responsibility. Again Jesus stood before him, awaiting his verdict. Once more Pilate protested that, having examined Jesus, he had found no fault in Him. Now he could say, "Neither has Herod found anything worthy of death in Him. My decision therefore is to release Him."

The Jews had a custom that at the Passover Feast the governor would release to them the prisoner whom they requested. Pilate now hoped that the populace would go over the head of their leaders and ask that Jesus be released to them. However, to his surprise and possible disappointment, when he presented Jesus to them they cried out, "Not this man but Barabbas." Now Barabbas was a rebel who had committed insurrection against the government. He had also been a robber and a murderer, and now he was to be released but Jesus was to be crucified. How typical of a sinful world. All who have robbed the Lord of His rightful inheritance in us are enemies of God and those who hate their brothers can be considered murderers at heart. Being sinners, all are servants of sin and prisoners to its power. This is the human race which Christ came to redeem.

At this juncture Pilate received a message from his wife pleading that he should have nothing to do with "that just Man." Rejecting her plea added further to Pilate's guilt. Protesting innocence of the crime that he was about to commit, he took a basin of water and washed his hands before the people. This was sheer pretense of course, and an attempted veneer to cover his guilt. The crowd of bloodthirsty Jews, however, were more candid than he and blatantly

198

invited that "his blood be upon us and our children." Pilate then released Barabbas unto them.

THIRD ROMAN TRIAL (*Matthew* 27:27-31; *Mark* 15:16-20; *John* 19:1-16)

The governor then turned Jesus over to his soldiers who took Him out into the common hall and scourged Him. This scourging was predicted by Isaiah (50:6). "I gave my back to the smiters, and my cheeks to them that plucked off the hair: I hid not my face from shame and spitting." The Romans scourged with knotted thongs of leather weighted with lead or bones. The Jews limited the stripes to "forty save one," but Roman practice knew no limit. "The plowers plowed upon my back: they made long their furrows" (Psalm 129:3). After stripping Jesus of His own garments for scourging, the soldiers then put a scarlet robe upon Him, mocking His claim to royalty. They also plaited a crown of thorns and placed it upon His head. They put a reed in His right hand and bowed the knee before Him saying, "Hail, King of the Jews!" They spat upon Him also and took the reed and smote Him on the head, piercing His sacred brow with the mock crown of thorns that He wore.

After the soldiers had satisfied their sadistic instinct, they took the robe off Him and put His own garments on Him again. They brought Him out to Pilate who once more presented Him to the people and said, "I bring him forth to you, that ye may know that I find no fault in him. . . . Behold the Man!" Again the mob called back, "Crucify him, crucify him." Once more Pilate tried to transfer his guilt, saying, "Take ye him, and crucify him: for I find no fault in him." The Jews then answered, "We have a law, and by our law he ought to die, because he made himself the Son of God." This was news to Pilate and it frightened him. He took Jesus again into the judgment hall and asked Him, "Whence art thou?" Jesus gave him no answer. Pilate wondered at this and reminded Jesus that he had power to crucify Him or to releaseHim. Whereupon Jesus answered. "Thou couldest have no power at all against me, except it were given thee from above." This is eternally true of all of God's children. Our heavenly Father watches and lets nothing come upon us but what He specifically allows. Jesus assured Pilate that the Jews who had delivered Him to the governor were guilty of a greater sin than he.

This conversation with Christ spurred Pilate on in his effort to release Him. The Jews then fell back on their ultimate argument: they hinted that they would report Pilate to Caesar, claiming that he was permitting the insurrection of this Man who was calling himself a king. This argument finally persuaded Pilate to release Jesus to them, for he would take no chances on losing his political position. Pilate showed that the life of an innocent godly Man, even possibly the very Son of God, was of less importance to him than his place as governor. He therefore delivered Jesus to the people, and they took Him away to crucify Him.

ON THE WAY TO CALVARY (*Matthew* 27:32; *Mark* 15:21; *Luke* 23:26-32; *John* 19:17)

As was the Roman custom, Christ's cross was laid upon His own shoulders and He went forth, bearing His cross. It chanced that a certain Cyrenian named Simon was passing by, coming out of the country. Either out of mercy for the exhausted Man or because of the necessity of providing aid in transporting the cross to the hill of crucifixion, the soldiers conscripted Simon to carry the cross for Jesus. Although the actual executioners were the men of the governor's guard, the Jewish leaders who had called for His blood and wrung the sentence of death from a reluctant Pilate were mainly responsible and they headed the procession to its ghastly objective. There also followed a great company of men and women who bewailed and lamented Him. The city was full of visitors at this Passover season, and the crowds thronged eagerly to any place which provided excitement. To the women who followed Jesus weeping, our Lord turned and said, "Weep not for me, but for yourselves, and for your children." How unselfish and noble of Him in His hour of personal pain to think of others who were in danger. He warned them that the time would come when childless women would be fortunate, for in those days, "shall they begin to say to the mountains, Fall on us; and to the hills, Cover us." The figure which He used, "If they do these things in a green tree, what shall be done in the dry?" was to say, "If they are doing these things to me, one who has no guilt, how much greater shall be the punishment of those who are guilty."

Two others, who were criminals, were led out with Him to be put to death at the same time. This fulfilled the Scripture, "He was numbered with transgressors" (Isaiah 53:12).

THE CRUCIFIXION (*Matthew* 27:33-36; *Mark* 15:22-25; *Luke* 23:33, *John* 19:17, 18)

To fulfill the Levitical type of the sin offering which Jesus was now about to become, they took Him "without the camp" (Leviticus 4:12). Hebrews 13:12 also tells us that He suffered "without the gate." Thus we know that the place of the Crucifixion was outside the gates of Jerusalem. It was called Golgotha (a Greek transliteration of an Aramaic* term meaning *skull*), and Matthew, Mark, and John referred to the site as such. Luke simply used the Greek term which meant *skull*. This could refer to the shape of the hill, or the fact that it was commonly used as the place of crucifixion. Calvary, our popular term for the site of the crucifixion, comes from the Latin and translators of the King James Version applied it to Luke's account. Christ's presence and death there has transformed it from a place of ignominy and shame into the most sacred spot of all Christendom.

Some sympathetic persons who were present, possibly of the women who had bewailed His death, offered Him a drink which doubtless included some narcotic to ease His suffering. However, He would not shrink from the bitterest dregs of that cup that His Father had given Him to drink and so He refused the potion.

TITLE AND GARMENTS (*Matthew* 27:35, 37; *Mark* 15:24, 26; *Luke* 23:38; *John* 19:19-23)

Pilate had instructed that a title be placed on His cross to identify Him. It read: JESUS OF NAZARETH, THE KING OF THE JEWS. Although Pilate may have meant it as humor or spite, God intended it that all the world might know that this Man was His Son and the rightful King over His chosen people. The title was written in three languages, Hebrew, Greek, and Latin, that all might read and understand. This great sacrifice was indeed on behalf of all the world (John 1:29). The Jews protested to Pilate concerning this title, but he refused to change it.

To complete Christ's humiliation and embarrassment, they stripped Him of all His clothes. The soldiers divided them among themselves. But when they came to the seamless robe they did not cut it up but gambled to see who would receive it. Unconsciously they ful-

---

*Aramaic is a Semetic language, closely related to Hebrew. When the Jews returned from captivity to Palestine, Aramaic became their everyday language.

filled the Scripture found in Psalm 22:18, "They part my garments among them, and cast lots upon my vesture."

Lesson 41

RIDICULED (*Matthew* 27:39-44; *Mark* 15:29-32; *Luke* 23:35-37)

A curious heartless throng surrounded Him. They wagged their heads and reviled the Lord. They reminded Him of His claim to be able to destroy the temple and build it again in three days, and challenged Him to save himself. Here was a chance, they said, for Him to demonstrate His deity by coming down from the cross. Years before this Satan himself had challenged Christ to demonstrate that He is the Son of God. He refused both temptations. The soldiers who crucified Him and the thieves who were crucified with Him joined in the mockery.

The chief priests and the scribes and the elders who were standing by also vented their spite and hatred for Him. With unconscious truthfulness they said, "He saved others; himself he cannot save." He would not save himself, for He was giving His life to save others. Rankling under the shame to them of the title that was over His head, they said, "If he be the King of Israel, let him now come down from the cross." They promised to believe on Him if He did. How empty was such a promise, however, in the face of the fact that they had seen so many of His marvelous miracles, including the raising of persons from the dead, and yet did not believe on Him. They put to Him the ultimate challenge. "He said, 'I am the Son of God.' If he is, let God deliver him now, for he trusted in God." How true this was. He trusted in God to answer His prayer, "Father . . . glorify thy Son, that thy Son also may glorify thee." And He did not trust in vain.

LAST WORDS (*Matthew* 27:45-47; *Mark* 15:34; *Luke* 23:34, 43,46; *John* 19:26-30)

Jesus hung on the cross for about six hours, from nine in the morning until three in the afternoon. During this time He made seven utterances which were so significant they were a complete picture of the heart and ministry of Christ. The first, middle, and last of these utterances were prayers. First and last He was talking to His Father. The first three were on behalf of others, the last three for himself. The fifth statement was particularly human, and the sixth was essentially divine. The fourth or central statement was representative of the sinning world for which He died.

Shortly after His crucifixion began He prayed, "Father, forgive them; for they know not what they do." This was a magnificent demonstration of the true love which He had in His heart for His enemies. Jesus was conscious of their blindness and cited it to His Father, possibly as a reason why they should be forgiven. It can be noted that this prayer was answered, when Peter preached to those who "by wicked hands had crucified and slain" the Lord and witnessed the conversion of thousands of them (see Acts 2).

To the last, and even in His intense suffering, Jesus had an ear for the call of penitent people. One of the thieves who was crucified with Him turned to Him and said, "Lord, remember me when thou comest into thy kingdom." Here is a double confession. He called Jesus, "Lord." He also expressed faith in Christ's Kingship and the coming glory of His kingdom. He did not ask for special favors, as John and James had done, but merely that the Lord would remember him at that hour. Long before that hour, even at that very moment, the Lord remembered him and promised him, "Today shalt thou be with me in paradise." Christ thus was already dispensing the salvation which He was in the act of purchasing. Incidentally, He also revealed that He would shortly go to that place of departed spirits known as Paradise. He was to proclaim His great salvation to them and was to take a great multitude of the righteous dead to that new Paradise which He would establish around the throne of His Father (Ephesians 4:8; Philippians 1:23; 2 Corinthians 5:8; 12:4).

The prophet Simeon had told Mary, when she brought her Babe to present Him in the temple, "A sword shall pierce through thy own soul also" (Luke 2:35). And now that solemn word was being fulfilled. His mother was standing there, witnessing the intense suffering of her Son. She could do nothing but pour out her heart in sympathy and in love for Him. He reciprocated that love and did something for her. He had doubtless been the support of His mother since the death of Joseph, and now He made provision for her further care. John, His beloved disciple, was standing there also, so Jesus said to His mother, "Woman, behold thy son!" And to John he said, "Behold thy mother!" And from that hour John took her into his own home. To the last, Jesus discharged His duty as a dutiful son. He honored His mother and made practical provision for her. He was obedient to the commandments of God to the very last.

At the sixth hour darkness settled over all the earth and remained until the ninth hour. (In our terms this would be from twelve noon until three in the afternoon.) It was about the ninth hour that Jesus cried with a loud voice, "My God, my God, why hast thou forsaken me?" This was the darkest hour, not only of that day, but of the whole life of Christ. It was doubtless at this moment that His Father laid on Him the sin of the whole world. Habakkuk had declared, "Thou are of purer eyes than to behold evil, and canst not look on iniquity" (Habakkuk 1:13). This is the answer to Jesus' question as to why His Father turned away from Him at that critical moment. In the sinners' place He cried, "My God, My God," and not "My Father." For the moment He was suffering the sinners' doom, darkness, and banishment. At the last day they who reject Christ as Substitute will be punished with everlasting destruction from the presence of the Lord (2 Thessalonians 1:9). Jesus tasted death for every man (Hebrews 2:9), and that was sufficient to pay the price.

After this, knowing that all things were now accomplished that the Scripture might be fulfilled, Jesus said, "I thirst." David had described His thirst in Psalm 22:15. "My strength is dried up like a potsherd; and my tongue cleaveth to my jaws; and thou hast brought me into the dust of death." Again, in Psalm 69:3 and 21, He said, "My throat is dried," and "In my thirst they gave me vinegar to drink." By His cry, "I thirst," He called attention to the fact that this jot and tittle of the Scripture was being fulfilled. He was not too proud to admit His human dependence upon others, to let them know His need so they could supply it. In response to His cry, they filled a sponge with pure vinegar and put it to His mouth.

Jesus came now to the great official proclamation: "It is finished." As a boy of twelve, He was "about His Father's business." At the height of His ministry, He said, "I must work the works of him that sent me, while it is day" (John 9:4). He also told His disciples, "My meat is to do the will of him that sent me, and to finish his work"

(John 4:34). He had reported to His Father, in His high-priestly prayer, "I have finished the work which thou gavest me to do" (John 17:4). This now was the official proclamation to all worlds that His life's mission, the redemption of the world, had been accomplished and was now finished.

Finally He cried with a loud voice, "Father, into thy hands I commend my spirit." Again David had anticipated His words (see Psalm 31:5). The broken communion with His Father, which He suffered in the dark hour when He cried, "Why hast thou forsaken me?" had now been restored, and He would be His Beloved Son forever. He had commended His body, soul, and spirit to His Father for His whole earthly mission, and now that perfect consecration was to continue without interruption and without end. Having said this, He bowed His head and died.

Lesson 42

INVISIBLE ACCOMPLISHMENTS AT CALVARY (*1 John* 2:2; *John* 1:29; *Romans* 6:6; *Galatians* 2:20; 6:14; *Hebrews* 2:14; *Matthew* 8:17; *Colossians* 2:14)

"Sitting down they watched Him there." What did they see? Some saw the Prophet of Galilee whom many had hoped would be their Messiah. Others saw an unfortunate Man being crucified as a criminal. John, and possibly Matthew of the Gospel writers, was there and recorded the literal events as he saw them. They were joined later by the Apostle Paul in seeing some spiritual facts which were not apparent to the people who sat down to watch Him then.

John recorded (1:29) that this was the Lamb of God which would take away the sin of the world. This was equivalent to Isaiah's statement (53:6), "The Lord hath laid on him the iniquity of us all." Unseen to mortal eyes but felt deeply by the Son of God, particularly in the intensity of those hours of darkness, the sin of the world was real and heavy. John also tells (1 John 2:2), and Peter joins him (1 Peter 2:24), that when Jesus died the individual acts of sin, even the sins of the whole world, He bore in His own body on the tree. This means that in addition to the great principle and fact of sin in the world, which was laid upon Christ, there were also the individual sins of the whole world laid upon His body there. How thorough and wide was God's provision for the atonement of our sins.

In Romans 6:6 Paul referred to our "old man" as the body of sin. He declared that this also was crucified with Christ. His personal testimony, as given in Galatians 2:20, confirms this statement. "I am crucified with Christ." Our self-life (Matthew 16:24), another name for the "old man," was taken with Jesus to the Cross. Thus all the inherent sins of the natural man were crucified with Christ,

207

and it merely remains that we should reckon ourselves to be "dead indeed unto sin" (Romans 6:11).

The father of John the Baptist prophesied that we would be "delivered out of the hand of our enemies" (Luke 1:74). Another of the great enemies of mankind is sickness and disease. Matthew recorded (8:17), "Himself took our infirmities, and bare our sicknesses." This was a quotation from Isaiah the prophet, who predicted that in the great atonement Jesus would be wounded for our transgressions, bruised for our iniquities, would carry our griefs and our sorrows, and that with His stripes we would be healed (Isaiah 53:4, 5). Thus we see that deliverance from sickness and disease was included in the atonement of our Lord, for these evil things too were laid upon Him when He died upon the cross. Again it is but for us to accept the deliverance which He has purchased.

Paul specifically records in Colossians 2:14 that the handwriting of ordinances which was against us He took out of the way, "nailing it to his cross." This means that the Mosaic law also, a burden which Peter said (Acts 15:10) was a yoke which we are not able to bear, was included in the great burden which rested upon our Lord as He bowed His head and died.

To Paul we also are indebted for the revelation that by the cross of our Lord Jesus Christ the world too was crucified (Galatians 6:14). This means that the power of the world was broken when Jesus died. This is why Jesus said, "In the world ye shall have tribulation: but be of good cheer; I have overcome the world" (John 16:33). There is no need, therefore, for us to love the world and the things that are in the world, for by a benefit of Calvary the power of the world is broken.

The king of all evil is Satan. In the thorough conquest of Calvary the Father included complete victory over the devil himself. Jesus announced in John 12:31, "Now is the judgment of this world: now shall the prince of this world be cast out." The next verse, referring to His being lifted up from the earth, definitely identifies the breaking of Satan's power by the work which Jesus would perform on the cross. The writer of Hebrews makes it very plain. Jesus became partaker of human flesh and blood "that through death he might destroy him that had the power of death, that is the devil" (Hebrews 2:14). Thus we know that by Jesus' work on the Cross the authority and power of Satan was broken over the lives of those who accept

Calvary's benefits. Like Samson of old, Jesus accomplished more in His death than in His lifetime.

HIS SIDE PIERCED (*John* 19:31-37)

The day upon which Jesus was crucified was called "The Preparation." This was the day before a Sabbath and in this instance it was before a Sabbath which was called "a high day." The Jews were anxious that the bodies of these crucified people should not be hanging on the cross on a Sabbath Day. Moses had commanded that if a man be hanged on a tree his body should not remain all night upon the tree, for he that is hanged is accursed of God (Deuteronomy 21:22, 23). Paul cited this verse in Galatians 3:13 as proving that Jesus was made a curse for us. The Jews therefore asked Pilate that the legs of the three persons on the cross might be broken to hasten their death so that they might be taken away. With permission to do this, the soldiers broke the legs of the two men who had been crucified with Jesus, but when they came to Him they saw that He was dead already, so they did not break His legs. This again was the fulfillment of Scripture (Exodus 12:46; Numbers 9:12; Psalm 34:20).

To satisfy himself that Jesus was really dead, one of the soldiers pierced His side with a spear and immediately there came out blood and water. This not only satisfied the soldier but proved to all the world that Jesus was really dead and had not merely swooned. The issuing of blood and water from His pierced side was evidence of a broken and collapsed physical heart. This also was a fulfillment of prophecy (Zechariah 12:10), "They shall look upon me whom they have pierced." They pierced Him on Calvary, but they will look on Him again as the Pierced One when He comes in the clouds of heaven, "and every eye shall see him, and they also which pierced him" (Revelation 1:7).

TEMPLE VEIL RENT AND GRAVES OPENED (*Matthew* 27:51-56; *Mark* 15:38-41; *Luke* 23:47-49)

Paul tells us that the handwriting of ordinances was nailed to His cross (Colossians 2:14). When Jesus died the great veil of the temple, which hung between the Holy Place and the Holiest of All, was rent in twain from the top to the bottom, demonstrating this tremendous spiritual victory. The veil was an exceedingly heavy piece of tapestry 60 feel long, 20 feet wide, and as thick as the palm of the hand (Edersheim, Vol. II, p. 611). by rending it God showed that the way into the Holiest was now opened wide (Hebrews 9:8; 10:19, 20). The veil had typified His flesh, which was now rent and torn.

At this time there was also an earthquake, and the rocks were rent asunder. Many graves were opened, and bodies of the saints arose and came out of the graves after His resurrection and appeared to many people in Jerusalem.

These phenomena greatly impressed the Roman centurion who was in charge of the crucifixion. He and his soldiers feared greatly and cried out, "Truly this was the Son of God." The women who had followed Jesus from Galilee and had ministered to Him were also standing by. Among them was Mary Magdalene, Mary the mother of James the less and Joses (Judas, not Iscariot), the mother of James and John, Salome, and of course the mother of Jesus himself. They all beheld the things which were done and smote their breasts and returned into the city.

THE BURIAL (*Matthew* 27:57-61; *Mark* 15:42-47; *Luke* 23:50-56; *John* 19:38-42)

Lest His body be thrown vilely away, as was the custom in the case of crucified criminals, His Father had planned that this sacred body which had been especially prepared for His Son, and through which He had done His Father's will so perfectly, should be tenderly cared for and preserved for the resurrection morning. A certain rich man of Arimathea named Joseph, who was "an honourable counsellor" and who was a secret disciple of Jesus, went in boldly to Pilate and asked that Jesus' body be given to him. Pilate marveled to hear that Jesus was already dead and so called the centurion to make sure. This the centurion certified (another evidence to all the world that He really died), so Pilate gave the body to Joseph. He was then joined by Nicodemus, the one who had come to Jesus by night, and together they took the body of Jesus and wound it in linen clothes with spices, as was the manner of the Jews for burial. Nicodemus contributed a mixture of myrrh and aloes, about an hundred pounds weight.

Now in the place where Jesus was crucified there was a garden, literally at the foot of the hill called Calvary. This garden belonged to Joseph, and he had prepared on the side of the hill a new tomb hewn out of the rock. He evidently had prepared it for his own use, but as yet no man had ever laid therein. They took Jesus to this tomb, placed Him therein, and rolled a great stone to the door of the sepulchre. Mary Magdalene and the other Mary beheld where He was laid. They later returned with prepared spices and ointments, after resting on the Sabbath Day.

THE WATCH SET (*Matthew* 27:62-66)

The next day, after the day of the preparation, the chief priests and Pharisees sought an audience with Pilate. They said, "Sir, we remember that the deceiver said while he was yet alive, After three days I will rise again." This statement of Christ, made a number of times to His disciples, had evidently been told by them to others, and it made quite an impression on the scribes and Pharisees. (It seemed to have made more of an impression upon them than upon the disciples themselves.) The Pharisees went on to ask Pilate therefore to set a guard at the grave where Jesus was buried. They feared that the disciples might come and steal Him away and tell the people that He was risen from the dead. They admitted that such an announcement would greatly stir the people and, according to them, "the last error shall be worse than the first." They were admitting that a possible resurrection would have a tremendous impact upon the people. They were wrong, however, in thinking that Christ's disciples would lie. Pilate instructed the chief priests and Pharisees to set a watch themselves and make it as sure as possible. They went to the grave and sealed it with a royal seal and appointed a group of soldiers to stand guard.

Lesson 43

PART 12—RESURRECTION

THE RESURRECTION (*Matthew* 28:2-4)

"For as Jonas was three days and three nights in the whale's belly; so shall the Son of man be three days and three nights in the heart of the earth" (Matthew 12:40). Jesus had said also (Matthew 16:21) that after He was killed He would "be raised again the third day." The Jewish day began at sundown in the evening. Sometime therefore after that hour, as the first day of the week began, Jesus was raised from the dead by the glory of the Father (Romans 6:4). It was not necessary to roll the stone away for Jesus to rise, for He appeared and disappeared through closed doors after His resurrection. the stone was rolled back and the tomb opened that the disciples and the world might see. The Father had glorified His Son in His resurrection, and Jesus had indeed not trusted in vain.

There had been an earthquake at the time of His crucifixion, and now again an earthquake accompanied His resurrection. An angel from heaven came and rolled back the stone from the door of the tomb and sat upon it. He shone with the brilliance of heaven, and for fear of him the guards trembled and fell prostrate. Evil men had fallen to the ground when they came to arrest Jesus, and now once more they fell at the appearance of His angel.

THE WOMEN COME TO THE TOMB (*Matthew* 28:1, 5-8; *Mark* 16:1-8; *Luke* 24:1-12; *John* 20:1)

As it began to dawn toward the first day of the week, a group of women who had prepared spices started on their journey to the tomb. These included Mary Magdalene and "the other Mary," the wife of Alpheus and mother of James and Joses, and Salome. It

212

appears that Mary Magdalene was the leader among these women as Peter was among the disciples. It would also appear that she went on ahead of the other women, arriving there before them.

Mary saw that the stone was rolled away and ran back immediately to tell Peter and John. Assuming that Jesus' body had been removed, she announced, "They have taken away the Lord out of the sepulchre, and we know not where they have laid him."

At this point the other women arrived and entered the open tomb. They saw an angel sitting on the right side and they were afraid. The angel said to them, "Do not be afraid. I know that you are looking for Jesus, who was crucified. He is not here, he is risen. You can see the place where they laid him is now empty. Go back and tell his disciples and Peter that they will find him in Galilee where he awaits them." Whereupon the women fled from the tomb in great fear.

They apparently met other women, including Joanna, and returned with them once more to the tomb. Again they entered the open sepulchre, and two men appeared unto them in shining garments. These angels repeated the message of the previous one and reminded the women of Christ's own prediction that the third day He would rise again. Then they remembered His words.

PETER AND JOHN COME TO THE TOMB (*John* 20:2-10)

When Peter and John heard the news from Mary that the Lord was missing from the tomb, they arose immediately and ran to the place where Jesus had been buried. John, the younger, outran Peter and arrived first. He found the stone rolled away. Stooping down, he looked in and saw the linen clothes lying but he did not himself go in. Herein was a miracle and an evidence of Jesus' resurrection. If He had been taken away by others, they would of course have taken Him all embalmed as He was. But here were His graveclothes collapsed, as if the body had dissolved. When Peter arrived at the tomb he went boldly inside and saw the linen clothes as John had seen them. He noticed also that the napkin which had been about Jesus' head was not lying with the clothes but was folded in a place by itself. This indicated the deliberate action of the risen Christ. When John came into the tomb he understood and believed Christ's saying that He would arise from the dead.

APPEARANCE TO MARY AND THE OTHER WOMEN (*Mark* 16:9-11; *John* 20:11-18; *Matthew* 28:9, 10)

The first one to whom Jesus appeared after His resurrection was Mary Magdalene. After delivering her message to Peter and John, she evidently returned to the tomb. By the time she arrived Jesus' disciples had returned to their own home. At first she stood outside the tomb, weeping. Then she stooped and looked inside. Again the two angels were there, sitting one at the head and one at the feet where the body of Jesus had lain. They asked her why she was weeping. She answered, "Because they have taken away my Lord, and I know not where they have laid him." She did not know that He had arisen but assumed that someone had removed His body. As she turned away from the tomb she came face to face with a man she thought was the gardener. He too asked her, "Why weepest thou? whom seekest thou?" She answered, "Sir, if thou hast borne him hence, tell me where thou hast laid him, and I will take him away." This remark revealed her love but overlooked the fact that she, a woman, would not be able to carry His body. This uninhibited remark was so spontaneous and human that it is an evidence of the truthfulness of the record.

Jesus replied by simply calling her name. The tone and tenderness of His voice immediately identified Him to her. She replied, "Rabboni," which is to say, "Master." He then instructed her not to touch Him. This could be interpreted, "You do not need to detain me." He then reminded her that He had not yet ascended to His Father to complete the work of redemption by presenting His blood at the holy altar in heaven. However, He would ascend. He instructed her to go and tell His brethren. He reminded her that His Father was their Father and His God was their God. She then went and told the disciples that she had seen the Lord and that He had spoken these things to her.

As the other women returned from the tomb on their way to tell the disciples, Jesus met them too. He revealed himself to them by saying, "All hail." "And they came and held him by the feet, and worshipped him." Jesus then told them not to be afraid but to go and tell His brethren to go into Galilee, for there they would see Him.

THE WATCH REPORT (*Matthew* 28:11-15)

When the soldiers who had been watching the tomb saw that it was empty, they went into the city to report to the chief priests. These Jews hurriedly assembled the elders to counsel together as to what should be done next. Their decision was to give a large sum of money to the soldiers and instruct them to tell that while they slept the disciples had come by night and stolen away Christ's body. It evidently did not occur to them or the soldiers that this lie was so palpable that its very ridiculousness would react against them. How could they know what had happened while they slept?

APPEARANCE TO PETER (*Luke* 24:34)

That evening when the disciples were gathered together, they commented, "The Lord is risen indeed, and hath appeared to Simon." There is no further record concerning this appearance. When the women came to the tomb that morning and the angel gave them Jesus' message, they were instructed specifically to tell "his disciples and Peter." This indicated that Peter held a unique relationship to Christ at this particular time. He had shamefully denied his Lord, cursing and swearing as he did so. But Jesus had prayed for Peter that his faith would not fail, and had referred to the time when he would be converted. Jesus set about that conversion immediately after His resurrection. He appeared personally and privately to Simon. We can only conjecture what He said. The relationship between them, however, had been restored sufficiently for Peter to be included in the number of the disciples to whom Jesus revealed Himself that night.

Lesson 44

APPEARANCE TO TWO DISCIPLES ON WAY TO EMMAUS (*Mark* 16:12, 13; *Luke* 24:13-35)

Sometime during that Resurrection afternoon two of the disciples went to a village called Emmaus, about seven and one-half miles northwest of Jerusalem. They were talking together of the things which had happened. As they were walking along, Jesus drew near, possibly from a side road, and joined their company. They did not recognize Him, for "their eyes were holden that they should not know him." He detected that they were sad and asked them what they were talking about. Cleopas, one of these disciples, answered Him, "Are you a stranger in Jerusalem and the only one who does not know of the things which have happened in these days?" He said, "What things?" Then they told Him what was in their hearts. One called Jesus of Nazareth had been a prophet, mighty in deed and in word before God and the people, but the chief priests and rulers of the Jews had crucified Him. They themselves had trusted that He was the Messiah and would have redeemed Israel. But now! It was the third day since He was crucified. However, certain women of their company had gone to the sepulchre early in the morning and found it empty. They said they had seen a vision of angels who told them that Jesus was alive. Certain of their brethren had also gone to the sepulchre and found that it was as the women had said.

At this juncture Jesus began to talk to them from the Scriptures. He explained how Moses and all the prophets had specifically predicted that the Christ would suffer these very things before He entered into His glory. He chided them and called them "fools, and slow of heart to believe." As they drew near the village Jesus "made as though he would have gone further." (How typical of the Christ who never thrusts himself upon men uninvited!) But they did invite Him to stay with them that evening, for the sun was low. He responded to their invitation and went in to abide with them. As they sat down to eat together "he took bread, and blessed it, and brake, and gave to them." this evidently was His accustomed procedure, and at that moment their eyes were opened, and they knew Him, and He vanished out of their sight. Then they remembered that their hearts had burned within them while He talked with them by the way. Whereupon they returned to Jerusalem immediately and found the disciples gathered together. They told them all that had happened as they walked along and how they had recognized Jesus as He broke the bread.

APPEARANCE TO TEN DISCIPLES (*Luke* 24:36-45; *John* 20:19, 20)

Even while the disciples were speaking together Jesus himself appeared in the midst of them and said, "Peace be unto you." They were terribly frightened and imagined they were seeing a spirit. He calmed them and showed them His hands and His feet, and invited them to handle Him and see that "a spirit hath not flesh and bones, as ye see me have." Joy arose in their hearts, but they also wondered greatly and could hardly believe. He then asked them for some food, and when they had given Him "a piece of broiled fish, and of an honeycomb," He took it and ate it before them. This evidently was sufficient proof to convince them, and so He began speaking to them. As with the two on the way to Emmaus, He pointed out to them through the words of Moses and the Prophets, and in the Psalms, what had been written concerning Him. He upbraided them also for their unbelief and hardness of heart because they believed not them that had seen Him after He was risen. He then opened their understanding that they might understand the Scriptures.

THE PLAN OF SALVATION (*Luke* 24:46-49; *John* 20:21-23)

Jesus then sketched for them the plan of salvation. It had come to pass as the Word had predicted: He had suffered death on the cross and had risen again from the dead the third day. Now repentance and remission of sins were to be preached in His name among all nations, beginning at Jerusalem. "You are witnesses of these things and are the ones who should do this preaching. Also, I will send the Holy Spirit, whom my Father has promised, but you must wait in the city of Jerusalem until he endues you with power."

Here are the links in redemption's chain: from God the Father,

who devised salvation's plan and did His part in raising Christ from
the dead; to Christ, who suffered and died as the Redeemer of the
world; to the Holy Spirit, who would provide spiritual power; to
the disciples, who should preach the gospel and be witnesses of the
Christ; on down to all nations of the world who are the great objects
of redemption's plan. The Father and the Son had completed their
parts. The Holy Spirit would surely come in due time. The world
was waiting to hear redemption's story. All now depended upon the
faithfulness of the disciples. They were the connecting link between
Christ and a world He died to redeem. "As my Father hath sent
me, even so send I you."

And when He had said this He breathed on them, saying, "Receive ye the Holy Ghost." This may have been said in anticipation
of the time when he would send the promise of His Father upon
them and they would be endued with power from on High. John
had said (John 7:39) the Holy Ghost was not yet given because that
Jesus was not yet glorified. Jesus had been glorified in His resurrection but had not as yet been received back into the glory of
His Father in heaven. It may also be that they received the Holy
Spirit in His regenerative power at that very moment, for we are
born again when we are born of the Spirit.

When He sent them and breathed on them, saying, "Receive ye
the Holy Spirit," He added, "Whose soever sins ye remit, they are
remitted unto them; and whose soever sins ye retain, they are
retained." This was a reference to the remission of sins that He had
just told them should be preached in His name among all nations.
They, the disciples, were witness of these things. But the remission
of sins which they would preach would be "in his name." Therefore,
the remitting and retaining of sins would in reality be the work of
Christ, although its proclamation and pronunciation should be by
His disciples. He was committing to them the preaching and the
propagation of the salvation which He had purchased.

APPEARANCE TO ELEVEN DISCIPLES (*John* 20:24-29)

It so happened that Thomas was not with the disciples that first
evening when Jesus appeared to them. The next day they told him
they had seen the Lord. He did not have the evidence which they
enjoyed, and he said, "I cannot believe your word alone. I must
see for myself and feel of his hands and his side."

Jesus could not leave one sheep outside of His fold, so there was a postponement of the appointment in Galilee until Thomas could be included among those who had seen and welcomed the Lord. Eight days after the first resurrection appearance, setting the great precedent for meeting Christ on the first day of the week, Jesus appeared once more to His disciples who were gathered together, and Thomas was with them. Again the doors were shut, but He stood in their midst and said, "Peace be unto you." He immediately turned to Thomas (for this was particularly why He was revealing himself to them) and invited him to take his finger and feel His hands and to take his hand and feel His wounded side. "And be not faithless, but believing." His presence and the proof that He presented overwhelmed Thomas. His reply was, "My Lord and my God."

Here evidently Jesus thought of "them also which shall believe on me through their word" (John 17:20). He said, "You, Thomas, have believed me because you have seen me. Blessed are they who, though they have not seen, yet will believe."

Lesson 45

APPEARANCE TO SEVEN DISCIPLES (*John* 21:1-23)

The scene now moved to Galilee, where Jesus had said He would meet them. Seven of His disciples were at the Sea of Tiberias when Jesus revealed himself to them. Simon and Thomas were there, for Jesus had made sure when yet in Jerusalem that they were still among His very own. There were also James and John, Nathanael, and two others of His disciples. At Peter's suggestion they had all gone fishing, which was their old trade. They toiled all night but caught nothing. As they came back toward the shore they saw a man standing there who called out to ask if they had caught anything. They replied, "No." He then told them, "Cast the net on the right side of the ship, and ye shall find." They did so and took so many fish into their net that they were unable to pull it into the ship.

They immediately remembered the time at the very beginning of their discipleship when Jesus had told them where to let down their nets. On that occasion they had enclosed so great a number of fish that the net broke. John immediately said to Peter, "It is the Lord." Whereupon Peter pulled his fisherman's coat about him and cast himself into the sea to swim to shore. The other disciples also wanted to be near the Lord, so they loosed a little ship and towed it to land. They dragged with them the net full of fish. When they arrived they saw that Jesus had already prepared a fire of coals and that fish and bread were on the coals. He told them to bring some of the fish that they themselves had caught. Again Peter was the first to respond. He drew the whole net to land and found that it contained 153 fish. Jesus then invited them to come and eat and He placed before them the bread and the fish which He had prepared.

After they had eaten, Jesus engaged Peter in conversation. Fellowship had been restored between them personally and privately. But Peter had denied the Lord publicly and proper repentance and restitution must be made. Peter had boasted that he loved Christ more than the other disciples and that he would never forsake Him. So Jesus asked him plainly, "Simon, do you still love me more than these?" Peter assured Him of his love. He had now been purged of his pride and so made no comparison between himself and the others. Jesus responded, "Feed my lambs." This was a reference to the shepherd ministry which awaited Peter and all the apostles. Special attention is here given to the lambs of the fold, the new converts and also the little children.

A second time Jesus asked Peter if he loved Him. Now He too omitted the comparison. Peter again replied in the affirmative and reminded the Lord that He knew what was in his heart. Jesus now told him, "Feed my sheep." This of course refers to the more mature sheep of the flock of God. The word "feed" here is better translated "tend." This calls attention to other phases of pastoral ministry than the direct ministry of the Word.

For the third and last time, to match the number of times Peter had denied Him, Jesus asked him, "Lovest thou me?" This touched Peter to the quick and completed the work of repentance and restoration. Again he reminded the Lord that He knew everything, thus expressing faith in Christ's omniscience. Again Jesus told him, "Feed my sheep." This was as much as to say that true love for Christ will be expressed by taking care of and providing for all His sheep, including the old as well as the young.

Jesus then turned to make a prediction concerning Peter's death. It was to be similar to Christ's own. Others would stretch forth his hands and take him where he would not have chosen to go. He then instructed Peter, "Follow me." These are the very words He had used when he called Peter in the first place (Matthew 4:19). This, therefore, was a renewal of Peter's call.

Peter then revealed a characteristic that is so human. He turned and pointed to John, who had been his close companion in the years they had followed Jesus, and asked the Lord, "What shall this man do?" We are always so concerned about the duty of others. Jesus replied to him, as He does to us, "What is that to thee? follow thou me."

APPEARANCE IN GALILEE (*Matthew* 28:16-20; *1 Corinthians* 15:6, 7)

Following His appearance to the seven at the Sea of Tiberias, Jesus went to a mountain in Galilee to keep the appointment to which the angels had referred at the empty tomb. The eleven disciples met Him there and worshiped Him. (It could have been that this was the occasion to which Paul referred when he said that our Lord was seen of above five hundred brethren at once.) It was here Jesus gave them His final words of instruction and encouragement. He assured them all power was given unto Him in heaven and in earth. He promised them also that He personally would be with them as they went to teach all nations. And then He repeated, "Go ye therefore, and teach all nations, baptizing them in the name of the Father, and of the Son, and of the Holy Ghost; teaching them to observe all things whatsoever I have commanded you." This commission and the assurance of His presence and power were to extend to the end of the world. It is therefore our own personal instruction and assurance today.

APPEARANCE TO JAMES AND ALL THE APOSTLES (*1 Corinthians* 15:7; *Mark* 16:15-18; *Acts* 1:4, 5, 8)

Jesus had told His disciples to tarry in Jerusalem, so they now traveled to that city. It was perhaps here that He was seen of James. This could have been the James who was the brother of John, the first of the apostles to become a martyr. He was killed with the sword by Herod the king, who then proceeded to imprison Peter also. Herod was thwarted in this latter design by the prayers of the church and by the intervention of an angel of the Lord (Acts 12:1-7). Or this appearance could have been to the James who became a moderator of the church at Jerusalem, the one who presided over the great council recorded in Acts 15. Reference is made to him also in Acts 21:18. Jesus might have appeared to him by way of preparation for his coming leadership.

In Jerusalem the apostles assembled together and Jesus was with them. He then "commanded them that they should not depart from Jerusalem, but wait for the promise of the Father, which, saith he, ye have heard of me. For John truly baptized with water; but ye shall be baptized with the Holy Ghost not many days hence. . . . Ye shall receive power, after that the Holy Ghost is come upon you: and ye shall be witnesses unto me both in Jerusalem, and in all

Judea, and in Samaria, and unto the uttermost part of the earth"
(Acts 1:4, 5, 8).

He then said unto them, "Go ye into all the world, and preach
the gospel to every creature. He that believeth and is baptized shall
be saved; but he that believeth not shall be damned. And these
signs shall follow them that believe [them that believe on me through
your word—your converts]; in my name shall they cast out devils;
they shall speak with new tongues [an anticipation of that manifestation on the Day of Pentecost]; they shall take up serpents; and if
they shall drink any deadly thing, it shall not hurt them; they shall
lay hands on the sick, and they shall recover."

Lesson 46

"He showed himself alive after his passion by many infallible proofs, being seen of them forty days, and speaking of the things pertaining to the kingdom of God." The Holy Spirit has indeed given us "many infallible proofs" of Christ's resurrection.

1. *The credibility of the records.*

    a. The unpretentious way in which they were told (e.g., "touch me not").
    b. The accounts were written by the same men who, under inspiration, wrote the highly moral record of the life and teachings of Christ. They all, except John, suffered martyrdom as proof of their sincerity and integrity.
    c. The veracity of their records was universally accepted and not once challenged for many centuries.

2. *The empty tomb.*

    The enemies of Christianity were not able satisfactorily to account for the empty tomb. If they had taken away His body they would have produced it to disprove the disciples' claim concerning the Resurrection. If the disciples had taken His body away, they would have had no enthusiasm to preach and to suffer for their claim that He had risen.

3. *The completeness of His revelation to His disciples after He arose.*

    a. Their eyes were witnesses. They beheld a miracle which was a repetition of one performed by Him before His death.
    b. Their ears were witnesses. They heard and recognized the same loving accents of His voice.

   c. Their hands were witnesses. They felt His hands, His side, and His form.

   d. Their minds were witnesses. He taught them with the same authority and power.

   e. Their hearts were witnesses. Their affections were stirred again to the depths.

4. *The transformation of the disciples.*

It was common knowledge that there was a tremendous change in the disciples after the Resurrection. It is inconceivable that belief in falsehood could have produced so great a change.

5. *If He did not rise there must have been some evidence that He did not do so.*

Not one shred of such evidence could their anxious enemies find.

THE ASCENSION (*Mark* 16:19; *Luke* 24:50, 51; *Acts* 1:9-11)

Again the hour had come. Forty days had elapsed since His resurrection. The conclusion of Christ's earthly ministry was at hand. He had summarized that ministry to His disciples as recorded in John 16:28, "I came forth from the Father, and am come into the world: again, I leave the world, and go to the Father." He had come into the world by a supernatural incarnation. Angels had heralded His birth. Now He was to leave the world by a supernatural ascension. Angels would herald His going away.

He chose Mount Olivet, on whose southern slope the village of Bethany lay, as the place of His ascension. Zechariah had predicted that He would return to the Mount of Olives to resume His contact with this world (Zechariah 14:4). He therefore went to the Mount of Olives to break off that contact. All was in readiness, so He lifted up His hands and blessed the assembled disciples. As He did so, He was parted from them and carried up into heaven, and a cloud received Him out of their sight.

As the disciples were looking toward heaven where He had gone, there appeared before them two men in white apparel. They gave the glad announcement which has served as a beacon star and the blessed hope of the Church ever since. "This same Jesus, which is taken up from you into heaven, shall so come in like manner as ye have seen him go into heaven." His manner of going was visible to their eyes, was accompanied with clouds, in the presence of angels, and was from the Mount of Olives. In like manner He shall return. Every eye shall see Him. He will come in the clouds of heaven, with the holy angels, and His feet shall stand at that day upon the Mount of Olives which is before Jerusalem on the east (Revelation 1:7; Mark 8:38; 14:62; Zechariah 14:4).

OUR IDENTIFICATION WITH CHRIST (*Galatians* 2:20; *Colossians* 2:12; 3:1; *Romans* 6:4, 6; *Ephesians* 1:4, 19, 20; 2:5, 6)

As we joined the people who watched Christ on the cross we saw some of the invisible accomplishments of that triumph. These had to do with what Jesus was effecting there on our behalf. Now we can extend our vision to include the full extent of what Jesus did on behalf of those who believe on Him. In the eternal counsel of God, we were chosen in Him before the foundation of the world. In the fullness of time He took our sins to the cross and we were crucified with Him. Furthermore our identification with Christ follows on to our being considered as "buried with Him." But not for long, since, with Christ, we were raised again. The Scripture distinctly declares that "like as Christ was raised up from the dead by the glory of the Father, even so we also should walk in newness of life." Jesus said, "Because I live, ye shall live also" (John 14:19). "If any man be in Christ, he is a new creature" (2 Corinthians 5:17). Our identification thus extends to His resurrection, and by faith we see ourselves, who were dead in trespasses and sins, made alive with Christ. This is not all. In the same wonderful spiritual sense we were caught up together with Him and made to sit with Him in heavenly places. Since we are risen with Christ, we are enjoined to "seek those things which are above, where Christ sitteth on the right hand of God." This spiritual identification with Christ will emerge at last into a visible reality for, "When Christ, who is our life, shall appear, then shall ye also appear with him in glory." So great is the wonder of God's eternal purpose in the plan of redemption.

CHRIST'S ARRIVAL IN HEAVEN (*Psalm* 24:7-10; *Hebrews* 1:3; 4:14; 6:20; 8:1; 9:12, 24; 10:12; 12:2)

A preview of the triumphant hour when Christ returned to heaven was given to David. He has described it for us in Psalm 24. He calls for the gates of heaven, the everlasting doors of the eternal kingdom, to swing wide to let the King of glory in. He asks, "Who is this King of glory?" and answers, "The Lord strong and mighty, the Lord mighty in battle . . . the Lord of hosts, he is the King of glory." The angels of heaven have maintained great interest in the mission of Christ into this world. "When he bringeth in the first begotten into the world, he saith, And let all the angels of God worship him" (Hebrews 1:6). A heavenly host of angels sang His praises in the hearing of the shepherds on the night when He was born (Luke 2:9-14). They ministered to Him on the mount of temptation (Matthew 4:11) and also in the Garden of Gethsemane (Luke 22:43). They desired to look into the gospel which was preached with the Holy Ghost sent down from heaven (1 Peter 1:12). No wonder that they gather about and break forth into exultant praise when the King of glory comes home.

In fulfillment of the high-priestly type of entering into the Holy Place to offer atonement for the people (Leviticus 16:15, 16), Jesus "by his own blood . . . entered in once into the holy place, having obtained eternal redemption for us" (Hebrews 9:12). He was not like Aaron who had to enter twice, once for his own sin. This Man had no sin for which to atone. His atonement for us was not to be repeated year after year, for His blood was applied once for all to the heavenly mercy seat (Hebrews 10:12).

From this triumphant consummation of the redemption of the world, Jesus proceeded to take His place with His Father on His throne. "I also overcame, and am set down with my Father in his throne" (Revelation 3:21). He sits today on the right hand of the Majesty on high. However, it is recorded that His martyr Stephen, when dying, "saw the Son of man standing on the right hand of God" (Acts 7:56). Jesus evidently arose to welcome His first martyr home. "After he had offered one sacrifice for sins forever, sat down on the right hand of God; from henceforth expecting till his enemies be made his footstool" (Hebrews 10:12, 13).

Lesson 47

HIGH-PRIESTLY MINISTRY (*Hebrews* 4:4-16; 7:28; 9:24)

The emergence of the high priest from the holy place was signaled by the tinkling of the bells on his garment (Exodus 28:34, 35). When Christ emerged from offering His own blood as eternal atonement for sin, He became seated on His Father's throne as indication of His Father's acceptance of that atonement. He then began His great high-priestly ministry. The first prayer He offered to His Father was in fulfillment of His own promise, "I will pray the Father, and he shall give you another Comforter" (John 14:16). This prayer was answered when the Comforter descended upon the waiting disciples on the Day of Pentecost. Again we are told (Ephesians 4:8), "When he ascended up on high he led captivity captive, and gave gifts unto men." In His ascension He had taken with Him the saints of Paradise, which before His resurrection was located in the heart of the earth. (Samuel said, "Why hast thou disquieted me, to bring me up?" (1 Samuel 28:15.) The gifts that Christ gave to men upon His ascension to heaven were apostles, prophets, evangelists, pastors, and teachers (Ephesians 4:11). Clearly, this giving of gifts was and is a continuous process through the Church age.

The high-priestly ministry of Christ on His Father's throne is in three capacities: Mediator, Intercessor, and Advocate. As Mediator, He stands between God and man as the great Daysman which Job longed for (Job 9:33). Incidentally, there is only one mediator, as declared by Paul (1 Timothy 2:5). As Intercessor, "he ever liveth to make intercession for them" (Hebrews 7:24, 25). A brief picture and example of this intercession is provided us in His prayer recorded in John 17. There He prayed that the Father would keep and preserve believers from the evil that is in the world, that He would sanctify them (set them apart for ministry in the world), that they

228

might have His joy fulfilled in them, that they might be one as He and the Father are one (as a testimony to the world), and that they might share the glory and the love which had been His from before the foundation of the world. As Advocate (lawyer), He stands in our defense to counteract the accusations of the devil which are made before God day and night (1 John 2:1; Revelation 12:10).

THE SECOND ADVENT (*1 Thessalonians* 4:16-18; *Revelation* 1:7)

There is in the heart of our Lord a great expectation as He engages in His high-priestly ministry. He is looking forward to the time when He will come again and receive us unto himself. He also is expecting that His enemies will be made His footstool. When He died on the cross He trusted that His Father would raise Him from the dead and He did not trust in vain. And now He is trusting that His Father will give Him the expectation of His heart. Again he will not trust in vain. He will return to His own and His enemies will be vanquished.

The second return of Christ will be in two phases. First of all, He will "descend from heaven with a shout, with the voice of the archangel, and the trump of God." The dead in Christ will rise, and the living saints will be raptured, and they together will meet the Lord in the air. "Come my people, enter thou into thy chambers, and shut thy doors about thee: hide thyself, as it were, for a little moment, until the indignation be overpast. For, behold, the Lord cometh out of his place to punish the inhabitants of the earth for their iniquity: the earth also shall disclose her blood, and shall no more cover her slain" (Isaiah 26:20, 21). The righteous dead will be resurrected, and the righteous living will be translated in response to the voice of their Beloved who will come personally to receive them unto Himself. After the joyful reunion with departed loved ones and our meeting with Christ face to face, the saints will appear before the judgment seat of Christ. There they will be judged by their Lord concerning the things which they have done in the body and be rewarded according to their works (2 Corinthians 5:10; Revelation 22:12).

Following the rapture of the saints, there will be on earth a time of "tribulation, such as was not since the beginning of the world to this time, no, nor ever shall be" (Matthew 24:21, 22). The Punisher of the inhabitants of the earth will be none other than the Lord himself. They will flee to the mountains and rocks and say, "Fall on us, and hide us from the face of him that sitteth on the throne, and from the wrath of the Lamb" (Revelation 6:16, 17). This period of Christ's wrath will culminate in the great battle of Armageddon. "I will tread them in mine anger, and trample them in my fury; and their blood shall be sprinkled upon my garments, and I will stain all my raiment. For the day of vengeance is in mine heart, and the year of my redeemed is come" (Isaiah 63:3, 4). The kings of the earth and of the whole world who are gathered together to make war with Him will be slain by His sword (Revelation 16:14; 19:19, 21).

THE MILLENNIAL REIGN (*Revelation* 20:4-6)

"When the Son of man shall come in his glory, and all the holy angels with him, then shall he sit upon the throne of His glory" (Matthew 25:31). Thus will begin His millennial reign. First He will judge the nations still living on the earth. He will be reconciled to His brethren, the Jewish people, who will look upon Him whom they pierced, and mourn for Him (Zechariah 12:10; Revelation 1:7).

The Jews, restored to Palestine, will be established there as described in detail in Ezekiel, chapters 40 through 48. Nature itself will be redeemed from the curse. "The wolf also shall dwell with the lamb, and the leopard shall lie down with the kid; and the calf and the young lion and the fatling together; and a little child shall lead them. . . . They shall not hurt nor destroy in all my holy mountain: for the earth shall be full of the knowledge of the Lord, as the waters cover the sea" (Isaiah 11:6, 9). "He shall have dominion also from sea to sea, and from the river unto the ends of the earth. . . . Yea, all kings shall fall down before him: all nations shall serve him" (Psalm 72:8, 11). "He shall judge among many people, and rebuke strong nations afar off; and they shall beat their swords into plowshares, and their spears into pruninghooks: nation shall not lift up sword against nation, neither shall they learn war any more" (Micah 4:3). This happy state will continue for one thousand years.

THE GREAT WHITE THRONE JUDGMENT (*Revelation* 20:11-15)

When Jesus was on earth He said, "The Father judgeth no man, but hath committed all judgment unto the Son" (John 5:22). And now the time for the great judgment of all the earth has arrived. "I saw a great white throne, and him that sat on it, from whose face the earth and the heavens fled away; and there was found no place for them." The dead, small and great, will stand before that throne and be judged according to their works. "And whosoever was not found written in the book of life was cast into the lake of fire." "The fearful, and unbelieving, and the abominable, and murderers, and whoremongers, and sorcerers, and idolaters, and all liars, shall have their part in the lake which burneth with fire and brimstone: which is the second death" (Revelation 21:8). This is the Bible's brief summary of the punishment and final disposal of all evil. "For he must reign, till he hath put all enemies under his feet" (1 Corinthians 15:25).

ETERNITY (*Revelation chapters 21 and 22*)

"Behold, I make all things new." "And I saw a new heaven and a new earth: for the first heaven and the first earth were passed away." A holy city will come down from God out of heaven and the tabernacle of God will be with men. All tears and death and sorrow and crying and pain will be forever passed away. The Lamb of God will be the Temple of that beautiful city and also the Light thereof. The throne of God and of the Lamb shall be in that city and His servants shall serve Him. "And they shall reign forever and ever." "Then cometh the end, when he shall have delivered up the kingdom to God, even the Father" (1 Corinthians 15:24). This is the endless end, the infinite Omega (Revelation 22:13).

STUDY QUESTIONS—UNIT 4

LESSON 36

1. Did Jesus wash Judas' feet?
2. What was Christ's new commandment?
3. What were the two outstanding features of Christ's words of comfort recorded in John 14?

LESSON 37

1. Name the degrees of fruit-bearing mentioned in the parable of the Vine and the Branches.
2. What did Jesus say would be the attitude of the world toward His disciples after His departure?
3. Did Jesus pray for us in His high-priestly prayer?

LESSON 38

1. In His prayer in Gethsemane from what did Jesus shrink?
2. What did Jesus say to Judas when He approached to betray Him.
3. Before whom was the first Jewish trial conducted?

LESSON 39

1. At the second Jewish trial, what was the chief charge brought against Jesus, which He confessed?
2. Why was it necessary to have a third Jewish trial?
3. What was the verdict at the first Roman trial?

LESSON 40

1. Wherein was Barabbas a type of the world?
2. Before whom were the second and third Roman trials conducted?
3. List three details of the physical abuse which Jesus suffered before His crucifixion.

LESSON 41

1. What was the darkest hour and deepest suffering Christ underwent when He was on the cross?
2. List the seven utterances which came from His lips at that time.

LESSON 42

1. Name four of our invisible enemies which were crucified with Jesus.
2. What did the rending of the temple veil signify?
3. What happened during the earthquake when Jesus died?
4. Cite four Old Testament prophecies which were fulfilled when Jesus died on the cross.

LESSON 43

1. Who arrived first at the tomb on the Resurrection morning and to whom did Jesus first appear?
2. What message did the angels give to those who came to view the empty tomb?
3. Why did Jesus appear privately to Peter?

LESSON 44

1. Give the four links in redemption's plan as given by Jesus that first Easter night.
2. What special equipment did the Father plan to provide for the disciples?
3. Which disciple was absent that first night and what did Jesus do about it?

LESSON 45

1. Which disciple was the special object of Christ's attention when He appeared to the seven disciples at the Sea of Tiberias?
2. Where was the Great Commission given?
3. What were the last words of Jesus before His ascension?

LESSON 46

1. Cite three "infallible proofs" of Christ's resurrection.
2. List four ways in which the Bible says we are identified with Christ.
3. Which Psalm especially describes Christ's arrival in heaven after His ascension?

LESSON 47

1. Name the three phases of Christ's high-priestly ministry in heaven.
2. Describe the two phases of Christ's future return to this earth.
3. Who will be the judge at the Great White Throne Judgment?
4. Describe briefly the eternal state.